LIFE On Your Own

McGraw Hill **Glencoe**

New York, New York   Columbus, Ohio   Chicago, Illinois   Woodland Hills, California

CONTRIBUTORS:

Linda Perrin, Yardley, Pennsylvania
Amy Livingston, Highland Park, New Jersey
Gayle McDowell, Peoria, Illinois
Patricia Clark, Mahomet, Illinois
Annette Gentry Bailey, Washington, Illinois
Suzanne Murdico, Wesley Chapel, Florida

PRODUCTION, DESIGN, AND PHOTO RESEARCH:

Art Direction/Design/Photo Research: Eric Hoffsten and Brock Waldron/Bill SMITH STUDIO

COVER:

Design by Bill SMITH STUDIO

ILLUSTRATIONS:

Pages 90, 93/Articulate Graphics
Pages 236/Marina Terletsky

Glencoe

The *McGraw-Hill* Companies

Send all inquiries to:
Glencoe
8787 Orion Place
Columbus, OH 43240

ISBN 0-07-861584-4

Printed in the United States of America

6 7 8 9 10 WDQ 14 13 12 11 10

Contents

SECTION 1: Taking Charge of Your Life

Look Out, Changes Ahead..7

Welcome to the REAL WORLD: Getting Priorities Straight...............9

EXPLORE more: What's in a Goal?...12

Putting It to Work..16

Welcome to the REAL WORLD: Choosing a Roommate....................18

How Will You Manage?..22

Balancing Act...26

Going With the Flow..28

Welcome to the REAL WORLD: Going It Alone..................................29

Putting It All Together: What's the Plan?...30

SECTION 2: People Skills

Talking Together...33

Family Matters...38

Friends Forever..42

More than Friends..46

See You Tomorrow...51

Welcome to the REAL WORLD: Roommate Woes.............................53

On the Outs..54

Putting It All Together: Staying Connected..56

SECTION 3: Consumer Smarts

Getting the Most for Your Money..59

The Power of Ads...61

So Many Stores, So Little Time...64

Welcome to the REAL WORLD: Is It a Bargain?...............................68

Getting the Best Deal..69

EXPLORE more: Choosing a Cell Phone Plan....................................72

Dollars & Sense...76

Returns & Exchanges..77

Welcome to the REAL WORLD: Returning an Item...........................78

Understanding Warranties...79

When You have a Consumer Problem...80

Recognizing Fraud...82

Protecting Your Privacy...83

Welcome to the REAL WORLD: An Easy Target...............................85

Putting It All Together: What's the Best Buy?....................................86

SECTION 4: Financial Know How

Money Matters 89

Paying Your Dues..91

Managing Your Money 94

Welcome to the REAL WORLD: Lending to a Friend 96

EXPLORE more: Saving Strategies 98

You Can Bank on It..101

Using Plastic 105

Top Billing 109

EXPLORE more: Bill Paying Options 112

Preparing for the Worst 114

Looking into the Future...116

Putting It All Together: Your Money and Your Life 120

SECTION 5: A Place to Call Home

New Digs 123

Apartment Hunting..125

EXPLORE more: Making the Right Choice 130

Make Room for Roommates 132

Budget Decorating..136

Taking Care of Your Place 140

What Could Go Wrong? 144

On the Move...146

Welcome to the REAL WORLD: Weeding Out 149

Putting It All Together: Setting Up Housekeeping 150

SECTION 6: Going Places

Getting There 153

Your Own Wheels 155

Welcome to the REAL WORLD: Accepting a gift 157

Wheeling & Dealing...158

EXPLORE more: Comparison Shopping 160

Indispensable Insurance 165

Safety First..166

Car Troubles..168

TLC for Your Vehicle 169

Putting It All Together: Buying a Car 170

SECTION 7: It's Your Health

Get into the Habit...173

Adjust Your Attitude..174

Welcome to the REAL WORLD: When to Say No 176

Are You a People Person? 177

Fit for Life 179

EXPLORE more: Joining a Gym 182

Watching Your Weight 186

Eating Disorders 190
Welcome to the REAL WORLD: Helping Out a Friend 191
Know the Risks 193
Safety First 195
Fighting Off Disease 199
Navigating the Health Care System 202
Putting It All Together: Go for the Goals 204

SECTION 8: Eating Well

Helping Yourself 207
EXPLORE more: Energy Bars 210
Plan Ahead 212
Shopping Smarts 214
What's Cooking? 217
Eating Out 222
EXPLORE more: Out to Lunch 223
Welcome to the REAL WORLD: Your Ideas 225
Putting It All Together: Ready, Set, Cook! 226

SECTION 9: Looking Your Best

What to Wear? 229
Your Clothing Needs 230
EXPLORE more: Traveling Light 233
Fashion Sense 234
Going Shopping 237
Treat Your Clothes Right 240
Welcome to the REAL WORLD: Wash and Whoops! 243
Putting It All Together: Work Clothes 246

SECTION 10: Navigating Your Careers

Life after High School 249
The World of Work 252
EXPLORE more: Learning About Careers 255
Looking for Work 258
Applying Yourself 264
Selling Yourself 268
Do You Want the Job? 272
Welcome to the REAL WORLD: Making Tough Choices 273
EXPLORE more: Company Benefits 275
On the Job 276
Lifelong Learning 277
Putting It All Together: Get a Job! 278

Glossary
.... 280

Index
.... 285

Taking Charge of Your Life

Look Out, Changes Ahead

WHAT COMES TO YOUR MIND WHEN YOU HEAR THESE WORDS: graduation; your future; living on your own? Do they bring thoughts of opportunities or difficulties? Feelings of excitement or fear? For most teens, high school graduation brings a mixed bag of thoughts and feelings. Many teens can't wait to leave home and head out on their own. Others prefer to take their next steps a little more cautiously, and some need a gentle push out of the nest.

No matter how you feel about moving toward independence, one thing is sure: You'll experience more changes over the next several years than at any other time in your life. You'll probably find yourself training for a career, working different jobs, moving out of your family home, finding a place of your own, and forming new relationships. These changes will be easier to deal with if you're prepared and have some idea of what maybe ahead.

So how *do* you prepare for all these changes? The key is to develop a strong sense of who you are—your values, your goals, and your priorities in life. Although you've been learning to understand yourself for years, it's time to make sure you're really who you want to be. At the same time, realize that knowing yourself is a life-long discovery. Your life experiences will continually change who you are.

It's also essential to improve some core skills—your ability to make decisions, solve problems, and manage resources like time, money, and information. These skills help you make wise choices become more and more independent.

> ## YOU'LL EXPERIENCE MORE CHANGES OVER THE NEXT SEVERAL YEARS THAN AT ANY OTHER TIME IN YOUR LIFE.

DID YOU KNOW?

Common Values

Certain values reflect basic human worth and dignity. They are common to most cultures and include:

- Fairness
- Caring
- Respect
- Honesty
- Integrity
- Responsibility
- Trustworthiness
- Self-discipline

Listen to that Voice

If you're in a situation where you hear a little nagging voice inside of you saying, "Don't do it," take time to think about what you're hearing. That voice is your conscience talking to you. Your values help guide this powerful warning system, giving you a sense of right and wrong. Be eager to listen to that little nagging voice!

WHAT'S IMPORTANT TO YOU?

The word *values* gets thrown around a lot these days. Everyone from teachers to politicians seems to be talking about the importance of having strong values. But what does this actually mean?

Your values are the things that you place value on—the things that are most important to you. Each person has a unique set of values. For example, some people care a great deal about being successful in their careers, while others place more importance on their relationships with friends and family. Most people share a few basic values, such as honesty, responsibility, and respect for others. However, the amount of weight placed on each of these values differs from person to person.

Your values are sometimes described as your "moral compass." If you've ever used a compass while hiking or sailing, you know that it's a tool with a magnetized needle that always points north. Using a compass helps you keep track of which way you're going so you don't get lost. Your values give direction to your life in much the same way. By using them to guide your actions and decisions, you can avoid losing your way

WHEN VALUES CONFLICT

There may be times in your life when your values come into conflict. Suppose that a friend confesses to you that she has cheated on a test and asks you not to tell anyone. What would you do? The value you place on the friendship may make you want to protect your friend, but the value you place on honesty and fairness may make you want to tell someone about the cheating. When you face a dilemma like this, think hard about what values are most important to you. In this case, you might try to be true to all your values by urging your friend to confess her actions to the teacher and be willing to accept the consequences.

WHAT WILL YOU FOCUS ON?

Many of your values are likely to be abstract ideas—friendship, health, honesty, and so on. How do you make those values part of your life? You do it by setting priorities—by devoting most of your time and energy to the tasks, relationships, and activities that are most important to you. If you value health, for example, you'll make an effort to exercise regularly and eat the proper foods. If you value your relationship with your family, you'll find a way to spend time with them. Your values are put into action through your priorities.

Getting Priorities Straight

MEGAN CAME BACK FROM CLASS to find her friend, Sean, sitting in the common area of their dorm playing a video game.

"I thought you said you were going to the library," said Megan. "Don't you have a big English paper due on Friday?"

Sean looked guilty. "Yeah, and I've got about 50 pages of reading for sociology, too. But there's not much point in starting on all that now—I've only got 20 minutes before I have to be at swimming practice."

Megan made a face at him. "Sounds to me like you've got more important things to worry about than beating your high score in that video game."

"Yeah, you might have a point there," admitted Sean.

YOUR IDEAS

1. What do Sean's actions say about his values? Priorities?

_____

_____

_____

_____

_____

_____

2. If you were Sean, what would you make your top priority? Why?

_____

_____

_____

_____

_____

_____

SETTING YOUR PRIORITIES HELPS YOU SPEND THE MOST TIME AND ENERGY ON WHAT YOU TRULY VALUE.

PUTTING YOUR LIFE IN ORDER

Why do you need priorities? Simply put, because you can't do everything! Imagine that you are trying to get straight As in school while playing a sport, learning music for jazz band, and organizing a school-wide food drive. Suppose that a local civic group has asked you to speak about teen life at their next meeting and you still want to relax with family and friends. You'll never be able to do it all—there just aren't enough hours in the day!

At some point, you'll probably feel forced to decide what you really care about and what is less important to you. Trying to do everything just doesn't work. Setting your priorities helps you spend the most time and energy on what you truly value. When you figure out your priorities before you make commitments, you'll be less likely to collapse from trying to do too much—and won't feel like it was another situation where you couldn't say "no."

Like values, priorities differ from person to person. They also change over time. Right now, your priorities probably include things like school and being with your friends. Ten years down the road, your priorities might include your career, your marriage and children, or your personal finances. It's normal for priorities to shift as your life changes.

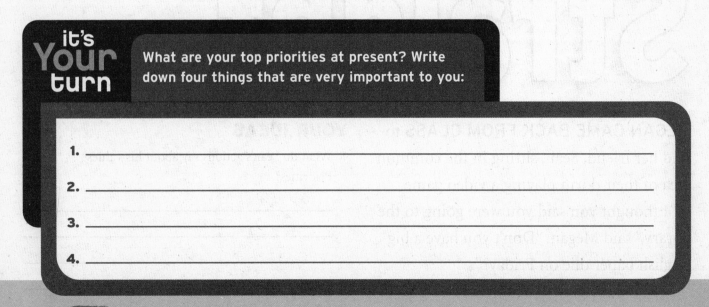

it's Your turn

What are your top priorities at present? Write down four things that are very important to you:

1. _____
2. _____
3. _____
4. _____

SETTING YOUR DIRECTION

Close your eyes for a minute and think about what you'd like to be doing in ten years. What kind of career will you have? Where will you live? Do you see yourself as single, dating, or married? Do you want children? The things you imagine as part of your life are your dreams. You can make many of your dreams come true if you're prepared to turn them into goals.

A goal is more than just something you'd like to achieve someday; it's something you consciously work toward. Goals give your life direction and purpose. They are a source of motivation. Without them, it's easy to be in the mode of "for the moment," not making progress toward independence, a future, your passions or your dreams.

THIS WEEK, NEXT WEEK...

Goals can be short-term or long-term. A short-term goal is something you want to achieve fairly soon, like finishing a book you're reading or completing an art project. A long-term goal is something that you want to achieve at some point months or even years in the future. Going to college or becoming a carpenter might be long-term goals.

In some cases, your short-term goals can contribute to your long-term goals. Think of it this way, if your long-term goal was to get a job as a computer programmer, then completing a computer course in school would be a short-term goal that would help you reach your long-term goal. On a still shorter timescale, a short-term goal to finish an assignment for your computer class would help you reach your goal of passing the course.

QuickTip

Break It Down

If a long-term goal seems overwhelming, break it down into a series of short-term goals. Suppose you're about to move into a new apartment and you're overwhelmed by all that you have to do. If you break the job of moving into specific tasks—notifying people of your new address, packing up your CDs and books, setting up new phone service, and so on—then you can deal with each task one at a time until you're done.

it's Your turn

Write down three short-term goals. They might relate to your schoolwork, sports, your family and personal life, or anything else that is important to you.

1. _____
2. _____
3. _____

Now write down three longer-term goals. These might relate to your career or further education plans, where you want to live, your personal life, or anything else that you hope to achieve in the longer term.

1. _____
2. _____
3. _____

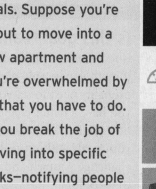

What's in

YOU'RE MORE LIKELY TO REACH YOUR GOALS if you approach them with a positive, but realistic, attitude. Here are a few useful questions to ask yourself:

Is this goal realistic? If your career goal is to become a professional baseball player, even though you've only played in Little League, you probably need to set your sights on something you have a better chance of achieving. On the other hand, don't aim so low that you reach your goals without really trying. It's good to challenge yourself and give yourself something to work for.

Is this goal specific? It's easier to work toward a goal when you know exactly what you want. For example, instead of just thinking, "I want to be in better shape," you might decide, "I want to be able to run a mile in eight minutes by the end of the summer." Then you can give yourself a timeline to reach this goal and measure your progress toward it.

Does this goal match my values and priorities? If you're thinking about a career in finance, but your values center more on people and relationships than on money, you might want to reconsider your goal. Maybe another field, like social work, would suit you better.

How long do I need? Figure out whether your goals are short-term or long-term, and come up with a general idea of when you'd like to meet them. If you set a long-term goal, think about what short-term goals might help you on the way to achieving it. It's OK to start out with short term goals.

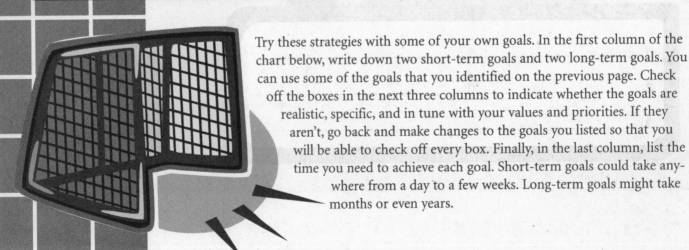

Try these strategies with some of your own goals. In the first column of the chart below, write down two short-term goals and two long-term goals. You can use some of the goals that you identified on the previous page. Check off the boxes in the next three columns to indicate whether the goals are realistic, specific, and in tune with your values and priorities. If they aren't, go back and make changes to the goals you listed so that you will be able to check off every box. Finally, in the last column, list the time you need to achieve each goal. Short-term goals could take anywhere from a day to a few weeks. Long-term goals might take months or even years.

a Goal?

Goals	Realistic	Specific	Matches values and priorities	Time needed
Short-term:				
Long-term:				

*Make sure you date the chart

Return to this chart in a couple of weeks and see how you did in working toward your goals.
Record your progress below:

1. Did you achieve your short-term goals? **Yes / No**
If not, why not?

_____

2. How could you change either the goal or your behavior to help yourself achieve it?

_____

_____

3. How have your activities in the past two weeks helped you work toward your long-term goals?

_____

4. What additional steps could you take to help reach these long-term goals?

_____

_____

IF YOU'VE GOT IT, USE IT

Suppose you've set a short-term goal to bake a batch of brownies for an upcoming bake sale. What will you need to meet this goal? For starters, you'll need a recipe. Then you'll need the ingredients—flour, sugar, cocoa, and so on. You'll need bowls and spoons for mixing and an oven for baking, and finally, you'll need some basic cooking skills (along with reading skills to read the recipe).

All these things—and in fact, anything that you use to help you meet a goal—are resources. Which of the following types of resources do you tend to use the most?

Human resources. Knowledge and skills are human resources. In the above example, your cooking skills are a human resource that you need to bake brownies. If you don't know anything about cooking, you might ask an older friend or parent, for help. That person's knowledge is a human resource as well.

Material resources. These are physical objects used to reach a goal. The ingredients, tools, and kitchen equipment described in the example are all material resources. Material resources also include all forms of technology, such as computers, cars, and telephones.

Community resources. Your community may offer various resources such as schools, parks, and hospitals that are available to the public. You may be able to use some of these resources to work toward your goals. Networking (person to person) within the community is also a great resource.

Natural resources. These resources include air, water, soil, plants, minerals, and sources of fuel. Imagine trying to bake the brownies without a source of heat. You'd wind up with one big gooey mess!

MAKING THE MOST OF YOUR RESOURCES

There are several ways you can make the most of the resources available to you. You can expand, conserve, exchange, and substitute resources. The table below shows how these strategies work.

Strategy	What it means	Examples
Expand resources	Increase the amount you have of a given resource.	• Work extra hours so you will have more money to spend. • Take a class to increase your knowledge on a subject.
Conserve resources	Use your resources more efficiently.	• Keep your car tuned up so it uses less gas. • Do several errands in one trip to save time.
Exchange resources	Trade a resource you have with someone else who has a resource you need.	• Offer to lend your friend a suit in exchange for your friend getting rid of a virus on your computer.
Substitute resources	Use a resource that you have a lot of instead of one that is in short supply.	• Use walnuts in place of pecans in a recipe because you don't have enough pecans.

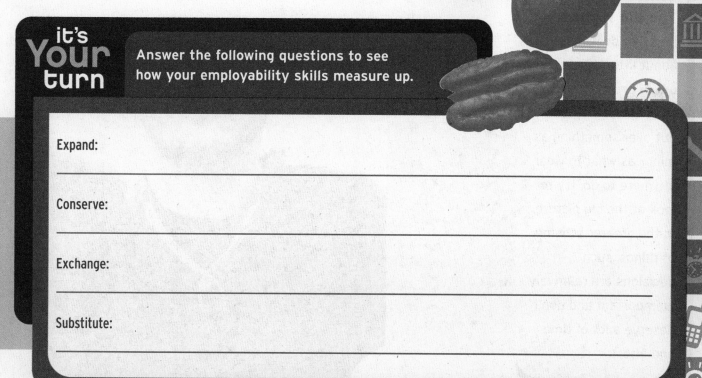

it's Your turn

Answer the following questions to see how your employability skills measure up.

Expand:
_____

Conserve:
_____

Exchange:
_____

Substitute:
_____

Making decisions also means making poor choices sometimes—even if you think things through carefully. Accept that you're going to make mistakes from time to time and do your best to learn from them. As you gain skill in making good decisions, you'll become more confident in your abilities and, most likely, make fewer poor choices.

Putting It to Work

YOUR VALUES, PRIORITIES, AND RESOURCES don't do anything for you by themselves; it's the way you apply them in real-life situations that makes a difference. Understanding how your values, priorities, and resources influence the decisions you make and the problems you solve goes a long way in choosing what is best for you and others.

DECISIONS, DECISIONS

You make lots of decisions every day, often without even thinking about it. Every morning, for instance, you decide what to wear and what to have for breakfast. You probably don't give these choices much thought because, in most cases, they don't matter all that much. On the other hand, some of the choices you make, like what classes to take in school, will have a major impact on your future. These kinds of decisions require more time and effort. You want to make sure you weigh all your options carefully and pick the one that's best for you.

In the face of many choices, you might feel paralyzed. A lot of high school seniors feel this way about choices regarding their future—jobs, further schooling, relationships, travel. Sometimes young people decide to put off making choices until later. Their refusal to decide turns out to be a decision in itself—and not necessarily the one they would have made if they had faced the decision head-on.

The Big Picture
Don't let decisions about little things get out of proportion. If you start to get stressed out over something as minor as what to wear or where to go, try to look at the big picture. In the greater scheme of things, such decisions are relatively unimportant and don't deserve a lot of time and effort.

How-To

Let's Decide Making an important decision can feel monumental. How can you be sure that you've thought of everything? Using a step-by-step process to break the decision into manageable pieces can help. Try following these steps:

Step 1	Step 2	Step 3	Step 4	Step 5
Identify the decision you need to make. This may seem obvious, but it's still important. If you want to understand your choices, it helps to spell out exactly what you're trying to decide.	List your options. Brainstorm a list of all the possible choices you can think of. Don't rule out anything at this point. If you're not sure about your options, you may need more information. Try doing some research or talking to people whose opinions you respect.	Assess the pros and cons of each option. Think your choices through carefully, and try to figure out all the possible outcomes of each one—both for you and for any other people involved.	Choose the best option. Sometimes there is no perfect choice. You may find that all of your options have drawbacks. In this case, pick the choice that will have the best overall outcome. Then figure out what you need to do to put this choice into action—and do it.	Evaluate your decision. After a suitable period of time, ask yourself, "Did I achieve what I wanted to achieve?" and "If not, why not? What could I have done differently to get a better result?" This step will help you use what you learned to make better decisions in the future.

QuickTip

Did It Work?

When evaluating a decision, ask yourself these questions:

- What went well?
- What did not go well?
- What would I do differently another time?
- What did I learn from this experience?

The Flip of a Coin

Flipping a coin to make a decision is about the same as not making a decision at all. It's a cop-out. Of course, for minor decisions (Do I want iced tea or lemonade?) a coin toss would work. Most decisions, though, deserve more than a flip of fate.

Choosing a Roommate

WHEN MAX DECIDED TO MOVE away from home and find an apartment, he knew he would need a roommate to share the rent. He put an ad up at his workplace, and had two responses from interested people. The first one, Joel, seemed shy and was considered a loner by most of the employees. Joel worked full-time and said he'd have no problem paying the rent. Max just wasn't sure if he wanted to live with someone who didn't talk much or want to do things together. The other person, Ryan, was really friendly and outgoing. Max had a great time hanging out with him. The problem was, Ryan was a temp at work and had no intentions of getting a steady job. When Max asked Ryan about his finances, he just said, "No problem, I always manage to get along somehow." This gave Max serious doubts about whether Ryan was responsible.

YOUR IDEAS

1. If you were Max, which roommate would you prefer and why?

_____

_____

_____

_____

_____

_____

_____

_____

2. What other options might Max have aside from rooming with Joel or Ryan?

_____

_____

_____

_____

_____

_____

_____

_____

WHAT'S YOUR PROBLEM?

The decision-making process works well when you have a specific choice to make and you know what your options are. But what do you do when you have a situation that's complex and that requires you to make several interrelated choices? These kinds of situations usually involve thinking about your values and your sense of right and wrong—not just the facts.

Suppose, for example, that you're trying to decide if you should go to college and, if so, where you want to apply. You know that this decision could change the course of your life. It's also a very complicated one because there are many choices and factors involved—what you want to study, how far from home you want to go, how much it will cost, what your parents say, what your friends are choosing, and so on.

FIGURING IT OUT

Obviously, the decision-making process isn't going to be enough to deal with a situation like the one just described. In that situation, you don't need to make just one decision—you have to make a whole series of related decisions, and you need to think about how each choice impacts yourself and others. In a situation like this you need to use problem-solving skills.

You've probably figured out that decision-making and problem-solving skills are related, but they're not the same. Decision making is a matter of choosing the best option for a single issue; problem solving is more a matter of figuring out how to work through several issues that are tangled together. To complicate matters, each issue usually has more than one solution.

The chart below shows some examples of situations in which you would use each type of skill. As you can see, many situations call for both decision-making and problem-solving skills.

Decision making	Problem solving
You want to join a club, but you aren't sure which one.	You want to have a strong résumé for college applications. You're currently not participating in any after-school activities.
It's your turn to cook dinner, and you don't know what to make.	It's your turn to cook dinner, and there's nothing in the fridge.
You're going to a dance, and you don't know what to wear.	You have to get home from a dance, and the person who was going to give you a ride isn't there.

LOOKING FROM DIFFERENT ANGLES

Solving problems takes time, thought, and effort. Besides figuring out the main issues or root causes of the problem, you need to gather and evaluate information about the problem, consider options, make the best choices, and develop a plan of action. Then after you think the problem is solved, you'll want to look back on the outcome and determine if you got the results you desired.

When you're doing all of this—and sometimes solving more than one problem at a time—you'll find that it helps if you think about the problem from these four angles:

- **Look at the context.** Context refers to all of the conditions surrounding the problem or situation. They're what make the problem unique. You might think about the people involved, your finances, and other aspects of the situation you need to be aware of. No two problems are identical because the conditions are always different and the people involved see only their own perspective.

- **Know what you, and others, want.** What do you desire? What do you want the outcome to be? What needs to happen so that everyone involved is satisfied that the problem is successfully solved? These questions help you focus on the end result and don't let you get sidetracked into less important aspects of the problem.

- **Consider how you can go about getting what you want.** "There's more than one means to an end." The quoted saying basically encourages you to use different ways and methods to reach your desired outcomes. To do this, you'll need to look at your resources, including the people who can help you.

- **Continually evaluate the consequences.** Every choice has positive and negative consequences attached to it. If you keep assessing the consequences and making any necessary changes in how you're solving the problem, you'll be more likely to reach the best outcome.

ETHICS CHECK

You'll find that some problems and decisions seem more complicated than others because they involve ethical issues. They require you to consider what is fair, right, and just for all the people involved. When you face an ethical issue, ask yourself these questions:

How would I feel if someone did this to me? Suppose you've made plans with a friend for Friday night, but then someone you like calls and asks you out. Thinking about how you'd feel if one of your friends bailed out on you will help you see how your choice affects others.

What would happen if everyone did this? Say you're having a snack at the beach, and you're tempted to bury the wrapper in the sand. One wrapper may not seem like a big deal, but thinking about the effect of thousands of buried wrappers will probably make you think twice.

Would I do the same thing in another situation? You forgot your lunch money at school, but you think maybe you can just sneak into the cafeteria and grab something. If you think about whether you'd steal food in a store, you'll probably reconsider your decision.

Which choice does the most good for the most people? The answer to this question isn't always obvious, but thinking about it can help put the decision in perspective. The most ethical decision is usually the one with the most positive consequences for the most people.

 it's Your turn

Think of a situation in which you faced an ethical issue similar to the ones described on this page. What happened? How did you deal with it? What did you learn?

_____

_____

_____

_____

_____

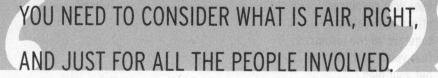

" YOU NEED TO CONSIDER WHAT IS FAIR, RIGHT, AND JUST FOR ALL THE PEOPLE INVOLVED. "

QuickTip

Leave Wiggle Room

When making a schedule, try to allow extra time to accomplish your task in case things don't go smoothly. That way, if one task takes a little longer than you had planned, you don't have to reschedule everything else.

How Will You Manage?

PROBLEM-SOLVING AND DECISION-MAKING SKILLS CAN HELP YOU in a lot of different situations. However, those skills alone don't actually solve anything or meet your goals. You also need to *manage* your decisions, problems, and goals. That means you use all your skills and resources effectively and in a timely manner.

Two of the most important resources you'll need to manage are time and information. There are only 24 hours in a day, but how you use them will determine what you accomplish and how you feel about it. Information, on the other hand, is not limited. Sorting through mounds of different sources to pick out the facts that you need can be a real challenge.

The Management Process When you have something you want to accomplish, you may not know where to start. The management process is a series of four steps you can use to turn a major task into something you can handle.

Step 1

Make a plan. Identify specific goals and the resources you will need to meet them. Use this information to make a to-do list, showing each step you'll need to take to reach your goal. Think about problems that might come up and try to develop contingency plans—steps you could take if these problems arise.

Step 2

Get organized. Check out your to-do list and figure out how much time you'll need for each task and which tasks should be done first. Use this information to make a schedule, giving yourself a deadline for each task. Try to organize the tasks in a way that uses your resources effectively. Gather together all the resources that you'll need to carry out your plan.

Step 3

Put your plan into action. As you carry out your plan, keep track of your progress. Be prepared to switch to a contingency plan if a problem comes up.

Step 4

Evaluate the results. After you've met your goals, think about how well the process worked. Did you achieve everything you wanted to? If not, did you meet your top priorities? If something went wrong, what could you do to avoid similar problems in the future?

TOO LITTLE TIME OR TOO MUCH

Does it ever seem like there just aren't enough hours in the day for everything you want to do? You can't make the day any longer, but you can make better use of the time you have. The key is organization. Some people like to keep their entire schedule laid out in a book or electronic organizer. For others, jotting things down on scraps of paper works well. There's no right or wrong way to plan your life—it's a matter of finding a system that works for you.

The first step, and possibly the most important, is to keep track of all the things you intend to do. Some of these will be things you *need* to do, like homework or household chores. Others will be things you *want* to do, like e-mailing a friend or practicing your guitar.

To keep track of all these tasks, make a to-do list. Then keep the list someplace where you can refer to it and update it often. Once you have everything written down, you can set priorities. If you don't have time to do everything, ask yourself: "What are the most important tasks to get done?"

Sometimes you are faced with the opposite problem of too much time. Have you ever been on a vacation with your family to visit your grandparents in a retirement facility? On the trip, your parents announce that instead of staying at a hotel, you are all staying at the retirement complex—you may have too much time on your hands!

it's Your turn

Make a sample to-do list for yourself. In the spaces below, list five things you need to do and five things you want do this week. If any task has a specific deadline, add it in parentheses. Then place a special mark, such as a star or an arrow, next to the three tasks that are your highest priorities for the week.

NEED TO DO

1. _____
2. _____
3. _____
4. _____
5. _____

WANT TO DO

1. _____
2. _____
3. _____
4. _____
5. _____

QuickTip

Dovetailing

A trick to fit more tasks into your schedule is to dovetail them. Dovetailing is when you fit two or more activities together to save time and resources. For example, you can run several errands in one trip rather than multiple ones. Or you can talk with a friend about a homework assignment and make plans for an upcoming movie night in one phone call rather than two.

Finally, you can schedule specific times for specific tasks. Some parts of your day, like the time you spend at school or the dinner hour at home, are already scheduled. You'll need to find time in between these filled-in blocks for all the other things you need and want to do. Look at your to-do lists and try to guess how much time each task will take. Try to fit them into time slots where they'll be most convenient. Also, be sure to note things that need to be done by specific times, like washing your sports uniform by Monday's game. Listing tasks on a calendar or day planner is a good way to keep priorities straight.

Time Traps

Have you ever felt like you don't know where the time goes? Those lost hours may be slipping into a time trap—something that prevents you from using time effectively. Two of the most common time traps are procrastination and overscheduling.

Procrastination means putting something off until later—especially something you don't really want to do. When you put things off, you may have to rush through them at the last minute—and you probably won't do as good a job as if you had taken your time. One way to avoid procrastination is to tackle your least favorite tasks first, while you're still fresh.

Overscheduling is taking on more than you can handle. You either end up leaving things undone, or you try to do everything and don't do any of them well. To avoid this problem, don't take on new projects unless you can handle them. Learn to be honest with yourself!

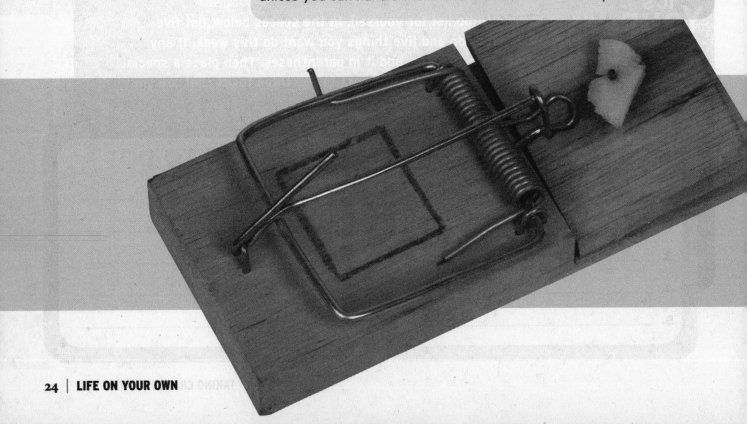

GETTING YOUR FACTS STRAIGHT

Suppose you need to find a hardware store in your area. Where would you look? You'd probably start by checking a phone directory. If a recipe for blueberry muffins is what you need, you turn to a cookbook, and to find out what day they pick up the trash in your new neighborhood, you might check a community Web site. As you can see from these examples, different information sources are useful for finding different types of facts. One of the keys to using information effectively is to know where to look for it—and to know which sources you can trust.

Not all information sources are reliable. This is especially true of the Internet, where anybody can post just about anything. So how can you tell whether a source is trustworthy? First of all, check to see where the information is coming from. If you find a statistic in a news article, see if the author mentions the statistic's source. If no source is given—or if the source is a person whose qualifications seem sketchy—then you shouldn't rely on the information. On the other hand, if the information appears to come from a reliable organization or a qualified expert, you can probably trust it. If you want to make extra sure, you can double-check the facts against other sources that you know are reliable.

Think It Through

Suppose you come across a magazine article that makes an interesting argument. You're not sure whether to believe it, though, because you don't know whether the author's facts are reliable. How can you be sure? Try asking these questions:

- Is this statement based on facts that can be checked, or is it opinion?

- Is there enough evidence to support the statement?

- Does the evidence support the statement, or could there be another explanation?

- Is the information balanced, or does it slant toward one point of view?

- Does the author overlook certain facts that don't support his or her conclusions?

- How could I check the author's facts?

Balancing Act

THINK ABOUT ALL THE ROLES YOU PLAY IN YOUR DAILY LIFE—son or daughter, sibling, student, worker, athlete, friend, and so on. These roles have demands and expectations that will sometimes collide. Suppose, for example, that you have a major paper due for school, but the night you're planning to work on it, your best friend has a personal crisis and wants to talk with you. You would be torn between your roles as student and friend.

These clashes can occur just for a day or for a period of time. Here's an example: Austin has the lead in the school musical, so he puts his time and energy into his role and cuts back on studying. When his grades start to slip, he finds that he has to put more effort into his studies. In this case, he doesn't want to reduce his focus on the musical, so he decides to work extra hard at both studying and drama. This is a short-term balancing act that he needs to balance equally.

Just like Austin, you'll need to strike a balance among different roles at different times. You'll have to think about how much of your time and energy you're willing to focus on each one. This decision is a very personal one, based on your values, priorities, and goals.

it's Your turn

List three roles that you have. For each role, describe a situation in which you experienced a conflict. Identify the values, priorities, and goals that influenced how you handled the conflict.

Roles	Situation creating role conflict	Influencing values, priorities, and goals

It's inevitable that your roles will clash periodically. When that happens, how do you usually feel? Most likely, you feel stressed out because your life seems out of control. To avoid situations like this, keep an eye on your roles, commitments, and priorities as you go. It's better to maintain a balance than to lose balance and have to regain it.

Maintaining a balance means that you set reasonable expectations for yourself. Don't take on more than you can handle. You can't expect to get perfect grades, be a star performer, look after your younger siblings, and always have time for your friends. You have to decide which of your roles and commitments is most important at any given time. And if you discover that you've taken on too many commitments, work your way out of the least important ones.

Timing Is Everything

Have you ever had a day when life seems out of control? Maybe you had scheduled your life so tight that you had no extra time and space to handle the emergencies and interruptions that came your way. Give yourself a daily buffer zone—the space between yourself and your physical, mental, and emotional limits. That way you'll have a little breathing room.

Check the Net

Family Friendly

Balancing work and family life is a challenge almost every employee faces. Many workplaces create policies and services to help employees who need child care, time off to deal with family illness, or before- and after-school programs. Use the Internet to find more information about these policies and services.

KeyTerms: family-friendly workplaces, flextime, telecommuting, on-site child care

Going With the Flow

QuickTip

Dealing with Loss

Change and transition may involve loss. If dealing with loss, try:

- Expressing your feelings to a trusted person
- Journaling your thoughts and feelings
- Accepting that you are entitled to feel how you feel.
- Giving yourself permission to mourn
- Taking care of yourself—doing what you need to do.

By now, you've realized that the changes you'll be experiencing can be exciting and also scary. To some extent, dealing with change is a matter of being able to go with the flow. In order to adjust to change, you need to accept it. It helps to focus on the positive side of all the changes in your life. Most likely, as your responsibilities increase, so will your freedom. You won't have your parents to cook dinner for you, but you'll be able to choose what you want to eat. And while you may not be seeing your old friends as often, you'll be meeting lots of people who could become new friends.

At the same time, you don't need to let go of every part of your past. Having some continuity in your life—some familiar things that don't go away—can help you stay centered when the rest of your life is changing.

However, the best way to deal with change is to know who you are, where you're headed, and how to make wise choices along the way. Lay your groundwork now to build a firm foundation for your future.

Change and Transition

Changes such as a move, new job, or different school often occur suddenly. Transition, on the other hand, takes time—it's more of a process. When you go through a transition you have to say goodbye to the way things were, deal with an in-between state of uncertainty and confusion, and then learn to live in your new "normal." Whether it's change or transition, give yourself permission to navigate the internal chaos in a way that is as comfortable as possible.

Support Systems

When you're trying to adjust to changes in your life, it helps to have a good support system—people and groups you can turn to for help. They might include family, friends, employers and coworkers, and religious or community organizations. Here are some examples of how support systems help people through a period of change:

- When Sandy moved into a new apartment, she couldn't afford to buy furniture. Her parents loaned her a few pieces to use until she could buy her own.

- Tim's mother had surgery and needed full-time care at home for a while. Tim's boss agreed to let him rearrange his work schedule so that he could spend more time at home.

- When Betsy moved to a different city, her friends took turns visiting her so that she wouldn't be lonely.

Going It Alone

WHEN FRAN LEFT HOME AND HEADED OFF TO COLLEGE, she was really excited. She was looking forward to being on her own and getting to try new things. After her first couple of weeks, though, she's starting to feel lost. Her classes are a lot harder than she expected, and the workload is much heavier than it was back in high school. She's also having trouble making new friends. She doesn't have much in common with her roommate, and she can't figure out how to meet people she likes. She really misses her family and all her old friends back home. She's beginning to wonder if maybe it was a mistake to go away in the first place.

YOUR IDEAS

1. What advice would you give Fran on her situation?

_____

_____

_____

_____

_____

_____

_____

_____

2. Who might be able to help her deal with the changes in her life, and how?

_____

_____

_____

_____

_____

_____

_____

_____

PUTTING IT ALL TOGETHER

WHAT'S THE PLAN?

You're on the verge of big changes in your life. To deal with them, you're going to need a plan. Complete the information below.

1. What do you want to achieve in the next few years? Do you want a college education? A rewarding job in a specific field? **LIST** your five top priorities on the lines below. Then **RANK** them from highest to lowest by numbering them from 1 to 5.

_____

_____

_____

2. **CHECK** to see if your priorities are in line with your values. **COMPARE** the values you listed earlier with the list above. Do your priorities seem to reflect these values? If not, you may wish to reorder or change some of the priorities.

3. **USE** your priorities to set goals. In the chart below, **IDENTIFY** one long-term goal you have for your life. **INDICATE** how it reflects your priorities and values.

Long-term goal	Priorities	Values

4. **LIST** the resources you have in your life—your skills, education, people you know, things you own—everything that could possibly help you as you work toward your goals. Categorize and number them in the table below.

Human	Community

Material	Natural

5. WRITE a to-do list for your long-term goal below—one task per line. Be sure to break the goal down into shorter-term goals.

_____

_____

_____

_____

_____

_____

6. CIRCLE the resources you will use from the table above. Jot down the appropriate number of each resource next to each task on your to-do list.

7. WORK OUT a schedule for completing the tasks. Next to each task on the list, write a deadline. Keep in mind that you may need to complete certain tasks before you can start on others.

8. IDENTIFY two problems that might arise. List some sources of information and support systems that could help you solve the potential problems.

Problem 1 _____

Problem 2 _____

People Skills

Talking Together

HAVE YOU EVER WATCHED TWO PEOPLE who seem to be in their own little world when they are together? Some people connect with each other so completely that the rest of the world just disappears. They may use private jokes or special phrases that don't mean anything to anybody else. It's like they have their own language.

When you think about it, every relationship has its own special language. Whether it's your relationship with family, friends, teammates, or coworkers, you have a specific way of communicating with each of them. You wouldn't, for example, walk into class and greet your teacher with a "What's up?" the way you might with a friend. And you wouldn't talk about personal concerns with a coworker the way you might with a close friend. The way you communicate depends on your personality, communication skills, circumstances, and the way you relate to the different people in your life.

> **GOOD COMMUNICATION IS THE KEY TO ALL GOOD RELATIONSHIPS.**

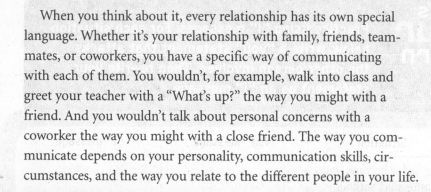

it's Your turn

Think about the different kinds of relationships you have. Fill in the chart below with the names of people you talk to regularly and your relationships to them. For each person, give an example of the way you communicate with that person that's different from the way you communicate with anyone else.

Name	Relationship	How we communicate

QuickTip

Mean What You Say

Make sure the tone of your voice matches your words. No one's going to believe you're really serious about something if you sound bored and uninterested or speak in a flip joking manner.

"I" Messages

An "I" message takes the following form: "I feel (a certain emotion) when you (act a certain way) because (this is what happens)." So instead of saying "Why do you always leave your dirty dishes in the sink? It's so bogus!" You could say, "I get really annoyed when you leave dishes in the sink, because then I can't use it without washing your things first." Using "I" messages will help you stay focused on the problem and keep negative feelings to a minimum.

GETTING THE MESSAGE ACROSS

Communication involves sending and receiving messages. It requires active participation. If you're talking to someone who isn't paying any attention—or if you don't pay attention to someone who's talking to you—then you're not communicating. To communicate effectively, you need to make sure that the messages you send get through to the other person. Look for body language that tells you the person is listening. And when it's your turn to listen, concentrate and give feedback.

You can't send a clear message if you don't really know what you want to say. The trick to expressing yourself clearly is first to clarify what you think and feel. If you need to criticize someone, be honest without being rude. Your message won't get through if you make people feel like they're under attack.

Anytime you have something to say that's likely to be hard for another person to hear, it helps to use "I" messages. "I" messages change the focus from the listener's behavior to the speaker's feelings—it's a way to communicate what you feel and think without being critical of someone else. They make it easier for your listener to see the situation from your point of view.

it's Your turn

Practice using "I" messages. For each situation below, write a "you" statement that attacks the other person involved. Then rewrite your statement as an "I" message.

Situation	"You" message	"I" message
Your sister borrows your favorite shirt without asking and spills ketchup on it.		
Your parents won't let you stay out past your usual curfew on homecoming night.		
Your roommate forgets to pay the phone bill, and the phone company cuts off your service.		

BEING A GOOD LISTENER

Communication is a two-way street. It's not enough to say how you feel; you also have to listen. That means more than just standing there and waiting until it's your turn to talk again. Listening is an active process of showing that you've heard the other person's words and understood the feelings behind them. It's most difficult to do when strong emotions are present. If you feel angry or upset at what the person is saying, try to control your emotions and concentrate on the message.

If your friend says, "You won't believe what happened to me!" you might raise an inquisitive eyebrow. If the story ends with, "I just hate when that happens." You can show that you're listening by making eye contact or using other non-verbal clues. Another way to show that you understand is to echo the speaker's thoughts. Phrases like, "It sounds like you feel…" or "Do you mean that…?" help clarify what the other person is saying.

WHAT YOU SAY WITHOUT WORDS

If anyone's ever given you the "silent treatment," you know how easy it is to send a message without saying a word. Turning away from someone or folding your arms, says clearly, "I don't want to deal with you." Facial expressions, gestures, and posture—can express your feelings as plainly as words do.

Your body language can reinforce your words—or it can contradict them. Making an alert expression, sends a clear message that you're interested in the conversation. On the other hand, if you say, "Yeah, I'm listening," while leafing through a magazine or watching TV, your words are at odds with your actions. Which do you think your listener is more likely to believe?

What you say without words can also have a positive effect. Giving someone a hug without words attached, can show empathy during a difficult time.

QuickTip

Keep It Moving

A conversation is like a game of catch. If someone says something to you and you just answer, "Uh huh," it's like dropping the ball. The other person has to pick it back up to keep the conversation going. If you want to throw that ball back to the other person, offer your own thoughts or ask a question about what the other person said.

Body Talk

Body talk without verbal talk can create confusion. If you walk away in the middle of a conversation, what might the other person think? You could be angry, bored, or hurt. Use words to communicate your message to avoid misunderstandings.

A CRITICAL LOOK

One of the hardest things to tell another person is that he or she is doing something wrong. Sometimes, though, it's the only way to let a friend or coworker know that there's a problem is to say something. In a situation like this, try to be honest without being mean. Tactfully summarize the problem and focus on ways to fix it. Choosing the right time and place also helps. If either of you are angry or upset, the conversation probably won't end well. Pick a time when you're both calm and focused and a place where you'll have some privacy.

On the flip side, keep an open mind when someone finds fault with you. Recognize that the person cares enough about you to say something. Think about what you've been told. Instead of getting mad, use the criticism to your advantage and use it in a positive way.

CLEARING THE AIR

No matter how clear you try to be, misunderstandings still happen. They are most likely to occur when people are in a hurry, distracted, stressed, or highly emotional. If you think that someone may have misunderstood your words—or vice versa—try to play back the conversation in your head. Are you sure you said what you meant? Are you sure you heard what the other person was saying?

If you realize there's been a misunderstanding, there are several ways to clear the air. Start by acknowledging the problem. Then try to clarify what you (or the other person) really meant. You might apologize for not expressing yourself clearly or for misinterpreting the other person's words—even if it wasn't entirely your fault. Saying "I'm sorry" sends the message that you're not blaming the other person.

> MISUNDERSTANDINGS ARE MOST LIKELY TO OCCUR WHEN PEOPLE ARE IN A HURRY, DISTRACTED, STRESSED, OR HIGHLY EMOTIONAL.

Etiquette

WHEN YOU HEAR THE WORD "ETIQUETTE," the first thing that comes to mind may be a list of rules about table manners. In fact, etiquette is a set of guidelines for how to behave in many different social situations, not just meals. Etiquette can be helpful for figuring out what to do when you're in an unfamiliar or awkward situation, such as:

- Meeting someone for the first time.
- Recovering from saying something that you think may have offended someone.
- Extending sympathy to someone who has experienced a loss.

Many newspapers feature columns on etiquette, and similar columns are available online. In addition, a wide variety of books deal with etiquette in general or with specific social situations. Use at least two of these sources to find information on how you might handle the following situations:

1. Your coworker arrives at work for the first time since her father died.

_____
_____
_____

2. You've just been introduced to someone, but you didn't hear his name.

_____
_____
_____

3. You hold out your hand when greeting your supervisor. She does not extend hers in return.

_____
_____
_____

4. Your date leaves you alone with his or her parents.

_____
_____
_____

Family Matters

THE RELATIONSHIPS YOU HAVE WITH FAMILY will probably change as you become more independent and develop a life of your own. Maybe your parents or guardians are letting you make more of your own decisions. At the same time, they may expect more of you when it comes to participating in household needs or caring for siblings. They may even ask your opinion sometimes when they have decisions to make. Once you graduate from school, there will be even bigger changes.

UNDER YOUR PARENTS' ROOF

If you decide to continue living at home after you graduate, you may find yourself in an awkward situation. You may feel like an adult, but your folks still think of you as a kid. They may still expect you to be home by a certain hour or to let them know where you're going every time you leave the house. At the same time, they may expect you to help out around the house and even do some of the grocery shopping and cooking. You may start to ask yourself if living rent-free is worth the cost of free rent.

As with most problems in relationships, the key is communication. You may be assuming that "now that you're an adult," you should get to make your own decisions. But from your parents' point of view, you're still under their roof, and that means that they set the rules. The only way to resolve this is to sit down and talk it out. Talk about expectations on both ends—yours and your parents. You need to be on the same page before you can find a solution that everyone's happy with.

GETTING OUT

You may figure that once you're all done with school, it's time to leave the nest and stretch your wings a bit. But you may be surprised—leaving home could be harder than you expect. Some teens can't wait to be out on their own, but as the time gets closer, they find themselves putting off decisions they need to make about going to college or finding an apartment of their own. Leaving the only home you've ever known is a major change, and you shouldn't expect it to be easy.

Having you move out may be hard on your family, too. Your parents may not feel ready to let go, even if they know you're looking forward to being on your own. Parents are always parents no matter how old you are! Younger brothers and sisters may joke about how they can hardly wait to take over your room but actually feel abandoned when you leave home.

You can make this transition easier on yourself and on them by remembering that family is still family—that doesn't change when you move into a place of your own. If your family relationships have been close and strong, they will continue to be so—provided that everyone puts forth some effort. If you haven't had close relationships and desire them, leaving home is a good time to start building them.

QuickTip

Don't Mope

Homesickness can hit hard when you first leave home. One key to keeping homesickness at bay is to stay busy. The more time you spend on work, friends, and hobbies, the less time you'll have to think about it. You can always pick up the phone and just touch base! Sometimes, that's all you might need.

Strengthening Families

Family closeness doesn't disappear when you move into a place of your own, but you do need to make an effort. Here are some suggestions:

- Show appreciation to your family for who they are and what they do.

- Show that you can be trusted to use money, possessions, and resources wisely.

- Talk about what is going on in your life and how you feel about it.

- Respect your family's opinions, feelings, and needs.

- Support family members when they need help and assurance.

- Spend time with family whenever possible.

KEEPING IN TOUCH

Make a point of keeping in touch with family after you move away. If you still live in the same area, you could arrange to see them once a week. For example, you might start a tradition of meeting for Sunday brunch, going over for dinner, or watching your favorite TV show together on a weeknight.

If you move to another city, keep in touch by calling and sending letters or e-mails. You might set a specific time to call home each week so you don't forget. The conversations don't have to be terribly significant. You can just talk to your family about what's going on in your life, and ask them about what's new with them. It's the effort to maintain contact that counts.

COMING HOME

After you move out, you and your family will need to figure out how you want to handle return visits. For example, will you still have a key to your parents' house? If so, can you just pop in whenever you want, or do you need to call first? Will you be allowed to do your laundry, raid the refrigerator, or spend the night? Try to work through these issues with your parents and agree on some ground rules. They may not like the idea of your dropping in unannounced any more than you'd like to have them show up at your place without asking!

If you can come home only once or twice a year, there may be questions about how you're expected to spend your time. For example, when Jared came home on furlough from the army, he wanted to visit all his friends. His parents were upset because they hardly got to see him. When they talked it out, they realized that no one was really being fair—Jared was spending no time with his parents, while his parents expected to have him all to themselves. They ended up agreeing that, for the remainder of his leave, he would spend the daytimes and dinner with his parents and see his friends later in the evenings.

DID YOU KNOW?

Home Alone Being alone isn't the same as being lonely. When you're alone, you're on your own, but you may be content to have some time to yourself. When you're lonely, you feel isolated, unhappy, and in need of friendship. To avoid future feelings of loneliness, get into the habit of spending time alone now. You might realize you're a better friend than you thought!

RIPPLES OF CHANGE

Once you're out on your own, you need to remember that life is also moving on for your family. You can't expect everything to be the same when you come home. Your old bedroom may now be home to the family computer—or to one of your siblings. At the same time, the family itself will be going through changes. Your siblings continue to grow and change, and your parents may develop new interests. You may also have to deal with one of the most devastating changes that can happen in a family—divorce or separation.

A divorce in the family is painful, even if you've seen it coming. On top of that, it makes your life a lot more complicated. Coming home for visits is tricky when your parents live in two different places. And if one parent remarries, you may also find you have a step-parent and new relations to deal with. Changes like this take time to adjust to. As always, keep those channels of communication open. Be prepared to talk together and work through any problems posed by divorce or other family changes.

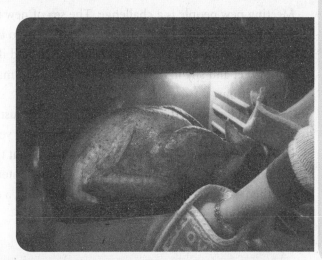

Home for the Holidays

If your parents divorce—or if you or one of your siblings marries—coming home for holidays can become complicated. You now have two whole families—or more—who feel entitled to a share of your time. You may end up making a holiday "tour" of all your family members, which can be exhausting if they don't live close together. Or you may choose to compromise by alternating years with each of your families.

it's Your turn

Staying close while you're far away takes effort. Imagine that you're going to be teaching in a foreign country for the next year. List five ideas for staying in touch with your family during that time.

1. _____
   _____
2. _____
   _____
3. _____
   _____
4. _____
   _____
5. _____
   _____

QuickTip

QuickTip

Friends Forever

IF THE CHANGES IN YOUR FAMILY RELATIONSHIPS are difficult, your changing friendships can be downright bewildering. You know that family will always be family, but how do you know when it's worth the trouble of trying to hold onto an old friendship? On the other hand, how do you go about making new friends in a new place?

MAKE NEW FRIENDS...

Meeting new people is a challenge. The sea of new faces on a college campus can seem overwhelming. New coworkers may seem to be all business, giving you no way to get to know them on a personal level. And if you're a person who tends to be quiet and shy in new social situations, you may find it difficult to start conversations.

A good way to start out with someone you've just met is to ask questions about the other person's interests. If you find an interest you have in common—say, baseball—then you'll have something to talk about the next time you run into that person. You may be able to build on this shared interest by doing something together, like going to a baseball game. Over time, a casual contact can blossom into a friendship.

...BUT KEEP THE OLD

When you were little, did you have a favorite toy or blanket that you literally loved to pieces? An old friendship can give you that same feeling of warmth and security. Even if it seems to be falling apart, you can't bear to let go of it. So moving away from a close friend can leave you feeling torn. How can you stay friends with someone you'll no longer see regularly?

Like family relationships, long-distance friendships can last if both people are willing to make the effort. Visit your old pals whenever you get the chance, and in between, call and e-mail to keep up on what's going on in each other's lives. Share memories of your times together, but don't focus just on the past—make sure they also know about what's going on in your present. Otherwise, it can feel like you no longer have ties to each other in the here and now.

Take an interest in how your friends' lives are changing, too. Listening to them talk about their new friends and interests, you may feel like these aren't the same people you used to know. Know what? You're right. No one stays the same, including you. But if you take the time to learn about the new things going on in your friends' lives, you can all continue to grow without growing apart.

QuickTip

Staying Connected

At this point you and your friends may be relocating all over the country. Sending a group e-mail is a quick and easy way to stay in touch. Don't let this be your only form of communication, though. Remember that your friends are individuals, with individual concerns and interests, so they'll need individual attention from time to time if you want to keep the friendship alive. It's also a great to hear a real voice!

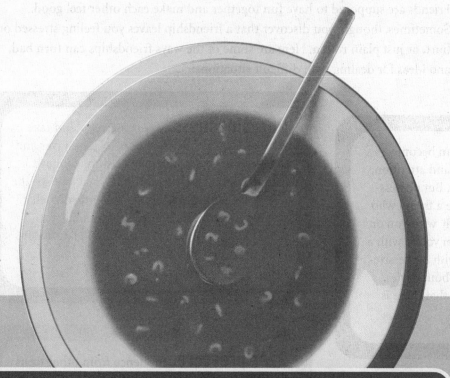

Lean on Me

It has been said, "To have a friend, to be a friend." If you want your friends to have time for you, make time for them! Take chicken soup to a friend who's sick, give a ride to someone whose car is broken, bake some mini loaf breads and attach a note "thinking of you." Comfort friends when they're down and cheer for them when they succeed. Actions can often be reciprocal.

WHEN FRIENDSHIPS GO WRONG

Friends are supposed to have fun together and make each other feel good. Sometimes, though, you discover that a friendship leaves you feeling stressed out, hurt, or just plain rotten. Here are some of the ways friendships can turn bad, and ideas for dealing with difficult situations:

Possessiveness. Friends can become possessive of one another's time and attention, sparked by jealousy or insecurity. But possessiveness snuffs out joy. If you have a friend who constantly wants to do things only with you or monopolizes your attention when you're with a group, you're probably dealing with possessiveness. Handle it by clearly setting boundaries. That friend needs to understand that there is plenty of you to go around!

One-sidedness. Friends give to and take from a relationship. When one person gives and the other does not, the relationship will have problems. The person who gives may not see the relationship as satisfying. If you find yourself playing this role, you'll need to decide if you want to continue the relationship. Relationships need to be two-sided.

Unrealistic expectations. Sometimes friends want to change each other. It's only possible to change yourself. If a friend is habitually late or doesn't return borrowed items, you will need to find ways to deal with those traits. While they need to know what your expectations may be, you have to understand that we are who we are.

Peer pressure. Influence from other teens may be positive or negative. Peers can encourage you to get involved with new activities or develop new skills. They can also influence you to do something that conflicts with your values or that you know is wrong. To deal with negative peer pressure you need a strong value system, clear priorities, and trust in your own judgment. Use your refusal skills to resist negative peer pressure. And listen to that inner voice.

Refusal Skills

When people try to persuade you to go against your values, character, and better judgment, use these refusal skills to resist the negative pressure:

- Decide in advance what you will do when your face negative pressure.
- In the moment, take time to collect your thoughts.
- State your position firmly and clearly.
- Make sure your body language reinforces what you say.
- Stay in control. Reject the action, change the subject, or suggest an alternative.
- If all else fails, walk away.

GOING SEPARATE WAYS

Sometimes it's possible to overcome problems and make a friendship work. Other times, though, you realize you just don't want to deal with the problems anymore. Friendships can also end because two people simply grow apart. For example, you may realize that you and your old buddy from camp no longer have anything other than your memories holding you together. Regardless of the reason, when a friendship isn't working anymore, it's time to think about ending it.

Ending a friendship isn't easy. Some people simply let the relationship fade away, calling and getting together less and less often. Others try to "break up" with a friend by explaining honestly why they think the friendship isn't working. This approach requires tact, since it's hard to say, "I don't want to be your friend anymore" in a way that isn't hurtful. No matter how you end a friendship, you should try to be sympathetic to the friend's feelings.

DID YOU KNOW?

Growing Apart Many friendships end when one person goes away to college and the other stays home. College brings new experiences and interests—and new friends. Over time, the friends may discover that they live in different worlds and have less and less in common.

More than Friends

DATING IS VERY DIFFERENT AS YOU MATURE. High school students often develop a group of friends that go out together. That usually changes to more one-on-one dating after high school. One-on-one dating can be very short-term or it can develop into long term relationships. A boyfriend or girlfriend may simply have been someone you spent a lot of time on the phone with. As you get older, you may have more interest in dating somebody one-on-one. This kind of dating tends to be less casual and more intimate. When you spend time alone with someone, you have more time to talk together and get to know one another. If you like what you discover, a few dates may be the start of a long-term romance.

MAKING A DATE

Perhaps you've just met someone at a party, and you think the two of you might make a good couple. Or maybe you've known someone for a while and it occurs to you that this could be more than a friendship. But in order to find out, someone has to make the first move—and if you wait for the other person to do it, you might wait a long time. So why not take the plunge and ask the other person out?

When asking for a date, be as clear as possible about what you're planning. Mention a specific date, time, and activity, as in "Would you like to go to the circus together on Saturday afternoon?" This gives the other person a chance to back out if watching trapeze artists isn't his or her idea of a good time. The other advantage is that a "no" answer to this question is a lot less painful than a "no" response to "Want to go out some time?" There's really no way to turn down an offer like this that isn't a rejection.

On the flip side, if someone asks you out, your job is to give a clear yes or no. You're *not* obliged to give a reason—and if your reason is that you don't like the other person, it's probably best just to say "No thanks." On the other hand, if you really would like to go out with this person, but just not on that day or for that activity, you can always propose an alternative, like "I'm busy Saturday—could we go on Sunday instead?"

Dealing With Rejection

Not every person you ask out will be interested. If you think something about your approach may be putting people off, you might try to fix it. Don't assume, though, that if someone rejects you there must be something wrong with you. Sometimes people just don't "click" together. That clicking is often called "chemistry." Some people just naturally have that special connection with someone.

STEPPING OUT

What can you expect when you go out on a date? Most dates will involve some type of activity, which could be anything from a picnic to a concert. For a first date, it's probably not a good idea to make a meal the main event. A dinner date gives you plenty of time to talk, but if you haven't been out together before, it can be hard to keep a conversation going. You might find it easier to go out for a bite to eat after a movie—you can talk about how you liked the film and let the conversation develop from there. On later dates, when you know each other better, the talk will probably flow more freely.

Remember that dating is a learning experience. It's different from your other friendships because it involves attraction and romance. Learning how to deal with those feelings is part of the maturing process. As with other kinds of friendships, the keys are respect and communication.

Who Pays?

In the past, it was customary for a man to pay when taking a woman out. Nowadays, there are no hard-and-fast rules about who pays—it can be either person, or they can split the bill. So how do you know who will pay for the evening? A good guideline is that if you did the asking, you should at least offer to pay, since you're "taking out" the other person. Then your date can either accept or offer to pay half—or offer to pay for the next date.

DID YOU KNOW?

Who's in Control? In general, the person who cares the least about a relationship controls it. By the same token, the partner who has the stronger feelings is more likely to allow the other person to dominate the relationship. Understanding the power dynamics of relationships will help you set healthy boundaries.

No Excuse For Abuse

There are some problems in a relationship that you *shouldn't* try to work out. If you're seeing someone who abuses you physically or emotionally, you can't afford to try and change the person's behavior. The best thing to do is get out–fast. If you need help, talk to family members or to a counselor. No relationship is worth the torment of abuse.

PLAYING IT SAFE

What do you do if you drop off your date at the end of the evening and you get the question, "Want to come inside for a while?" What does that mean? It could mean a lot of things—it could mean just a cup of coffee and more conversation. On the other hand, it could be something more intimate. Never put yourself in a compromising situation. Make sure your date is getting clear messages. The big message becomes NO means no in all situations.

RESISTING UNWELCOME ADVANCES

Imagine you're at a party and a person is making unwelcome advances. What do you do? As you find yourself in new social situations, you also find yourself dealing with many different people—some who choose not respect your wishes. Two options are to ignore the advances or to leave the party. You could also let the person know how you feel. It's a good idea to decide in advance how you might handle such situations. Consider the words you will use and the ways you can make your body language support your verbal message.

it's Your turn

Brainstorm ideas for dealing with unwelcome advances, then complete the following chart.

Types of Advances	Words to Use	Body Language	Actions to Take
Inappropriate touching			
Suggestive language			
Invasion of personal space			

GETTING SERIOUS

After you've been dating someone for a while, the two of you may start to think about making a commitment. There are several levels of commitment, from deciding not to date other people anymore all the way up to the lifetime commitment of marriage. What they all have in common is that they require a willingness to stick it out and work through your problems.

Whether you commit to someone else depends on what you want out of the relationship. That's something only you can decide. However, you can usually spot certain signs that a relationship is likely to work:

Shared interests.
Do you enjoy doing the same things? Would you have enough to talk about if you were seeing each other every day?

Shared values and goals.
Do you want the same things out of life? Do you see eye to eye on the basic issues that are important to you?

Mutual support.
Do you take care of each other? Does your partner make you feel special and valued?

Honesty.
Can you be yourselves when you're together? Can you talk about anything at all without worrying about being rejected or laughed at?

Freedom.
Can you accept the idea of being apart and doing things independently sometimes? Can you allow each other to have other friends and interests without feeling threatened?

Trust.
Do you trust that other person? Do you know that they will be honest, kind and caring?

QuickTip

Take Your Time
No matter how right a relationship feels, don't be in too much of a hurry to get serious. You may think after one date that this is the person you want to be with forever, but one date isn't really enough time to make that call. Give the relationship time to develop. Everyone has the ability to be on good behavior for a time—give yourself time in a relationship. We all have "warts" and there's nothing like time to bring them out!

These questions can be helpful as guidelines; following your heart is essential, but so is using your head. Using all "heart" is not a safe bet! Even if all the signs indicate you're perfect for each other, if you don't feel ready to make a commitment, trust your instincts. You have plenty of time—there's no need to rush. It's better to take things slowly than to plunge into a commitment you're not ready for.

BREAKING UP IS HARD TO DO

Listen to any radio station and you're likely to hear a song about the pain of breaking up. Unless both people grow tired of their relationship, there's pretty much no way to break up with someone that isn't going to hurt. If you simply stop returning the other person's calls, he or she could go through weeks of uncertainty, not knowing whether you're still together or not. On the other hand, if you tell the other person flat out that you don't want to go out anymore, you may be asked why—and any answer you give could hurt even more.

The best you can do is to make it as quick, clean, and honest as possible. If you're the person who initiates the break, don't let the other person drag you into weeks of discussion about what went wrong. Once you've sent a clear message that it's over, you've done all you need to do—and it'll be less painful in the long run if you don't drag it out. If you're the one being dumped, do your best to accept it without arguing or attacking the other person. Trying to cling to the relationship is unlikely to change the other person's mind, and could be humiliating.

After any breakup, give yourself some time to heal. Do whatever it takes to cope with your feelings—cry, pound your pillow, "vent" to your friends, or write in your journal. Most of all, don't get involved in a new relationship until you're over the last one. Using another person as a safety net isn't fair to either of you.

> "THERE ISN'T A WAY TO BREAK UP WITH SOMEONE THAT ISN'T GOING TO HURT... THE BEST YOU CAN DO IS TO MAKE IT AS QUICK AND CLEAN AS POSSIBLE."

See You Tomorrow

SOME OF THE PEOPLE IN YOUR LIFE, like your teachers and classmates, aren't necessarily close friends of yours. You still have to get along with them, though, because you see them every day. After you graduate, you'll have the same kinds of day-to-day relationships with coworkers and maybe with roommates as well. Keeping these relationships running smoothly will make your day-to-day life a lot less complex.

PEOPLE YOU WORK WITH

Imagine you have a coworker who's very good at his job. He shows up early and stays late, always meets his deadlines, and consistently produces high-quality

work. But this same coworker is rude and snappish with others. He interrupts in meetings, yells at his assistants, and takes all the credit for any project he works on, no matter how many other people were involved. You might respect this person's work, but you sure wouldn't like him!

If you want your coworkers to like you as well as respect you, you have to go beyond the requirements of your job. You have to be able to work *with* others, not just alongside them. Making the effort to help coworkers when they're in a jam, listen to their ideas, and give credit where it's due will earn you a reputation as a team player. Be friendly and courteous with your coworkers, but don't pry into their personal lives. Keep office chatter casual and light. Avoid gossiping or spreading rumors about people you work with. Stay away from controversial subjects like politics and religion. These are personal issues that should be respected.

The Head Honcho

Your relationship with your boss is a special case. While you should treat all your coworkers with respect, you may want to maintain a little more distance with your supervisor. You need to respect that person's authority. Accept the assignments you're given and do the best you can with them.

Different Places, Different People

Whether you're at work, school, or in the community you will meet a broader variety of people than you did during your high school years. Sometimes it's hard to accept their differences. You may not agree with how they live or understand how they think, but you'll still need to get along. Work toward maintaining your individuality and respecting theirs.

RELATING TO ROOMMATES

If you decide to live with one or more roommates, you need to learn how to share your space. Whether your roommates are friends you've known for years or people you don't know, you need to be tolerant and flexible. Spend some time together learning about likes, dislikes, and personal styles. Agree to show respect, responsibility, and honesty in your relationship.

You will also need to establish a set of "house rules" for handling certain situations. Some issues to consider include:

Chores. Who will keep the shared areas of your home clean? Will each of you be responsible for specific tasks, or will you take turns with everything?

Finances. How will you divide up the rent, phone bills, utility bills, and so on? Who will be responsible for making sure the bills get paid on time?

Food and supplies. Will you share food and supplies or each buy your own? Is it okay to eat whatever you find in the fridge, or should you have a system to identify which items belong to which roommate?

Disturbances. How late can guests stay? What about loud music? Can guests stay over?

Shared items. Who gets first crack at the bathroom, telephone, shared computer, and so on? How long is it acceptable for one person to tie these items up?

Setting ground rules ahead of time should help you avoid major problems. You probably won't be able to anticipate every possible problem, though. If awkward situations come up, talk them out—don't store up your annoyance and let it all burst out at the worst possible moment.

DID YOU KNOW?

Rooming Together

About 30 percent of men between the ages of 18 and 24, and 35 percent of women in this age group, share a home with someone other than a spouse or their parents.

Roommate Woes

WHEN BRETT AND JOEL

agreed to share an apartment, they thought it would be a great way to save money. Since they moved in, though, they've discovered that they don't agree on a lot of things. Brett likes order and tidiness while Joel is comfortable with clutter. Brett likes to go to bed early and get up early while Joel tends to be a night owl and sleep in. Brett tends to go places to meet friends while Joel likes to invite people over. They can't even agree on what to watch on TV. They're both starting to wonder if it was a mistake to move in together in the first place.

YOUR IDEAS

1. What could Brett and Joel have done to prevent these problems?

_____

_____

_____

_____

_____

_____

_____

2. Do you think Brett and Joel can resolve their differences? If so, how?

_____

_____

_____

_____

_____

_____

_____

_____

_____

On the Outs

JAYNIE AND HER BEST FRIEND ERIN are in the middle of a huge fight. Jaynie has been spending all her free time with her new boyfriend, Chris, and ignoring her friends and her schoolwork. Erin has pointed this out to Jaynie. Jaynie thinks Erin is jealous of her relationship with Chris. The girls are now at odds over a boyfriend.

Conflicts like these can come up in any relationship. Because every person has a unique set of ideas, experiences, interests, and values, no two people will ever see exactly eye to eye on everything. These differences can lead to conflict when people clash over something they both care strongly about. The more time you spend with someone, the likelier it is that sooner or later, you'll have a conflict over something.

WHY PEOPLE FIGHT

A conflict is more than a simple misunderstanding that can be cleared up with a few words. It's a clash of opposing ideas or interests. Conflicts can occur over:

- Resources. Toby wants to watch an old movie on television, but his sister wants to watch a football game. Because there's only one TV set, they end up grappling over the remote.
- Jealousy. Louise and Moira both have a crush on the same guy at work. When he asks Louise out, Moira is furious and accuses Louise of "stealing" him.
- Power. Frank and Annette have been put on the same project at work, but they can't agree over who's in charge of it. They're making no progress because every time one of them does something, the other one undoes it.
- Ideas and values. Rick and Byron are working on a class project together. Byron takes some information off the Internet—cuts and pastes it in their joint report. When Rick questions Byron's part of the report—Byron's response is "the teacher will never know—it makes our report sound really good." Should Rick accept this? Should Rick refuse to use the copied writing? Should Rick go to his teacher and discuss the problem? Byron doesn't understand why this is such a big deal.

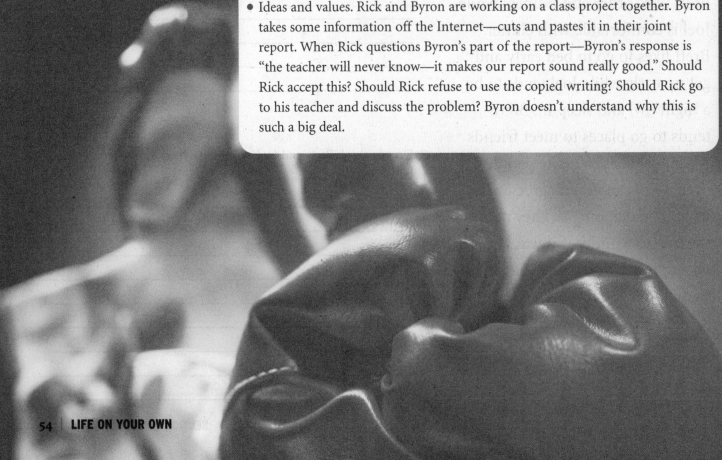

WORKING IT OUT

Obviously, it's best to avoid a conflict if you can. But if it's too late for that, the next best thing is to sit down and talk it out as calmly and rationally as possible. Start by making sure you understand what the conflict is really about. When you look at it carefully, you may find that there's more going on than meets the eye. On the surface, what may seem like a conflict over one thing may also be about another. There can be overlapping of issues.

Resolving a conflict means reaching a solution that everyone can accept. Doing this may require compromise, in which each person gives up something in exchange for something else.

With compromise, no one gets everything he or she wants, but everyone gets something. An even better result is a win-win solution, which benefits everyone involved. This is where you both come away feeling like you have won and the situation provided positive results for both of you.

QuickTip

Stay Focused

If you're trying to work through a conflict, use good communication skills. Listen to what the other person says; don't assume you know what he or she is thinking. Stick to the subject at hand and don't bring up past incidents that upset you.

How-To

Put a Relationship Back Together What if you experience a conflict that hurts a relationship you value? Use these steps if you want to put the relationship back together:

Step 1	Step 2	Step 3	Step 4	Step 5
Don't even think of sending other friends to patch up your relationship.	Instead, arrange to talk one-on-one with the person.	If that doesn't work, ask a friend with mediation skills to get involved and help you brainstorm possible solutions to the conflict.	If that doesn't work, ask a wise adult who knows you to suggest alternative approaches.	If that doesn't work, take a time-out. Maybe you both need time apart to consider the issues that caused the conflict.

STAYING CONNECTED

It's been three months since you graduated from high school, and now you're off to college in another state, hundreds of miles from home. You're excited but nervous at the same time. You're worried about losing touch with your friends and family back home and also about how you'll meet new people at school.

1. FIRST, think of all the people from home that you want to keep in touch with while you're away. On the lines below, list each person's name and relationship to you.

_____

_____

_____

_____

2. MAKE A PLAN for keeping in contact with each person on your list. Explain what method of communication you will use (e-mails, phone calls, etc.), and how often. If you plan to set a specific time for contacting someone on a regular basis, write that down too. Remember that you can—and probably should—use more than one method of communication for each person. For example, you might call your parents once a week and also visit them every two months.

Person	Method	How Often
_____	_____	_____
_____	_____	_____
_____	_____	_____
_____	_____	_____
_____	_____	_____
_____	_____	_____

3. One of the first people you'll meet at college is your new roommate. It's especially important to get along with this person, because you can't get away from each other! **EXPLAIN** how you feel about sharing living space. What actions would you take to establish a good relationship with your roommate?

_____

_____

_____

4. You and your roommate will probably want to set ground rules to help you avoid conflicts. **USE** the chart below to list the issues you need to reach an agreement on, such as noise and visitors, and what rules you would propose for each one.

Issue	Rule
_____	_____
_____	_____
_____	_____
_____	_____
_____	_____

5. After you arrive at school, you'll be meeting new people. It's easier to break the ice with new people if you think ahead about topics you could use as conversation starters. **LIST** several topics that you feel comfortable discussing. For each topic, **WRITE** one or two sentences that you could use to get a conversation started.

Topic: _____ **Conversation starter:** _____

_____

Topic: _____ **Conversation starter:** _____

_____

Topic: _____ **Conversation starter:** _____

_____

Topic: _____ **Conversation starter:** _____

_____

6. If you meet someone who interests you, how will you pursue the friendship? List possible activities you do in a college setting with someone you're just getting to know.

_____

_____

Consumer Smarts

Getting the Most for Your Money

EVERY DAY, YOU MAKE CHOICES about how to spend your money. Most of these decisions are fairly minor, like where to go for lunch or what magazine to read. Over time, though, all these little choices add up to big money—both for you and for the people you buy from.

Even if you're not feeling the money crunch now, it's likely you will once you're on your own. That's why it's so important to learn how to spend wisely. A good first step is to figure out what influences you to open up your wallet. Once you know why you choose to buy, you can learn smarter ways to shop so you can get the most out of every dollar.

WHY DO YOU BUY?

You walk into a store, lay down your money, and walk out with a CD by a hot new group. It seems so simple that you probably don't even stop to think about your reasons for buying. Did you buy the CD because you like this group, because your friends do, or because your older sister told you it was really good? Maybe you read an article about the band in a magazine or saw a poster advertising the CD at the store. As you can see, there are lots of reasons for buying something—some of them better than others.

NEEDS & WANTS

What's on the top of your list of things to buy? Perhaps you've been shopping for shoes, or maybe you're in the market for a new CD player. You've probably been in and out of stores, trying to find exactly what you want. But have you stopped to think about whether it's something you really need?

Good Choices?

Think back over the past two weeks. What were your major purchases? Why did you buy those items? Do you detect a pattern in your buying? Knowing the reasons behind your purchasing decisions can help you become a wiser consumer.

QuickTip

1, 2, 3
Keep a running list of what you need and what you want. Placing items in one category or the other will help you make your *needs* a priority. You'll also find that by the time some *wants* work their way to the top of your priority list, they won't seem so important!

In today's consumer environment, it's easy to blur the distinction between needs and wants. **NEEDS** are the basics you have to have, such as food, shelter, clothing, and transportation. **WANTS,** on the other hand, are things that you'd like to have, but that you could get along just fine without, like a new computer game.

Sometimes, one item fits into both categories. For example, you might need a jacket to keep you warm, but you might *want* the terrific $200-jacket with the designer logo. Being able to distinguish between needs and wants can help you avoid having a closet full of great clothes but no money for gas.

GOING ALONG WITH THE CROWD

Your new roommate wants to take you to a trendy store to decorate your dorm room. Your friends invite you to NBA games and concerts. You don't want to spend all your money on all this stuff, but you don't want to be left out either. So you go along with their plans, and your cash goes right along with you.

It's natural to want to fit in, but buying just to keep up your image isn't smart. You've heard about the downside of peer pressure before, but it's worth repeating: It's okay to say no! You don't have to have the same things as everyone else or go everywhere your friends go. There's nothing wrong with saying "Thanks, but no thanks." It's called being a smart consumer. If you blow all your money now on things you don't really want or need, you could be paying for those expenses for years to come.

JUST LIKE MOM

Sometimes, you choose to buy a certain product just because you're used to it. For example, maybe you always get the brand of socks that your mom buys or the toothpaste you've been using all your life. There's nothing wrong with that, of course, if it's really the brand you like best. On the other hand, maybe a different brand would be even better, or just as good and less expensive.

If you often buy things just out of habit, you might want to step outside the box and try something different. If you always buy apples in a big bag, and if some of them usually spoil before you eat them all, then buy a smaller bag next time. Break out of your routine, and you may be pleasantly surprised. If you're not, no problem—you can go back to the old standby.

DID YOU KNOW?

Do You Really Need It? The fashion industry works hard to convince you that you need new clothes every season. It's no accident that styles change radically from year to year. Don't fall into the "trend trap" of fashion and spend all your money on the latest styles. Either buy more traditional clothes that are timeless or create your own style instead.

it's Your turn

Write down five items you buy just out of habit. For each, list an alternative that might save you money:

I ALWAYS BUY

1. _____
2. _____
3. _____
4. _____
5. _____

I COULD TRY

1. _____
2. _____
3. _____
4. _____
5. _____

The Power of Ads

IF YOU THINK THAT ADS don't have much influence on you, take a closer look at the things you buy. Why did you grab that particular bottle of soda at the convenience store? Maybe you'd tried it before and liked it, but what about the first time you tried it? How did you even know that brand existed? Chances are, somewhere, sometime, you saw an ad for it.

Does that mean you're a fool for falling for an ad? Not at all! Advertising can be a useful way to learn about new products and services. The trick is to remember that ads all have one specific goal: to persuade you to open your wallet. This means that you have to view ads with a critical eye. Don't assume that a product must be terrific just because everyone in the ad seems to love it. Instead, think about whether it's really something that you want.

Is It an Ad?

Advertisers have clever ways of disguising their ads. Television infomercials, for example, appear to be regular talk shows—but the talkers are being paid to push a product. Magazine ads may look like regular articles—but the statement "Paid Advertisement" in fine print at the bottom of the page tells you otherwise. Recognizing ads in disguise is an important consumer skill to develop.

DID YOU KNOW?

Ad Revenues If it weren't for advertising, many magazines, newspapers, commercial television stations, and other media would not be able to operate. The revenue from advertisers enables these companies to provide information and entertainment at little or no cost to consumers. In general, the larger the audience for a publication or program, the more advertisers must pay.

HOW THEY SELL

Try to remember the last commercial you saw on TV. Can you remember what it was selling? If you can't remember, then it wasn't a good ad! One goal of an advertisement is to make you remember the product or service it's selling. Another is to make you think positively about a product so that you'll be more likely to buy it.

Advertisers know that feelings rather than facts drive many consumer decisions. That's why they create ads that appeal to your emotions. Here are some ways they do that:

Feel-good approach. These ads try to give the impression that using their product will make you happy, smart, beautiful, or popular.

Bandwagon approach. These ads try to convince you that everyone is using a certain product and you should "jump on the bandwagon" if you don't want to be left out.

Popularity promise. Ads for clothing or accessories might suggest that you'll fit in with a particular group and be more popular if you use their product.

Fear of rejection. Ads for deodorants or for breath fresheners may prey upon your fear of being embarrassed when on a date or out with friends.

Traditional values. Ads showing images of happy families hope to appeal to people who embrace traditional values.

DID YOU KNOW?

Yes I Really Use It!

There are rules governing endorsements. A celebrity who claims to use a product, for example, must actually use it. A so-called expert who endorses a product must have credentials to back up his or her expertise. Advertisers are not, however, required to reveal how much they pay the endorsers—or how many free products they give them.

Many ads feature images of beautiful people, gorgeous scenery, or cute animals. What do these images have to do with the products being sold? Often times, nothing at all—but the advertisers hope that the ad will create a link in your mind between these positive images and the product they are promoting. That way, you'll feel good about the product without even knowing why.

Have you ever seen a sports star advertising a certain brand of sneaker? Endorsements—statements from people about how much they like a particular product or service—are a popular advertising technique. Some of the people are ordinary consumers. More often, though, they are celebrities, being paid big bucks to promote the product or service.

TRICKS OF THE TRADE

You know that ads try to play on your emotions, but a few cross the line from manipulative into just plain misleading. Watch out for these sneaky tricks:

Bait and switch.

A seller advertises a product at a great price. This is the "bait" to get you into the store, where you hear that the sale item is sold out. The store then tries to convince you to "switch" to a more expensive product.

"Introductory" pricing.

The ad offers a service at an "introductory" cost. What it doesn't mention is that the price will shoot up after the first few months.

Not-so-free gifts.

An ad promises a "free gift," but then you find that you must buy something else to get it.

Phony sales.

The ad offers a great "sale" price that's actually just the same as the regular price.

Hidden catches.

An ad offers a great deal, but when you check it out, you find out there area a lot of extra charges and restrictions that the ad somehow forgot to mention.

Discount Delight

The ad reads 10, 20, or even 50 percent off. Does the offer apply only to certain items or to everything in the store? Is the discount taken off the item's original price, or its sale price? Get the details!

it's Your turn

Raise your awareness of advertising techniques. Watch TV and choose five ads to analyze. Complete the chart below. In the final column record your judgment of the ad as a useful tool for consumers.

Name of advertiser	Product or service	Advertising technique used	Overall judgment

It's Free

"Buy one, get one free," says the ad. Before you rise to the bait, compare prices. If an item's overpriced to start with, it's not such a bargain. And maybe you don't really need two large bottles of mayonnaise!

So Many Stores, So Little Time

WHAT'S YOUR FAVORITE WAY to shop? Do the salespeople at your favorite department store know you by name, or are you an online auction junkie? Maybe you love to page through catalogs or browse through the racks at local thrift shops. There are lots of different places to shop, each with its own advantages and disadvantages. Here's the scoop on some of your shopping options:

Store type	Selection	Service	Prices
Department store	Wide variety of goods, usually with several brands and models to choose from	Full service; may include services such as alterations	Vary by store, from upscale to discount
Specialty shop	One type of merchandise, such as clothing or music; there may be only a few brands in the store	Salespeople are usually knowledgeable about the store's products	May be higher than at other stores
Discount store	Nationally advertised brands available at reduced prices	Stores are less elaborate; customer service is minimal	May be significantly lower than other stores
Close-out store	Stores receive single batches of a product; once it's sold, they may not receive more	Varies by store	Lower than average
Factory outlet	Merchandise from one manufacturer sold at reduced prices; some goods may be slightly damaged, imperfect, or discontinued	Stores often located in outlet malls; returns may be restricted	Usually lower than average
Warehouse club	Wide range of products; selection of brands may be limited; many products sold in bulk	Stores open only to members; customer service very limited	Prices often very low, but members must pay a yearly fee
Second-hand store and thrift shop	Previously used items such as clothing or furniture, often donated to the store; selection and sizes are usually limited	Varies by store; money from sales may go to charity	Much cheaper than new merchandise

SHOPPING FROM HOME

Suppose that a book you've been waiting months for is finally published. You could go to the mall, fight your way through the crowds, and hope that there's still a copy left—or you could just use your computer to arrange to have a copy delivered to your home, and be done in ten minutes.

You can shop from home by telephone or mail, as well by using the Internet. The chart below compares the pros and cons of shopping from home.

Advantages	Disadvantages
You don't need to travel to a store.	You can't see, handle, or try on items.
You don't have to fight your way through crowds or find a spot in a parking lot.	You have to pay extra for shipping and handling.
The selection of goods is often larger and may include hard-to-find items.	You may have to wait anywhere from a few days to a few weeks for delivery.
In many cases, you can order at any time, day or night.	If you're not satisfied, you may need to pay an extra shipping fee to return the item.
You can compare prices from many sources more easily, making it easier to find the best deals.	The ease of shopping makes you likelier to be tempted into impulse purchases—things you didn't plan to buy.

If you decide that the benefits of shopping from home outweigh the drawbacks, make sure that the company you're dealing with is trustworthy. If you're not familiar with a particular seller, try talking to other people who have dealt with the company before. If you're shopping online, be absolutely certain that the Web site is secure before you type in your credit card number. The letters "shttp" or "https" in the Web address at the top of your screen, and the little padlock icon at the bottom, tell you that the site is secure. You may also want to check on the company's privacy policy to make sure they won't give your personal information to anyone else. (You'll read more about privacy issues later in this section.)

DID YOU KNOW?

Security Blanket Giving out your credit card information over the Internet may be safer than handing your card to a cashier in a store—provided you use secure sites. These sites use special software that encodes your information during transmission. That way, if outside parties intercept it, they can't read it.

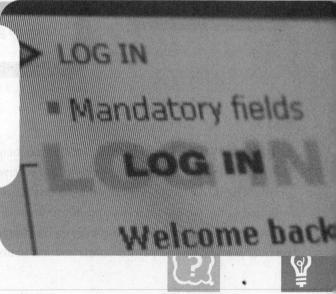

QuickTip

Going, Going, Sold!

You can find some great deals at online auction sites, but be careful! The things you buy usually can't be returned. Read the item description extra carefully, and contact the seller if you have any questions. Before you place a bid, check out the seller's feedback rating to make sure you're dealing with a reliable person. Make sure you understand the auction rules. Once you place a bid, you can't take it back, so don't get carried away in the excitement of the auction and bid more than you can afford.

When shopping from home, study the pictures and descriptions of the items you want to buy to make sure you know what you're getting. If you have questions, contact the seller by phone or e-mail. Also, check out the terms of sale. You should find out about the cost, delivery options, warranties, and how to reach the company if there's a problem. You should also make sure that you can return the items you're buying. Remember, a picture doesn't tell you how something looks close up, or how well it works. If the item isn't returnable, think long and hard before buying it. It may not be as good a deal as it seems.

Speaking of deals, be sure to take shipping and handling costs into account when you compare prices. You may find that the low price you find online is really higher than the price at a nearby store when you add shipping and handling.

GETTING IT USED

If you're looking for some real bargains, consider buying things secondhand. Something that cost $100 when it was new might sell two years later for only $25, and it might still be in perfectly good shape. You can find used items in thrift stores, secondhand shops, and antique stores. Other sources of used merchandise include:

Yard sales and garage sales. People hold these sales outside their homes to get rid of items that they no longer need.

Flea markets. People rent tables at these markets to sell new or used goods at low prices.

Estate sales. Much like garage sales but usually are described that way if the sale incorporates all the household goods.

Auctions. People place bids on used items, and the highest bidder takes the item home. Online auction sites work in a similar way, except that items usually take several days to sell instead of a few minutes.

Classified ads. Most newspapers include a "For sale" section in which people can advertise items that they want to sell.

DID YOU KNOW?

Online Payment Services Online payment services enable individuals and businesses to easily send and receive payments online. The buyer has the security that its credit card information is supplied to the payment service and not to the seller. The seller has the security of knowing he or she will receive payment. Using the services is a safe way to pay for online auction items.

When you buy things secondhand, you're not just getting a bargain—you're also helping the environment. By taking a used item off someone's hands, you're extending its life and keeping it out of a landfill. Also, since making new items uses up raw material and energy, you're conserving these resources when you buy something used.

Secondhand shopping does require extra work, however. Items that have been used before may be damaged, so you should inspect them very carefully to make sure they're still usable. If you don't discover a problem until you get the item home, it's probably too late—the seller is unlikely to let you return it.

On the other hand, you shouldn't be put off too much by small flaws. If you find a shirt that's missing a button, there's a good chance you'll be able to find a new, matching button to replace it. Even if you have to replace all the buttons, you'll probably still spend less than you would have spent on a new shirt.

How-To

Buying Secondhand. Buying secondhand is different from buying new. You're usually dealing with an ordinary human being rather than a company, and you probably won't be able to return the item once you pay for it. Follow these steps when buying a secondhand item.

Step 1	Step 2	Step 3	Step 4	Step 5
Do your research. Check the ads and find out what is a reasonable price for the item you want to purchase.	Inspect the item carefully. If it is an electrical appliance, ask if you can use an outlet so that you can switch it on. If it is an item of clothing, check for stains or tears.	Ask the seller what the selling price is. If it's more than you want to pay, ask if the price is negotiable. If it is, proceed to the next step. If it is not, decide if you want to pay the asking price. If not, walk away.	If the price is negotiable, offer what you consider to be a reasonable price. Say something like, "Would you accept ... for it?" Try to reach an agreement.	Pay for the item. With most secondhand purchases, you have to pay cash.

DID YOU KNOW?

Treasure Hunting Sometimes, it's possible to get something for nothing. In many towns, it's perfectly legal for residents to put unwanted items out on the sidewalk for others to take. You can take home useful stuff from the "sidewalk market" without paying one cent! (If you're not sure that something is really a throwaway, knock on the door and ask the homeowner.)

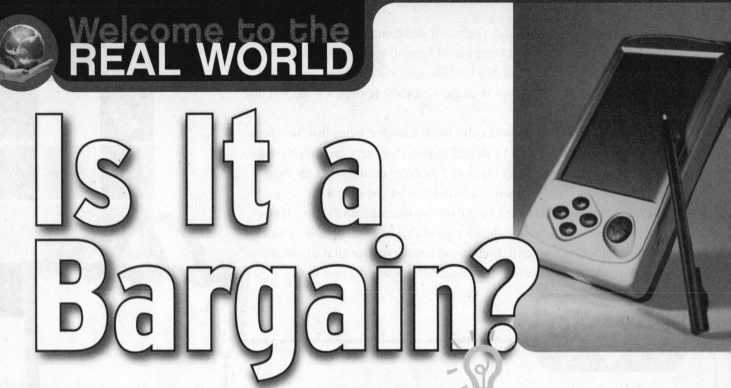

Is It a Bargain?

JACK'S NEW JOB as a sales rep requires a lot of travel. Every day he calls on six or more customers, in different locations. He decides to make his life easier by buying a PDA (Personal Digital Assistant). The electronic device will fit in his pocket and will allow him to keep all his contact information in one place. Jack does some research and discovers that PDAs are expensive! A good one with all the latest features costs more than Jack can afford, but he's not sure about buying a cheaper model. He mentions his dilemma to Carson, his roommate. Next thing he knows, Carson is on the phone talking to his parents. It turns out that they bought PDAs a couple of years ago, and while his mother uses hers all the time, his father does not and would be willing to sell it to Jack.

YOUR IDEAS

1. What factors does Jack need to take into account when deciding whether to buy the secondhand PDA?

_____

_____

_____

_____

_____

_____

_____

_____

_____

_____

_____

2. If you were Jack, how would you handle this situation? Why?

_____

_____

_____

_____

_____

_____

_____

_____

_____

_____

_____

_____

_____

Getting the Best Deal

WITH SO MANY SHOPPING OPTIONS, how can you make sure you get the most for your money? The key to successful shopping is to do some comparison shopping. Comparison shopping means more than comparing prices—that's just one part of it. You also need to compare features to make sure that you get the best quality for the dollars you spend. This is especially important when you shop for things you don't know much about. Consider trying these ways to gather information:

Talk about it.

Ask friends or family for recommendations. They might know which stores have the best selection or the best prices for the items you want. Checking out other peoples' recommendations can be especially helpful when you need to choose someone to provide a service.

Read the label.

Labels give information about a product such as ingredients (food and cosmetics), nutritional values (food), care instructions (clothes) or operating instructions (electronics). Always read labels carefully. For big purchases such as electronic gear, ask to see the user's manual as well. It gives much more information than the features listed on the box.

And the experts say...

Consumer publications such as *Consumer Reports* give detailed information on products that they have tested. Everything from cars to computers to cell phones to credit cards are evaluated and compared. These articles and reports are a great jumping-off point when researching which products to buy. They also help you know what questions to ask as you evaluate your options.

Navigating the Net.

The Internet offers a wealth of information on products and services. However, be alert for false or incorrect information. Check out the source of the information to separate facts from opinions. For product details, check manufacturers' Web sites.

In the news.

The news media—radio, television, Web sites, magazines, and newspapers—carry special features for the consumer. You'll find information on existing products and on new ones being developed. You'll also find reports about products on the market that are defective and have been recalled.

And those ads.

Remember to use ads to your advantage, rather than let them use you. Some ads provide useful information that helps you compare features in competing products.

SHOPPING MAVEN

Do you know someone who always seems to find bargains and pay less for purchases than you do? If so, you know a skilled consumer who understands how to work the system. As you read about smart shopping strategies below, identify the ones you use.

Shop the sales. Many retailers hold end-of-season and holiday sales events. You can get good bargains at sales, provided you keep a level head. It would be great to get 50 percent off that jacket you've had your eye on—but does it make sense to buy it at the end of the season? Make sure you really want any item that you buy on sale because you may not be able to return it. Also, notice which items are not on sale. Retailers hope that you'll also buy regular-priced merchandise when you shop the sales.

Use coupons. Some coupons enable you to get a percentage off the price of certain products. Others give you, say, "20 percent off any item in the store." You can find coupons in newspapers and magazines, in the mail, and on the Internet. Smart shoppers use coupons to buy items that they had planned to buy, but don't let coupons persuade them to make unplanned purchases.

DID YOU KNOW?

Are You Tempted?

You're walking through a department store, and there, right in the middle of the aisle, is a display of colorful T-shirts with a "50%" off sign. Of course you're tempted. And that's exactly what the store planned. It's no accident that enticing displays are placed where you can't miss them. Just as it's no accident that candy is placed near the checkout counters in supermarkets. A lot of effort goes into attempts to tempt shoppers!

Take advantage of rebate offers. Some manufacturers offer rebates, or refunds, on products such as appliances and electronic goods. To receive the rebate, you must complete a form and mail it to the manufacturer with proof of purchase. If you follow the directions, you should receive a check in the mail.

DON'T BE IMPULSIVE!

Are you one of those people who go into a store for one item and come out with six—mostly things you really don't need and can't afford? Retailers have many ways of tempting you to buy things you don't want, but smart shoppers know how to resist impulse purchases. Your best defense is to plan your purchases. Make a list before you go shopping, and stick to your list. If you see something that you hadn't planned to buy, but that looks like a real bargain, go away and think about it. Don't buy it on impulse. Return to the store later if you still want it.

SHOPPING FOR SERVICES

Consumers spend money on a wide range of services ranging from haircuts and dry cleaning to car repair and Internet service. Shopping for services is a little more complicated than shopping for goods. Here's why:

- You can't see what you are buying. You can't touch it or compare to other similar items.
- You may not be able to compare prices. A car mechanic, for example, may not be able to give you a price for a repair job until he actually does the job and assesses the damage.
- It's hard to know what quality of service you will receive. If you get estimates from two different carpenters, for example, how do you know who will do the better job?
- Buying goods is usually a simple transaction. Buying services may involve getting recommendations, estimates, references, and contracts.
- If you're not satisfied with a product, you can usually return it. You can't return, or undo, unsatisfactory services. In some cases, you can insist that the service is redone (dry cleaning is a good example).

For these reasons, it's worth doing some careful research when shopping for services—especially services that will cost a lot of money. You may not want to spend much time researching hairdressers; a bad haircut will grow out in a matter of weeks. But the same is not true of services such as painting, carpentry, or carpet installation: You may have to live with the results for years!

QuickTip

Use Your Network

A quick e-mail message can help you find good service providers—and avoid bad ones. If you need a service, send an e-mail to friends and relatives who might have useful experience. Just write something like, "I'm looking for a [fill in the blank]. Any recommendations? Anyone I should avoid?"

> "IT'S WORTH DOING SOME CAREFUL RESEARCH WHEN SHOPPING FOR SERVICES ... YOU MAY HAVE TO LIVE WITH THE RESULTS FOR YEARS!"

Choosing a

IF YOU HAVE A CELL PHONE, you probably know that it's worth shopping around for the best deal. But with so many options and plans to choose from, how do you decide which is the best deal for you? Here's how you go about comparison shopping.

FIRST, some facts you need to know:

- Most cell phone companies offer local, regional, and national plans. Each type is based on a designated calling area.
- If you make or receive calls from outside your designated area, you may be billed additional roaming charges.
- Many cell phone plans charge more for calls at peak calling times.
- Some plans allow you to prepay for a certain number of minutes instead of signing a contract for services. Are any plans offering a special deal?

NOW ask yourself these questions:

1. Who are the people I call most often?

_____
_____
_____
_____
_____

2. What percentage of my calls will be local? _____
Regional? _____
Nationwide? _____

3. Which companies provide service in the areas that I call regularly?

_____
_____
_____
_____
_____

Cell Phone Plan

NEXT determine if you need a local, regional, or national plan. Choose three companies that provide cell phone service in your area. Use the Internet or contact local service centers to find out about their plans and rates. Complete the chart to help you compare plans.

COMPARING CELL PHONE PROVIDERS

Type of Plan Selected	Provider A:	Provider B:	Provider C:
Monthly fee			
Number of minutes included in plan			
Charges for going over alloted minutes			
Additional charges and fees			
Special features of the plan			

Which provider would you choose?

_____

Explain why.

_____

_____

_____

_____

_____

_____

_____

HOW DO YOU CHOOSE?

There is a difference between choosing goods and services. Because you can't compare services in the same way that you can compare products, or goods, you need a different system for choosing any service provider. Here are some suggestions:

Get estimates. Once you've narrowed down your choices, ask the providers on your shortlist for written estimates. The estimates should list the tasks to be done, and the charge for providing the service. Compare the estimates carefully, making sure that they all include the same items.

Check qualifications. Make sure the person has the necessary training and experience, is licensed to do the work, and carries the required insurance. You can do this in a personal interview. An experienced service provider should have no problem producing the necessary documents.

Ask for references. Ask for the names of people the provider has worked for. Talk to several of them about the service they received and their overall satisfaction. Find out if there were any problems and, if so, how they were resolved.

Get recommendations. Don't choose blindly from the Yellow Pages. Ask around. If friends and family can't recommend a particular type of service provider, they will know someone who can.

Study the paperwork. For major service work you will receive a work order or a contract. You should study the paperwork carefully and make sure you understand everything in it before you sign. Once you sign, you commit to having the work done.

it's Your turn

Write down four kinds of services you might need to buy in the next few months. Beside each one, note the names of people you might ask for recommendations.

SERVICE	USEFUL CONTACTS

GETTING THE MOST FOR YOUR SERVICE DOLLARS

Once you choose a service provider, you want to make sure that you receive the best value for your money. The key to getting good service is good communication. Make sure you understand the process the provider will follow. If you don't understand something, ask. If there's a problem, work with the provider to find a solution. If you're not satisfied with some aspect of the service, explain what bothers you.

Make an effort to build a good business relationship with the provider. If you take an interest in the service you are buying, and show respect for the service provider's expertise, the provider will be more likely to make an extra effort if needed. Look at it this way: say you are a carpenter and have two customers who want you to work over a weekend. One customer always treats you with respect and shows appreciation for your skill and workmanship. The other one never seems to be satisfied and is always ready to criticize everything you do. Which one would you choose to work for?

Of course, if you are not satisfied with the service that you receive from someone, you should contact the provider and discuss the problem. Remember that service providers need repeat business and they need customers who will recommend them to others. Most will therefore make an effort to resolve a problem.

How-To

Evaluating a Service Evaluating a service means more than simply judging the end result. You can take steps along the way to determine if this is someone you would recommend to others.

Step 1	Step 2	Step 3	Step 4
Evaluate the relationship. Is this person pleasant to work with? Does he or she explain what is going on and keep you in the picture?	Evaluate the process. Does the provider work efficiently? Are you satisfied with the rate of progress? Does the provider stay on schedule? Does he or she have the right tools and equipment?	Evaluate the cost. Does the provider bring the job in at or under the originally estimated cost? If not, is there a good reason for the additional cost? Do you feel that you're getting value for money?	Evaluate the end result. Does it meet your expectations? Is the quality satisfactory? Would you work with this provider again?

QuickTip

The Incredible Vanishing Paycheck

Never go to a payday loan office to arrange a loan—the places that offer to give you money before you receive your paycheck. You could wind up paying 500 percent interest, in addition to the amount you borrowed!

Dollars & Sense

When you buy a product or service, you need to decide how to pay for it. The most common payment options are cash, debit cards, checks, credit cards, or a loan. These options are discussed in more detail in Section 4. Here's a summary of what they entail:

Cash is the simplest form of payment. Using cash can also help you keep your spending in check. However, you may not always have enough cash available to pay for big-ticket items.

A **debit card** is the closest thing to cash. The amount of the purchase is deducted from your bank account. If there's not enough money in your account to cover a purchase, your card will be refused or you will be charged a fee just like bouncing a check.

With **credit card** offers everywhere, it's easy to take buying now and paying later for granted. What the offers don't really stress is that you pay interest on any amount you don't pay in full when your credit card statement arrives. With unpaid balances and new purchases, the "real" cost of your purchases adds up fast. If you pay only the minimum balance each month, it could take years to pay off your balance. Credit card debt is one of the top financial problems teens and young adults face. If you don't have the willpower to use credit wisely, stick to cash and checks.

When you write a **check**, the money is deducted from your checking account balance once the merchant deposits it in the bank. Never write a check for more than you have in your account. It's illegal.

DID YOU KNOW?

You can use your **debit card** for both online and offline transactions. With online transactions, you enter your PIN number (supplied by the bank) into a keypad and the money is deducted from your account immediately. With offline transactions, you sign a receipt, just as you would with a credit card, and the money is deducted from your account within one to three days.

A **loan** is another form of credit. You agree to pay interest for a set amount of time (months or years) in addition to the amount borrowed. If you don't make your payments on time you can lose the item you purchased and also risk ruining your credit history. Read more about managing your finances in Section 4.

> "CREDIT CARD DEBT IS ONE OF THE TOP FINANCIAL PROBLEMS TEENS AND YOUNG ADULTS FACE."

Returns & Exchanges

HAVE YOU EVER TRIED TO RETURN AN ITEM to a store, only to be told that the store gives store credit only? That's fine if it's a store that you use often. But what if you're on vacation and unlikely to visit that store again? Then you may end up buying something you don't want, simply so that you can use the credit.

If you need to return or exchange an item because it doesn't fit, is missing parts, or just doesn't work, follow these tips:

Check a store's **return policy** *before* you buy. Is there a time limit on returns? Would you get cash back or credit toward another purchase? If you buy an item labeled "as is" or at a sale marked "all sales final," then you can't take it back.

Save your **receipts**. Get in the habit of filing them. You never know when you may need one. Saving receipts will also help you track your expenditures.

Some stores require that certain items (electronics, for example) be returned in their **original packaging**. If you buy an item that comes in a box, save the box.

Be **polite** and **patient**. You may need to visit several counters before completing the return.

If the salesperson is unreasonable about the return or exchange, don't argue. Ask to speak to a **manager**.

QuickTip

Storing Boxes

No room to store those large boxes that your computer and television came in? Break down the boxes, fold them flat, and store them under your bed. You can always tape a box back together when you need it.

Rules for Returning Clothes

When you buy clothes, *don't remove the labels* until you're positive you want to keep them. Leaving the labels attached proves that you did not wear a garment before deciding to return it. Some stores will not allow customers to return clothing from which the labels have been removed.

Returning an Item

SUSI BOUGHT THE BLUE

shirt, even though it was expensive, because it went perfectly with the jacket and pants she had just bought for her job interviews. The first time she washed it, she carefully followed the instructions on the label. When she put it on the next day she was horrified to discover that it had shrunk. She could no longer do up the buttons; it was too short; it looked awful.

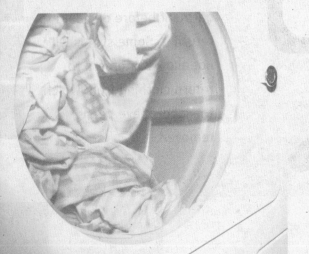

YOUR IDEAS

1. If you were Susi, what would you do next?

_____
_____
_____
_____
_____
_____

2. How would you prepare for returning the defective item?

_____
_____
_____
_____
_____

2. What arguments would you give for getting a refund?

_____
_____
_____
_____
_____
_____
_____

Understanding Warranties

MANY PURCHASES COME WITH A WARRANTY—a manufacturer's written promise to repair or replace a product if it doesn't work as claimed. Check any warranty before you buy. Some warranties apply only to certain parts of the product or only under specific conditions. For example, the parts on your computer may be covered by the warranty, but the labor to fix it may not.

If you make a purchase that comes with a warranty, follow the directions. You might have to mail in a card or register at a Web site to activate the warranty. You should then keep the warranty information, along with the receipt, in a safe place. To be able to make a claim against the warranty, you must use the product only as directed, and follow any suggested maintenance procedures.

When you buy an item such as a car, major appliance or a computer, you may be asked if you would like to buy an extended warranty—an agreement that offers additional coverage beyond what is included in the regular warranty. Study the terms of the extended warranty carefully before deciding whether to spend the extra money. If you are buying a reputable product, you probably won't need any additional warranty coverage.

Limited and Full Warranty

Take the time to read a warranty carefully to determine whether you're getting a limited or full warranty. A limited warranty may limit the terms of the warranty to the original owner of the product only, may not cover the full cost of any needed repair, and may not cover replacement of a defective product. A full warranty is more comprehensive and gives better protection.

DID YOU KNOW?

You're Covered Anyway If you buy a product that does not come with a written warranty, you may be covered anyway. The law states that products come with an **IMPLIED WARRANTY**. The implication is that a product must do what it is intended to do. Thus, if you buy a clock radio and discover that the clock does not keep good time, the seller is obliged to replace it or give you a refund, even if there is no written warranty.

When You Have a Consumer Problem

You take your car to the repair shop because it keeps stalling out, but two days after it is repaired you experience the same problem again. You buy a set of bookshelves that you must assemble yourself, but when you start to assemble it you discover that some of the parts are missing. You order a sweater from a Web site, but when it arrives it's not the color you requested. How do you handle problems like this?

The way you handle a consumer complaint depends on the problem. In general, you need to be able to explain what the problem is, produce your receipt, and decide how you want the problem resolved. Then you're ready to take action.

If your complaint is about a service, as in the case of the car repair, you would talk to the person who did the repair. If it's about an item you bought at a store, like the bookshelves, you would speak to the salesperson who sold you the item. For purchases made on the Internet or by telephone, you might have to send an e-mail or make a phone call. The Web site where you bought the sweater, for example, would probably provide instructions for dealing with problems.

No matter what method you use, you should be polite. Even though you may be annoyed, there's no point taking it out on the person you are dealing with. Just state the problem clearly and explain how you would like it to be resolved. In most cases, you'll find that merchants will do everything in their power to correct the problem. After all, it's in their interest to have satisfied customers.

it's Your turn

Explain how you would deal with the three problems cited above. Who would you contact? How would you make the contact? What would you say? Use the spaces below for your answers.

CONSUMER PROBLEM	HOW TO DEAL WITH IT
Unsatisfactory car repair	
Incomplete bookshelves	
Wrong color sweater	

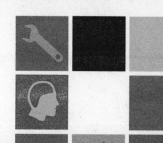

KEEP GOOD RECORDS

If you make a complaint by e-mail, save the messages you send and any that you receive in reply. If you complain by phone or in person, make detailed notes about the conversation, including the date, the person you spoke to, and what was said. That way, if you do not receive a satisfactory response to your problem, you have a record of all that has transpired.

PUT IT IN WRITING

If your initial attempts to resolve a problem don't work, you can write a formal letter of complaint. Address it to the store manager, service manager, or customer service department—whoever is relevant to your case. In your letter explain what the problem is, what steps you have taken so far to try to resolve it, and how you want the situation to be resolved. Enclose copies of your receipt and any other documents that support your case.

If you don't receive a response, write again and send a copy of your letter to the Better Business Bureau. If that doesn't work, you might choose to take legal action, but that should be a last resort.

How-To

Let's Negotiate There will be times in your life when you need to negotiate with someone to resolve a consumer problem. Understanding the steps in the negotiation process will help things go more smoothly.

Step 1	Step 2	Step 3	Step 4	Step 5
Identify the problem. Often people argue, not realizing they're talking about two different issues.	Take turns stating your concerns about the problem. Stay focused on the problem and don't make things personal!	Suggest solutions, considering both sides of the problem.	Discuss the possible solution to see if both sides can agree on one. If not, brainstorm additional solutions.	Agree to try the chosen solution. Make adjustments as needed.

Recognizing Fraud

IT'S A SAD FACT OF LIFE THAT FRAUD—dishonest behavior for personal gain—has been around for centuries. Only the methods have changed to keep up with modern technology. Millions of people become victims of fraud every year. To make sure you don't become one of them, be on the lookout for these kinds of deceitful practices:

Telemarketing fraud. Cunning "telemarketers" persuade victims to buy expensive products or services or to invest in schemes that will pay huge dividends. The victims send money but receive nothing in return.

Charity fraud. Preying upon human kindness, deceitful people ask for contributions to a charity, but keep the money for themselves.

Credit card scams. You get a call or an e-mail from someone who claims to be from a financial institution and who needs to verify your credit card information. What the person is actually doing is stealing that information. Banks never ask for such information by telephone.

Work-at-home scams. You see an ad that promises good wages for simple work that you can do at home. You must send a check to cover the cost of the start-up materials. The materials never arrive.

WARNING SIGNS

You can protect yourself from fraud by looking for warning signs. Be suspicious, for example, if a company or individual won't give a physical mailing address. A legitimate company would have offices somewhere. And don't be fooled by high-pressure tactics that suggest that an offer is good for "today only." Don't send money to anyone who asks you to pay up front for information about a money-making opportunity. Trust your instincts: if it seems too good to be true, it almost certainly is!

Check the Net

Check the Net

Fraud is a serious problem. Go online and find out how you can help combat fraud and file complaints about it.
KeyTerms: Federal Trade Commission, National Fraud Information Center, Internet fraud

DID YOU KNOW?

The Federal Trade Commission (FTC) has developed a new method of combating fraud and educating the public. It has posted fake sites on the Web that promise miracle products or terrific money-making opportunities. If you click on one of these sites you may be disappointed but wiser—instead of learning of a get-rich-quick scheme you read a warning about fraud.

Protecting Your Privacy

As a consumer, you give out personal information in many situations. When you open a bank account, apply for a credit card, or fill out a form on a Web site, you provide information about yourself and your finances. Companies can even gather information about you based on the Web sites you visit. In the practice known as online profiling, these companies use cookies, small files stored on your computer, to record information about you. They use that information to tailor online advertising to your interests.

Many consumers are concerned about giving out personal information, and about how that information is used. They don't want other companies to know about their purchasing habits. They don't want to be bombarded with catalogs and e-mails about gardening just because they bought gardening tools from a Web site. In other words, they want to protect their privacy.

Fortunately, the government is on your side. It has introduced laws requiring all companies involved in financial activities to send their customers privacy notices. The notices explain company policy regarding customer privacy, and give you the right to opt out of having your information shared with others. In general, if you don't opt out, the company will assume that it can share your information.

Health Care Privacy

Concern about consumer privacy extends to health care too. The Health Insurance Portability and Accountability Act, known as HIPPA, includes safeguards to protect the security and confidentiality of patient information. It requires health care companies to use secure systems for transmitting patient information and forbids the disclosure of some health information without the patient's authorization.

The Opt-in Option

Some companies have an opt-in policy. They agree not to send you e-mails or promotional materials unless you opt in, or specifically give your consent. If you choose to opt in, and then change your mind later, you can always opt out again.

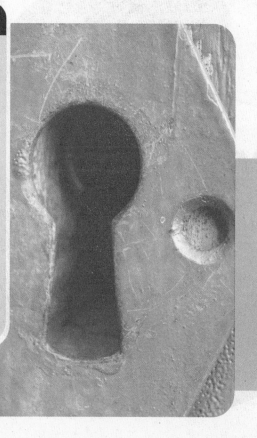

PREVENTING IDENTITY THEFT

One reason consumers are concerned about their privacy is that they fear identity theft—the illegal use of their personal information by a complete stranger. Identity theft begins when someone gains access to information such as your name, social security number, date of birth, credit card number, PIN number, and so on.

How does this happen? Identity thieves might steal your wallet or purse containing credit cards, steal your mail (lots of personal information there), or retrieve discarded papers from your garbage. They might watch over your shoulder when you use an ATM, steal personal information from the Internet, or use a number of other methods to gain information. Once they have the information, they might use your credit card to run up charges, open new credit card accounts in your name, and generally cause financial havoc for you. Victims of identity theft sometimes spend years setting the record straight.

To avoid identify theft take these precautions:

- Don't give out your **SOCIAL SECURITY NUMBER** unless you must, and then only to people or organizations you know you can trust.
- When you need to give personal and financial information over the Internet, check that you're at a **SECURE SITE**.
- **TEAR UP OR SHRED** bank statements, credit card statements, and any other documents that might contain account numbers and/or your Social Security number before you throw them away. Cut up expired credit cards.

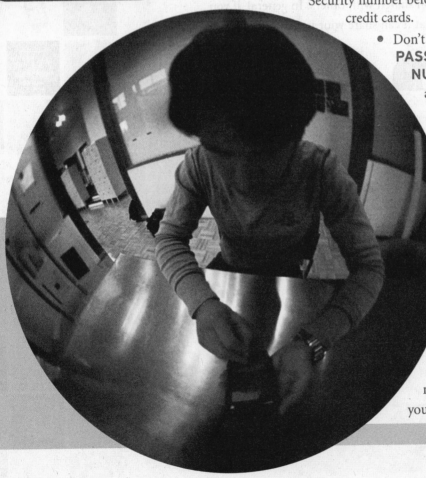

- Don't tell anyone your computer or online **PASSWORD**. Don't tell anyone the **PIN NUMBER** for your debit card. If you're afraid of forgetting the number and must write it down, keep it in a separate place from the card.
- Make sure no one is watching you when you use an **ATM**. Likewise, be aware of your surroundings when you use your **CELL PHONE**. Don't give out personal information by phone when somebody might overhear you.

If you ever suspect that your identity has been stolen you will need to act immediately. Your first steps should be to contact the police, your bank, and your credit card companies. They will advise you on the actions your should take next.

QuickTip

Keep a List

Be prepared for identity theft. Keep a list of account numbers from credit card companies, banks, and other financial service providers in a safe place at home. That way, if you become a victim of identity theft you can quickly call the companies and providers to stop action on your account.

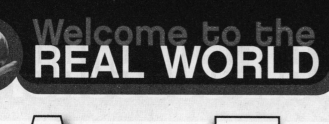

Welcome to the REAL WORLD

An Easy Target

IT ONLY TOOK A SECOND.

Tina put her purse down by her feet as she tried on hats in the store. When she went to pick it up, it had gone. The store manager was very helpful. He called the police and suggested that while Tina was waiting for them to arrive she list the contents of her purse. Here's what Tina listed: $60 in cash; checkbook; debit card; bank credit card; four store credit cards; gasoline credit card; Social Security card; driver's license. When the police arrived and questioned her, she admitted that she also kept the PIN number for her debit card written on a small piece of paper in her purse.

YOUR IDEAS

1. What made Tina an easy target for an identity thief?

_____
_____
_____
_____
_____

2. What changes should she make to the items she keeps in her purse?

_____
_____
_____
_____
_____

3. Based on what you learned in this exercise, what changes should you make to the way you store your personal documents?

_____
_____
_____
_____
_____

PUTTING IT ALL TOGETHER

WHAT'S THE BEST BUY?

You're moving into a new place and need to make some significant purchases, including a microwave, a mattress, and a TV. Your budget's tight, so getting a good deal's important. At the same time, you expect these things to last for years. It's time to put all you've learned to work. Choose one of the items you need and begin your research to decide what brand and model you will buy and where you'll buy it.

I'LL BUY A

_____
_____

1. **START** by researching consumer information about the type of item you'll be buying. For each resource you find, jot down the source of information and notes about available features, technical information, and other relevant points.

2. **TALK** to people you know who own one of these items. Ask them about their experience with the brand and model they chose. Ask for any suggestions they might have about what to look for and what to avoid.

3. **DEVELOP** a list of the features that are most and least important to you:

MOST IMPORTANT FEATURES	LEAST IMPORTANT FEATURES
_____	_____
_____	_____
_____	_____
_____	_____
_____	_____
_____	_____
_____	_____

4. Based on your research, **COME UP WITH A LIST** of questions to ask the salesperson:

5. What brands and models are available? Use the spaces at right to **RECORD** important information about five models you might consider:

6. **USE** sources such as ads, local stores, the Internet, and catalogs to check prices on these models. Also consider the pros and cons of buying from each source (such as shipping charges, free delivery, etc.). Use a notepad to record your findings.

7. DECIDE on your top choice of brand, model, and place of purchase based on the information you've gathered.

What would you buy?

_____

Give your rationale for your choice:

_____

_____

_____

_____

_____

_____

_____

_____

_____

_____

_____

8. EVALUATE the resources you used. Which would you rate as most helpful? Why?

_____

_____

_____

_____

_____

_____

_____

_____

_____

_____

_____

Microwave Brands and Models

Brand Name MODEL NAME

_____

_____

_____

_____

Price: _____

Brand Name MODEL NAME

_____

_____

_____

_____

Price: _____

Brand Name MODEL NAME

_____

_____

_____

_____

Price: _____

Brand Name MODEL NAME

_____

_____

_____

_____

Price: _____

Financial Know-How

Money Matters

SOME PEOPLE LIVE FROM PAYCHECK TO PAYCHECK. As soon as they get paid, they rush to the bank to cash the check so they can pay the rent and all the other bills that have been piling up. With no savings to fall back on, these people can find themselves in serious trouble if an emergency comes up.

If you don't want to get caught short, you need a plan for handling your money. By figuring out how much you need for basic expenses, you can find ways to set aside money for future needs and still have some left over for a few extras.

EARNING A PAYCHECK

You've probably worked for money by now, but do you realize that there are several different ways of being paid?

Hourly wage. When you work for a wage, the total amount you make is your hourly wage times the number of hours you put in. In some jobs, such as waiting tables, your hourly wage may be supplemented with tips from customers.

Salary. Salaried jobs pay a certain fixed amount per year. If you work for a salary, you earn the same amount no matter how many hours you work. Typically, you receive your paycheck at the end of each pay period, generally, every two weeks.

Commission. Salespeople who are paid on commission earn a percentage of every sale they make. Some salespeople work for commission only; others also earn a regular wage or salary.

Minimum Wage

In the United States, the Fair Labor Standards Act (FLSA) requires employers to pay their workers at least a minimum wage—an amount set by the federal government. Workers who earn tips can be paid less than the minimum wage, as long as they earn enough in tips to make up the difference. Full-time students and people under 20 years old can also be paid less.

Overtime (for hourly employees)

The law stipulates that hourly workers who put in more time than 40 hours a week must receive at least 1.5 times their regular hourly wage for the extra hours. Most salaried employees aren't compensated for overtime.

HOW TO READ A PAY STUB

When you receive your first paycheck from a new employer, you may be confused by all the information on it—especially all the numbers listed under "deductions." What are all these things being taken out of your pay? To understand the answer, take a look at the sample pay stub.

The top section, labeled "Identification," gives your name and other forms of identification and shows what period of time the paycheck covers. The sections labeled "Earnings" show how much you made during that particular pay period and how much you've made so far this year. If you earn an hourly wage, this part of the pay stub will also show how many hours you worked and your hourly pay. The last three columns are every worker's least favorite part of the paycheck—the deductions. A deduction is anything subtracted from your earnings.

Identification

Earnings

Deductions

Net pay

Totals

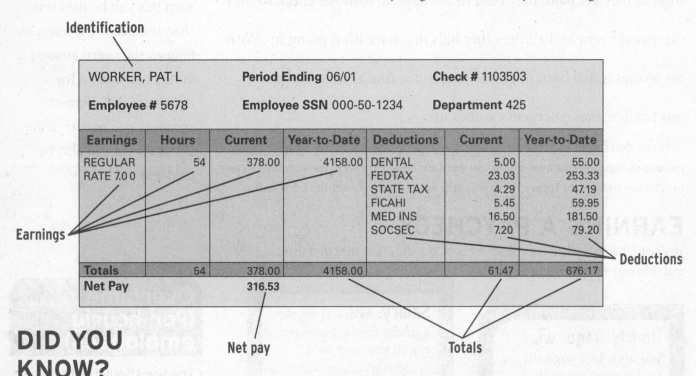

WORKER, PAT L		Period Ending 06/01		Check # 1103503		
Employee # 5678		Employee SSN 000-50-1234		Department 425		

Earnings	Hours	Current	Year-to-Date	Deductions	Current	Year-to-Date
REGULAR RATE 7.0 0	54	378.00	4158.00	DENTAL	5.00	55.00
				FEDTAX	23.03	253.33
				STATE TAX	4.29	47.19
				FICAHI	5.45	59.95
				MED INS	16.50	181.50
				SOCSEC	7.20	79.20
Totals	54	378.00	4158.00		61.47	676.17
Net Pay		316.53				

DID YOU KNOW?

Checks don't have to be paper.
It's possible to get paid without ever receiving a paper check. With a system called direct deposit, the employer deposits your earnings directly into your bank account. This saves you the trouble of going to the bank to deposit your check. You'll still receive a pay stub, along with a receipt showing how much money went into your account.

TYPES OF DEDUCTIONS

Several types of deductions may appear on a pay stub:

- **TAXES.** Employers must deduct a certain amount of your pay for federal income taxes. Depending on where you live, money may also be taken out for state and local taxes.
- **BENEFITS.** If your employer provides benefits such as a health plan or a dental plan, you will probably have to pay part of the cost. The money you contribute to the plans comes directly out of your pay.
- **SOCIAL SECURITY AND MEDICARE.** Social Security provides a source of income for senior citizens and disabled people. Medicare helps older Americans meet their health care costs. The taxes that support these two programs may appear on your pay stub with the label "FICA," which stands for "Federal Insurance Contributions Act."
- **SAVINGS PLANS.** Some companies offer plans that let you take money out of your paycheck and invest it so that you can save up for your retirement. You'll learn more about these plans at the end of this section.

Your pay stub will show the total amount that has come out of your paycheck for all these deductions, as well as the total amount you earned. The amount you have left after deductions is what you have *cleared*, or your net pay, which appears at the bottom of the pay stub.

Paying Your Dues

HAVE YOU EVER VISITED A NATIONAL PARK? Driven on an interstate highway? Your tax dollars also support programs that you can't see as easily, like national defense and Social Security. Many states take state taxes out of your paycheck. This varies from state to state. Check on the Internet to see what states don't take out state taxes.

Every worker who earns more than a certain minimum amount has to pay income taxes. In most cases, this is a two-stage process. Throughout the year, your employer withholds money from your paychecks to pay income taxes. This way, you pay your share in small doses. Before April 15th of the following year, you fill out an income tax return and figure out whether the amount you've paid in taxes is too much, too little, or just right. If you paid too little, you send the Internal Revenue Service a check to make up the difference. If you overpaid, the IRS sends you a refund.

DID YOU KNOW?

Better than a Refund Getting a tax refund may seem like a good thing, but all that it really means is that you've been paying too much in taxes all year long. In effect, you've loaned your money to the government and it's now paying you back—with no interest. Of course, you may end up paying too little tax during the year and having to write a check to the IRS at tax time, but that's not a bad thing—it means that the government has loaned *you* money with no interest!

QuickTip

HOW WITHHOLDING WORKS

Your employer figures out how much money to withhold from your paycheck based on the amount that you make and the number of allowances you claim. When you start a job, you fill out a simple form called a W-4 to provide the information that your employer needs:

- **PERSONAL INFORMATION.** This includes your name, address, Social Security number, and marital status.
- **HOW MANY EXEMPTIONS YOU ARE CLAIMING.** Exemption allowances are factors that affect the amount of tax withheld from your pay. For example, if you support a spouse or children, you can claim exemption allowances for them. The more exemptions you claim, the less tax your employer will take out of your paycheck.
- **WHETHER YOU'RE EXEMPT.** Being exempt means that your income is so low that you don't have to pay taxes at all. In this case, your employer won't withhold any tax from your pay.

SURVIVING TAX TIME

The phrase "doing your taxes" tends to strike fear in the hearts of many Americans. They see the whole process as a mass of complex forms that have to be filled out exactly right. It's true that there are forms involved and the instructions can be confusing, but don't panic—for a young, single person, the process isn't really that complicated. In fact, if you get everything you need ready ahead of time, you can probably get through the whole process in less than an hour.

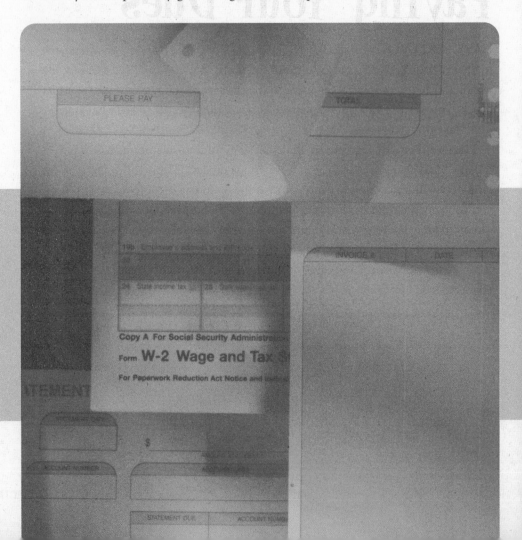

Before you sit down to do your taxes, make sure you have all these items:

Form W-2.
This important form shows how much you earned during the year and how much tax was withheld from your pay. You need one W-2 form for each job you held in the past year. Your employer(s) should send you the form by the end of January. Don't lose it! A sample W-2 form appears below.

Form 1099.
If you have a savings account or any other account that earns interest, your bank will send you a form 1099-INT, which shows how much money you made as interest. Other types of 1099 forms list income from other sources.

Form 1040 and instructions.
Form 1040 is the form you fill out to send to the Internal Revenue Service, the agency that collects taxes. There are several versions of this form. If you're filing your tax return for the first time, there's a good chance you'll be able to use the simplest version, Form 1040EZ. You can pick up tax forms from a library or download and print them from the IRS Web site.

Personal records.
You'll probably find all the information you need on the W-2 and the 1099. If not, you may need to refer to your financial records from the past year, such as pay stubs and bank statements.

Tools.
You'll need a pen to fill out the forms in ink, but you'll probably want to go through them in pencil first, in case you make a mistake. You may also want some scratch paper and a calculator for doing the math.

Check the Net

Check the Net

Filing Without Paper

You can file your tax return without touching a single piece of paper. One way to do it is to file online. Another option, if you use Form 1040EZ, is to file your return by telephone. Check the Internet to learn more about these services and how to use them.

KeyTerms: e-File, TeleFile

a Control number				
	OMB No. 1545-0008			
b Employer identification number 123456-78		1 Wages, tips, other compensation 9,672.00	2 Federal income tax withheld 745.00	
c Employer's name, address, and ZIP code ABC STORES 2001 RING ROAD LARGETOWN, NY 10001		3 Social security wages 9,672.00	4 Social security tax withheld 599.66	
		5 Medicare wages and tips 9,672.00	6 Medicare tax withheld 140.24	
		7 Social security tips	8 Allocated tips	
d Employee's social security number 000-98-7654		9 Advance EIC payment	10 Dependent care benefits	
e Employee's name, address, and ZIP code JESSE B. STUDENT 4567 LINCOLN ST. LARGETOWN, NY 10001		11 Nonqualified plans	12 Benefits included in box 1	
		13	14 Other	
		15 Statutory employee ☐ Deceased ☐ Pension plan ☐ Legal rep. ☐ Deferred compensation ☐		

16 State	Employer's state I.D. no.	17 State wages, tips, etc.	18 State income tax	19 Locality name	20 Local wages, tips, etc.	21 Local income tax
NY	00-98765	9,672.00	345.00			

Form **W-2** Wage and Tax Statement

Copy 1 For State, City, or Local Tax Department

Department of the Treasury—Internal Revenue Service

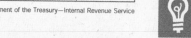

Managing Your Money

WILKINS MICAWBER, A CHARACTER IN THE NOVEL *David Copperfield*, makes the observation that a man who spends all but six cents of what he makes each year will be happy, but a man who spends six cents more than he makes will be miserable. This is an exaggerated way of making an important point: the number one key to financial success is to stay out of debt. To put it another way, don't spend money that you don't have.

Okay, that sounds simple enough—but that doesn't mean it's easy. Paying for everything you need without running out of money can seem impossible when your income is low. It takes a little planning to figure out just how much you *need* to spend each month, and how much you can *afford* to spend.

EASY COME, EASY GO

Suppose you earn $1,000 in a month. After spending $600 on rent and the electric bill, and another $150 on groceries, you have $250 left. With the extra cash, you decide to buy yourself some new clothes and CDs. You also go out to eat and see a couple of movies. Then the phone bill arrives and you realize you don't have enough left to pay it. You think, "This is impossible! I just don't make enough money to live on!"

That's not really true. You just don't make enough to live the way you've been living. To have enough for everything you need, you'll have to scale back. To do this, you'll have to make a distinction between what you *need* and what you *want*. In the example above, the rent and utility bill were expenses you had to pay in order to have a warm place to live. Those CDs, on the other hand, were something you could have lived without.

Sometimes, the line between needs and wants can be fuzzy. For example, look at the $150 for groceries in this example. That food bill may have included some things you could have done without, like magazines or candy. Also, think about the money you spent on clothes. You might really have needed a new pair of jeans, but you could probably have made do with a $30 pair instead of $60 designer jeans.

So how do you decide what you *really* need to spend money on and what you don't? You set priorities. In the example above, you might have decided that the rent, groceries, and bills should be your top priorities, followed by the clothes, then the CDs, and finally the restaurant meals and movies. Some of these same issues are covered in greater depth in later sections of this book.

> ## THE NUMBER ONE KEY TO FINANCIAL SUCCESS IS ... DON'T SPEND MONEY THAT YOU DON'T HAVE.

QuickTip

Need or Want?
To determine if a planned purchase is a need or a want, ask yourself a simple question: "Could I manage without this?" If the answer is yes, you're looking at a want, not a need.

it's Your turn

Where does your money go? On the lines below list five items that you bought in the last few weeks. Write the amount you spent on each item, and identify it as a need or a want.

Item	Cost	Need or Want?
1. _____	_____	_____
2. _____	_____	_____
3. _____	_____	_____
4. _____	_____	_____
5. _____	_____	_____

Total the amounts you spent on needs and on wants. Which was higher?

SAVING UP

Let's say that when you determine your priorities, you decide that you need to buy a car. The problem is, you just don't have enough money. If you're ever going to afford a car, you'll have to save up for it. Saving for the car will be one of your long-term financial goals.

To meet long-term goals, you have to set aside money for them. So if your current priority list is "rent, food, bills, clothes," your new list will be "rent, food, bills, savings for car, clothes." If you need at least $2,500 for a used car, and you put away $100 every month, then it'll take you a little over two years to save the money. If you save more each month, of course, you'll reach your goal sooner.

Other financial goals might take longer to reach. For example, you might spend ten years saving up for a down payment on a house or condo. You'll spend much of your working life saving for your retirement. Your parents may have been saving for years to afford to help with your college fees.

Saving to reach long-term goals takes discipline. It's likely that you'll have to cut back on the money you spend on wants. You may also need to reconsider your needs, and figure out ways to meet them for less money. It's up to you to decide how much you're willing to give up now so you can save for the future. You'll probably find, though, that saving is easier if you make it a habit. In time, you may not even notice the things you're doing without.

DID YOU KNOW?

Money for College If you think college is out of your reach because of finances, fill out the FAFSA, the free application for student aid. The federal government awards millions of dollars in grants and loans. Grants are financial awards that you don't have to pay back; loans are to be paid back in installments *after* you leave school. The money awarded is based on the incomes of students and their families and can be used for tuition at colleges and universities across America.

> IT'S UP TO YOU TO DECIDE HOW MUCH YOU'RE WILLING TO GIVE UP NOW SO YOU CAN SAVE FOR THE FUTURE.

Lending to a Friend

RAVI WAS WATCHING television when his roommate Jeff burst in.

"Hey Ravi," said Jeff, "can I borrow 50 bucks? That new video game I've been waiting for just came out, and I want to grab a copy before it sells out."

"I just loaned you 20 dollars last week!" protested Ravi.

"Look, it's only two more days until I get paid. I'll pay you back the 50 and the other 20. Give me a break, will you?"

Ravi sighed. He did have the money, but he was planning to save it. Still, if Jeff really was going to pay him back, would a couple of days make that much difference?

YOUR IDEAS

1. Should Ravi lend Jeff the money? Why or why not?

_____

_____

_____

_____

_____

_____

_____

_____

2. If he lends the money, what conditions could he give Jeff? If he doesn't, what reasons could he give?

_____

_____

_____

_____

_____

_____

_____

_____

_____

_____

How-To

Making a Budget   A budget will help you figure out how much you can save in a given period of time. You can make a budget to cover any time period, but a month is a good choice because so many expenses come up on a monthly basis. To set up your own budget, follow these steps.

Step 1

Estimate your income. Include all sources of income, such as wages, tips, and possible gifts. If your income varies from month to month, then estimate the average amount. Be sure to list your take-home pay, not your pre-tax earnings.

Step 2

Estimate your expenses. It may help to group your expenses into categories, such as rent, food, clothing, and entertainment. Some expenses, such as rent, are fixed—they cost the same amount each month. Other expenses, such as utility bills, vary from month to month. For these, you'll have to estimate the average monthly cost. Later, you can check your estimate and adjust your budget if you need to. Also, remember that some expenses (renter's insurance, dentist bills, a concert ticket) only come up once in a while, so include some extra "padding" in your budget.

Step 3

Plan for savings. If you plan to save whatever's "left over" at the end of the month, you may find that there's never anything left over. To make sure you'll actually save money, set aside a certain amount for savings in your monthly budget and treat it like any other expense.

Step 4

Balance the budget. Your total expenses shouldn't be more than your earnings. If your income happens to be greater than your expenses, you can bump up your savings or add in an extra expense for something you'd like to buy. If your expenses exceed your income, look for ways to cut back—or to supplement your income.

MAKING ENDS MEET

What if you work out a monthly budget and find that you're not making enough to meet your expenses, let alone save any money? Well, there are two basic ways to make your budget balance: make more money or spend less.

If you work at a job where you're paid by the hour, could you put in a few more hours? Other options are to take a second part-time job or to look for a new job that pays more. One possible drawback to this plan is that a new job sometimes brings new expenses along with the extra income. For instance, you might need to spend more on transportation, uniforms, or business clothes. For parents, working longer hours may mean paying more for child care. And of course, working more means that you'll have a little less free time.

Saving

THERE ARE THREE BASIC WAYS to save money on anything you buy:

1. **BUY IT CHEAPER.** Instead of spending $40 every six months on a new pair of dress pants for work, you find a discount store that sells them for $30.

2. **USE IT LESS.** You wear your new pants only for work, and change into an old pair as soon as you get home. Since you wear them half as much, you can make one pair last a year.

3. **MAKE IT LAST LONGER.** When you discover a hole in the pocket of your pants, you don't stop wearing them. Instead you fix the hole, doubling the life of the pants.

You can save even more money by combining two or more of these strategies. Take a look at how it all adds up:

• With strategy 1 only, you spend $60 a year on pants instead of $80.

  • If you combine this with strategy 2, each pair of pants lasts twice as long, so you only spend $30 for the whole year.

    • Add in strategy 3, and the pair of pants lasts twice as long as that—so the cost drops to $30 every *two* years, for an average of $15 a year. You've cut your spending by more than 75 percent!

You can't use all three of these methods all the time. For example, you wouldn't want to save on toothpaste by brushing your teeth less. However, you can use at least one strategy, and probably two, for almost anything you buy.

Use the chart below to apply these strategies to your own expenses. In row 1, name something you buy regularly, and list the amount you pay each month (or each year). Next, do some research to see if you can find the same product for less money. Consider shopping at a different store, buying a different brand, or buying on sale. List the best price you find in row 2. In rows 3 and 4, list ways you could cut your use of the product or extend its life, and note how much farther you could stretch your purchase this way. Finally, use row 5 to total up your savings.

Strategies

Product			
	Current cost:	Current cost:	Current cost:
Buy it cheaper			
	New Cost:	New Cost:	New Cost:
Use it less			
	New Cost:	New Cost:	New Cost:
Make it last longer			
	New Cost:	New Cost:	New Cost:
Total savings			

HOW TO SAVE

Almost everybody can find ways to cut expenses. For example, maybe you can trim your food or entertainment costs. If your budget shortfall is serious, you may need to reduce your fixed expenses—for example, by moving into a cheaper apartment or finding a roommate. Here are some general pointers for saving money in all areas of your budget:

Keep track of spending. Try this: for one month, write down every penny you spend, from your rent payment to the $2 you pay for a coffee drink. Don't be surprised to find you're spending a lot on things you don't really need. Impulse purchases add up fast!

Do it yourself. There are many ways to save money at home. Cooking your own meals, using a home dry-cleaning kit, and changing the oil in your car are just a few. Just be sure to stick to jobs you can handle.

Think before you spend. Wait a day or two before making a purchase. Ask yourself: Do I really need a digital camera to take on my trip? Could I get by with a disposable camera? Could I borrow my sister's camera? If you're replacing an item that's broken, first see if it makes sense to have the old one repaired.

Get it for less. Save money by choosing store brands, using coupons, watching for sales, and shopping at discount stores. Sometimes online shopping saves money too. Buy in bulk when it makes sense. Consider buying second-hand—you may be able to get what you need for a fraction of the cost of a new item!

Be creative! You can get more use out of old things by seeing them in a new way. A battered old chair might work just fine with a new slipcover. Pants with a hole in the knee could be turned into shorts. You can get cheap art for your walls by framing calendar pages or making something yourself.. Before investing in something new, look for a creative way to reuse something you have or expend some creative juices on a work of art.

You Can Bank on It

NOW THAT YOU'RE STARTING TO SAVE MONEY, you'll need somewhere to stash your savings. A piggy bank won't do the trick anymore. Your money will be safer in a bank, and even better, you can earn more money without lifting a finger.

USING A BANK ACCOUNT

Here's a refresher course on bank accounts: you put your money in the bank, which uses it to make loans. In exchange for the use of your money, the bank pays you a fee, called *interest*. The bank makes a profit because the people it lends money to pay higher interest rates than it pays to you. Most banks offer several types of accounts.

Savings. A basic savings account is the simplest type of account. When you have money to deposit, you take it to the bank and give it to the teller. When you want to take money out, you go to the bank and make a withdrawal. If you prefer, you can make deposits and withdrawals at an automatic teller machine (ATM).

Money market. When you open a money market account, the bank invests the money you deposit. This means that money market accounts pay higher interest rates than regular savings accounts. The catch is that you usually have to keep a certain minimum amount, such as $2,500, in the account. Most money market accounts limit the number of checks you can write on the account.

CDs. With a CD, or certificate of deposit, you agree to deposit your money for a certain length of time—anywhere from three months to five years—in exchange for a specified interest rate that is usually higher than other types of accounts are paying. If you withdraw your funds early, you pay a penalty, so don't commit to a long time period if there's a good chance that you'll need the money sooner.

Checking. With a checking account, you use checks to pay for things you buy, and the money comes out of your account. Using checks lets you make purchases without having to carry large amounts of cash. Of course you'd never want to send cash through the mail, so it's convenient to have checks to send.

The Real Deal

Before you choose any account, make sure you have all the facts. In particular, you should find out about:

- **Minimum balances.** You may need to keep a certain amount in the account. If you drop below that level, you'll be charged a penalty.

- **Fees.** Some accounts have a service charge—a fee the bank charges each month just to maintain your account. You may also be charged for each check you write or for each use of your ATM card. Avoid accounts with such charges!

- **Transaction limits.** Some accounts limit the number of withdrawals or other transactions you can make each month.

Checking accounts make it easy to use your money. Instead of going to the bank or ATM for cash every time you buy something, you can just write a check. Checks are preprinted with your name, the name of your bank, and your account number. You fill in the date, the amount, and the name of the person you're paying (the payee). Then you sign the check at the bottom. Your signature is proof that the check is from you and not from someone using your account illegally. The payee also has to sign, or *endorse*, the check on the back in order to deposit or cash it.

If you write a check for $100, you have to be sure that you have at least $100 in your account. If a check comes to your bank and there isn't enough money in your account to cover it, the check will "bounce" back to the payee's bank. Your bank will charge you a substantial fee for overdrawing your account (taking out more than you have). Most banks offer overdraft protection: if you have a savings account as well as a checking account, the bank will take money out of your savings to cover a check that would otherwise bounce.

To know how much you have in your account at all times, keep track of the checks you write. When you order personalized checks, you'll receive a booklet called a check register. Whenever you write a check or make any other transaction, enter it in the check register, as shown below. Then subtract (or add) the amount of the transaction to find your new balance.

CHECK NO.	DATE	CHECK ISSUED TO	AMOUNT OF CHECK	✓	DATE OF DEP	AMOUNT OF DEPOSIT	BALANCE 556 48
543	2/8	Pure & Fresh, Inc. (bottled water)	16 50	✓			16 50
							539 98
544	2/16	XYZ Center	59 95				59 95
							480 03
	2/18	Deposit				400 00	400 00
							880 03
545	2/20	City Electric	124 63				124 63
							755 40
546	2/21	123 Comm	35 96				35 96
							719 44
	2/22	ATM withdrawal	60 00				60 00
							659 44

DID YOU KNOW?

Proof of Payment A cancelled check provides legal proof that you paid for a product or service. Most financial institutions no longer send their customers cancelled checks. If you need the actual check, request a photocopied check from your bank. There may be a small fee attached to this service.

How-To

Balancing Your Checkbook Each month, you'll receive a *statement* that summarizes the financial transactions you made that month—your deposits, as well as the withdrawals and checks that were processed. Make it a habit to open your statement the day it arrives. Check your check register against this statement to catch any errors before they lead to problems. This is called balancing your checkbook, or reconciling your account. Here's how to do it:

Step 1	Step 2	Step 3	Step 4	Step 5	Step 6
Compare your check register with your bank statement. Mark each transaction that appears on the statement with a check mark. If the statement lists a transaction that you forgot to enter in your register—or a transaction made by the bank, such as a fee or an interest payment—record it in the register and do the math to update your balance. If your statement lists any transaction that you don't remember making, contact the bank to see if there's been a mistake.	Write down the amount listed on the statement as your closing balance (the amount you had at the end of the month).	Go through the register and find any deposits that aren't checked off. These are "outstanding" deposits, which means that the bank hasn't processed them yet. Copy down the date and amount of any outstanding deposit. Add all the amounts and add the total to the number you wrote down in step 2.	Go through the register again and find all checks and withdrawals that aren't checked off. Copy these down and add them the way you did with the outstanding deposits. Subtract the total from the number you got in step 3.	The number you got in step 4 should match the balance on the last line of your check register. If it doesn't, go back and see if you made a mistake when writing down or adding the numbers in steps 3 and 4. If you don't find one, check the math in your register.	If you can't find any mistake in your figures, try checking the math on the statement itself. It's possible—though very unlikely—that the mistake was the bank's. If you go through the whole thing over and over and still can't find the mistake, stop by the bank for assistance.

QuickTip

Double Whammy

When you use an ATM that isn't part of your bank's network, you may see a message on the display screen indicating that you'll have to pay a fee— maybe a dollar or two extra. That's not the whole story. Your own bank may charge you an additional fee for using someone else's ATM, so you get hit twice. To avoid this, plan your withdrawals so that you make them only at your own bank's ATMs.

VIRTUAL BANKING

Thanks to computers, you can do a lot of your banking without actually setting foot in a bank. You can make transactions at an ATM, over the phone, or online. You can even arrange to have certain transactions take place automatically at certain times.

If you have an ATM card, you can use it at almost any ATM, whether the machine belongs to your bank or not. To use an ATM, you have to enter your personal identification number, or PIN. The purpose of the PIN is to make sure that no one but you uses your card. To keep your PIN secure, memorize the number. Don't share your PIN with anyone, and make sure no one can read the digits as you punch them into the machine.

To put money into your account, or to take money out, you have to visit either an ATM or a real, live teller. But what if all you want to do is check your account balance or transfer money from one account to another? In that case, you can probably make the transaction from home with either a telephone or a computer. To access your account by phone, you dial a toll-free number and enter a PIN or password. Then you select the transaction you want to make from a list. With online banking, you go to a Web site and type in your name and password. The site gives you access to all your account information and lets you make transfers.

You can also arrange to have some transactions occur automatically, so that you don't even need to log on. For example, you can have your paychecks deposited directly into your account. You can also have money taken out of your account on a regular basis to make payments on a loan or to pay your electric bill.

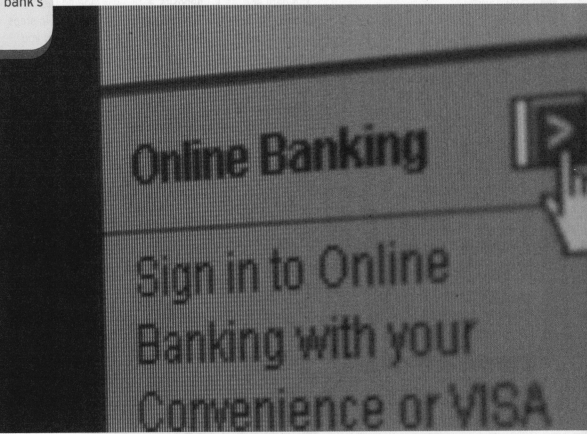

Using Plastic

DO YOU KNOW THE DIFFERENCE between a debit card and a credit card? You can use a debit card to make purchases at the grocery store or the gas pump and have the money taken out of your account—just as if you'd written a check. The term *debit* means "subtract." The money is subtracted from your account immediately.

A credit card looks like a debit card, but it doesn't work the same way. When you pay for something by credit card, the credit card company pays for your purchase. At the end of the billing cycle, the company sends a bill for all the charges you've made during the past month. You can take care of the bill online or with a check, paying for all your purchases in one lump sum instead of one at a time.

With most credit cards, you also have the option of paying off only part of the monthly bill right away and paying the rest later. Doing this is called carrying a balance. This option might be useful for unexpected expenses, such as a costly car repair, that you can't afford to pay for all at once—but it comes with a hefty price tag. If you don't pay your bill in full every month, you'll pay interest on the amount carried over. How much interest you pay depends on the card, but the annual percentage rate could be 18 percent or higher.

DID YOU KNOW?

One advantage of using a **credit card** is that if you see a purchase on your bill that you didn't make, you can dispute the charge. If the merchant can't produce a signed receipt to prove that you made the purchase, you won't have to pay it. This means if someone steals your card and uses it, you're protected from having to pay a huge bill. With a debit card, by contrast, the money comes straight out of your account. By the time you discover the card is gone, your money may be gone too.

Your Credit Rating

If you apply for a loan, the creditor will look at your credit history—the way you've handled your debts in the past. If you have a history of paying debts off promptly, creditors are more likely to trust you to pay back their loan. Organizations called credit bureaus keep track of people's credit history and produce detailed credit reports. Lenders buy the reports and use them to create credit ratings—assessments of whether a borrower is a good risk or not. If your credit rating is poor, you will be denied a loan when you want to buy a house or a car.

IT'S TO YOUR CREDIT

Using credit cards can help you financially—or it can hurt you. To see why, let's take a look at two roommates, Sonia and Megan. Sonia uses her credit card for everyday purchases, such as gas and groceries, and she saves all her receipts so that she can keep track of how much she charges each month. She's careful not to let her spending go over the amount she budgets for the month. When the bill comes, Sonia pays off the balance and starts off the next month with a clean slate.

Megan, by contrast, regards her credit cards as free money. When she sees something she wants for herself or to give as a gift, she doesn't worry much about its cost because she can just put it on the card. She has several credit cards, and her balance is dangerously close to the limit on all of them. When she gets her bills, she makes the minimum monthly payment on each. This means that she makes a hefty interest payment on every single purchase she makes. To make matters worse, Megan sometimes pays her bills late—so she ends up paying late fees as well.

It's easy to see that Sonia is saving money by using her card, while Megan is costing herself money. She may pay less each month than Sonia does, but she's digging herself deeper and deeper into debt. Even if she stops charging, the payments on the balances she already owes will continue to be a drain on her finances until she pays them off. If she keeps paying only the minimum, that could take years.

You don't want to fall into credit card debt. Don't buy things now, thinking that you'll pay for them later. Remember that having a credit card doesn't mean you can afford to spend more—it just makes it easy to spend more than you can afford. If you do use a credit card, figure out a maximum that you can afford to spend each month, and always keep your spending within that limit. If there's ever a time that you can't pay the full balance, pay as much as you can and get the balance paid off as soon as possible.

"HAVING A CREDIT CARD DOESN'T MEAN YOU CAN AFFORD TO SPEND MORE—IT JUST MAKES IT EASY TO SPEND MORE THAN YOU CAN AFFORD."

WHICH CARD?

Unless you have a bad credit history, you'll probably have no trouble getting a credit card. In fact, it's more likely you'll have to fight off the offers. Credit card companies work hard to attract young people, offering freebies and badgering students with high-pressure sales pitches. Before you sign up, shop around and find a credit card that fits your needs. Here are some factors to consider:

QuickTip

Chuck Those Checks

Your credit card company may routinely send you checks with a note urging you to "Use these checks for easy access to your credit account!" You have to read the fine print to learn that purchases made with the checks are treated as cash advances, which means you pay a higher interest rate than you do for regular purchases. On top of that, the credit card company may charge you a fee just for using the checks. So what's the advantage over using your card the normal way? You guessed it—there isn't any. The best thing to do is to shred those checks.

Annual percentage rate (APR).

The APR is the amount of interest you pay per year on your balance. With some cards, the APR is fixed; with others, it can vary from month to month. If you expect to carry a balance on your card, a low APR is a must. Don't be tricked by cards that offer an "introductory" APR to lure you in. Usually, this deal lasts for a few months, and then the company raises the rate.

Credit limit.

The credit limit is the maximum amount you can charge with the card. With your first credit card, you may start out with a fairly low credit limit, but if you pay your bills promptly, the company will probably raise your limit over time.

Grace period.

The grace period is the period of time allowed to pay your bill after you receive it. If you pay within the grace period, you don't have to pay any finance charges. Most cards have a grace period of 20 to 25 days.

Fees.

Some credit cards charge an annual fee of $15 to $55 just for having the card, even if you don't use it. For consumers who carry a balance, it may be worth paying the fee in exchange for a low APR. Otherwise, there's *no* reason to pay an annual fee—there are plenty of cards without one. Also, find out what fees the card charges for late payments or going over your credit limit.

Special features.

Many cards give you a bonus of some kind every time you use the card. For example, you could earn frequent flyer miles or discounts on certain purchases. Some cards give you cash back or make a contribution to a particular charity every time you use them.

Where you can use it.

Some businesses won't accept certain cards. Make sure the type of card you choose is good at the places where you'll want to use it.

DEALING WITH DEBT

Remember Megan, the credit card spendthrift? Well, suppose that her spending habits finally catch up with her. She finds she's maxed out all her cards. She's devastated when the store repossesses her computer because she's fallen behind on the payments. She can't even scrape together the cash to cover her regular living expenses. When Megan asks Sonia if it's okay for her to pay her share of the rent late, Sonia puts her foot down. She insists that Megan get help with her finances.

So what do consumers like Megan do when they find themselves in this situation? For starters, they can contact creditors and explain their problem. Creditors may be willing to help work out a plan to pay off the debts gradually. Megan could also seek help from a credit counselor—a professional trained to help people get out of debt and learn to control their spending. Credit counselors may require a certain amount be paid to the counseling service each month, which they use to pay off creditors on a schedule that they work out. They may also teach skills for managing money. Some credit counseling services are free.

Ultimately, though, changing habits is up to the individual. Shopping as a hobby is fine if you can afford it. If shopping becomes an obsession, it's time to find a new hobby. Compulsive shoppers need to stay out of the stores and not even pause at a shopping channel on television. Experts recommend that they stop buying anything on credit. The last thing they need is to pile on more debt. Paying off current debts becomes the top priority. They are advised to set aside a certain amount of money each month to pay toward their debts, and to pay that amount *before* any other expenses.

DID YOU KNOW?

Cash vs. Credit Studies show that people tend to spend more when they use credit cards than when they use cash. If you want to curb your spending you might want to take out your cash "allowance" for the week, and leave those credit cards at home. You'll be much more aware of how much you're spending if you actually count out the money as you spend it and see your stash get smaller as the week wears on.

QuickTip

Payment Plan

One way to make sure you pay your bills on time is to sit down and write out a check as soon as each bill arrives. If you can't get to them right away, put them in a spot where you won't be able to overlook them. You might want to set aside a specific block of time—say, after dinner every Monday night—to tackle the bills that are due. Write it on your calendar so you won't forget.

Top Billing

YOU COME HOME FROM WORK and take in the mail. As you head into the kitchen, you flip through the envelopes. Phone company, electric company, cable company—nothing but bills. In disgust, you throw the whole pile onto the table. You'll deal with them later.

Days turn into weeks, and the pile on the table gets bigger. You've forgotten about those bills on the bottom. Next thing you know, you get a second bill from the phone company—this time with a warning that you're a month behind in your payments. Not only do you now owe them for two months' worth of service, you have to pay a late fee as well! You didn't really let that bill go for a whole month—did you?

If this has happened to you before, you need a system for dealing with bills. If you let bills go unpaid, late charges may not be your only problem—you run the risk of having services, like your phone or electricity, cut off. Getting them working again is a lot more trouble than just paying the bill on time.

READ BEFORE YOU PAY

Okay, you're ready to tackle your bill pile. Before you actually write out any checks, open each bill and go through it item by item to make sure that the charges make sense. If it's a phone bill, for example, look at each call listed to see if you remember making it. (If you share a phone, your roommates probably made some of the calls.) If you're going through a credit card bill, check the bill against the receipts you saved from the past month. Do the numbers match? Are there any charges on the bill that you don't remember making? If you can't figure out what a charge is for, contact the company. It might just be a purchase that you forgot about, but it could also be someone else trying to use your credit card number without your knowledge.

Going through your bills also gives you a chance to see where your money is going. For instance, suppose you notice that your electric bill for July is twice as high as your bill for June. You realize that it's probably because you've been running the air conditioner nonstop. Once you see the cost, you might decide to save the air conditioner for only the hottest days and use a fan the rest of the time. You can also see whether you're paying for services you don't really need. Say your phone bill shows that you're paying a few extra dollars a month for a service like call waiting. How many times a month do you actually use it? Maybe you want to drop that service and save the money.

How-To

Paying a Bill Once you're satisfied that the bill is accurate, you can pay it—in person, online, or by mail. Here are a few easy steps for paying by mail.

Step 1	Step 2	Step 3	Step 4	Step 5	Step 6	Step 7
Usually there's a place on the bill to write the amount you're enclosing. Write the amount on the bill, then fill in the same amount on your check.	The bill will probably instruct you to "Make your check payable to XYZ Corporation." Write this name on your check. If there's no such instruction, then make the check out to the company name that appears at the top of the bill.	Look on the stub to see if it gives an "account number" or "member number." For a phone bill, this might be your phone number plus a few extra digits. Copy this number onto your check. (You can put it on the line at the lower left of the check.) Writing your account number on the check helps prevent errors in processing your payment.	Sign and date your check.	Tear off the payment stub and insert it into the return envelope provided with your bill. If you're using a window envelope, make sure the stub goes into the envelope correctly so the address shows through the window. Slip your check in behind the stub so it doesn't cover the address.	Before you seal the envelope, check to make sure you didn't forget anything. Some envelopes have a list of reminders (like "Did you remember to sign your check?") printed on the inside of the flap. Read through the list to make sure you did everything, then seal the envelope. Write your return address on the envelope or use an address label and add a stamp.	If your checking account doesn't have the funds to pay the bill immediately, jot the date you want to mail your payment (perhaps your next payday) in the space where the stamp will go. On that day, put a stamp on the envelope and drop it in the mail.

KEEPING TRACK

There—you've worked your way through the pile. The envelopes with your payments are in a neat stack. Figuring that you're finished with these bills, you grab the pile and head for the recycling bin. Whoa, hold on a minute! You might need those!

There are several reasons you should hold on to old bills. For example, a dispute could come up with the company. If your Internet provider sends you a letter saying you were supposed to pay $57 last month, it'll be helpful to be able to show that you were billed $35. You can also use your bills to work out average monthly payments when you prepare a budget.

A simple home filing system can help you keep track of your old bills and other important papers. You can use a file cabinet or a series of folders or envelopes stored in a plastic crate. Just make sure that each folder or envelope is clearly labeled so you don't have to sort through the whole stack to find what you want. Keep the most recent bills toward the front of each folder, since those are the ones you'll most likely need to look at. The table below lists a variety of documents you might want to store in your files, along with suggestions for how long to hold on to them.

Type of Document	How Long to Keep
ATM receipts	Until you've checked them against your monthly bank statement
Bank statements and canceled checks	6 years
Credit card receipts	Until you've checked them against your monthly statement. For large purchases and items that could require service, keep the receipts as a proof of purchase as long as you own the item
Credit card statements	3 years
Pay stubs	Until you've checked them against your W-2 at the beginning of the next year
Repair records and warranties	For the length of the warranty; keep vehicle repair receipts while you're the owner
Tax returns and related documents	7 years
Utility bills	3 months, or longer to establish a budget

Bill Paying

IF YOU WANT TO SAVE YOURSELF A STAMP—and some time—you can sign up for a service that lets you pay your bills electronically. This service is available through some banks, usually for a monthly fee, although it may be free to people with certain types of accounts. If your bank doesn't provide this service, you can sign up with a third party for a monthly fee. Some of your regular service providers, such as your phone company, may also give you the option of paying your bill online.

Another option is automatic payment. If you have a bill that is the same every month, such as health club dues, you can have your bank pay it every month on a certain date, so that you never even have to think about it. Individual service providers may also give you the option of having the amount you owe each month deducted directly from your account. Here are some pros and cons of this arrangement:

PROS
- You don't have to spend time writing checks.
- You don't have to worry about missing a bill.
- Your payment is received and processed more quickly.

CONS
- You might not get to look at the bill before you pay it. If there are any mistakes, you can't dispute them before the bill is paid.
- If you don't leave enough money in your checking account for the automatic payment, you could overdraw the account.
- Because you don't spend time examining your bills, you may not realize how much you're paying for some services.

To find out if online bill paying might be a good choice for you, ask yourself these questions:

1. Are you generally more comfortable with computers or with paper?

_____

2. How much time do you spend doing your bills each month?

_____

3. How much time do you estimate it would take you to pay them online?

_____

Options

4. Which of your regular monthly bills can be paid electronically? (If you aren't sure, contact the service providers to find out, or see if you can find the answer on their Web sites.) List them here:

_____   _____
_____   _____
_____   _____

5. Do any of these providers give you a way to pay your bills online at no charge? **YES / NO** If so, list them here:

_____   _____
_____   _____

6. Does your bank offer a bill paying service? **YES / NO**
If yes, what is the monthly cost? _____

7. What do you have to do to sign up? _____
_____

8. Check with at least two other providers other than your bank to find out what they charge for bill paying service. List the amounts here:

_____   _____
_____   _____

9. Which of your regular monthly bills can be paid automatically? List them here:

_____
_____
_____
_____
_____

10. Do the pros of automatic payment outweigh the cons (listed above) for you?
YES / NO

BASED ON YOUR ANSWERS to the questions listed, which would you choose?

A Online payment through a bank

B Online payment through a third party

C Online payment through the individual service providers

D Automatic bill payment

E Traditional payment with checks

Explain why.

_____
_____
_____
_____
_____
_____
_____
_____
_____
_____
_____
_____
_____
_____
_____
_____
_____

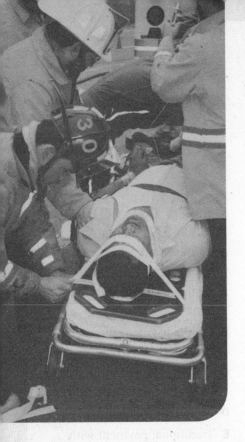

Preparing for the Worst

LET'S SAY THAT YOU'RE A RESPONSIBLE CONSUMER and you pride yourself on handling your money wisely. You always pay bills on time, you have no debts, and your savings account, though modest, is growing steadily. Then one day, everything changes: while driving home, you're involved in an accident. Your car is damaged, your leg is broken, and you must take time off work to recover. The last thing you want at a time like this is to see your hard-earned savings wiped out by bills from the hospital and the autobody shop. That's why you need insurance.

The basic idea behind insurance is this: you pay a regular fee, called a premium, to the insurance company. In return, the company agrees to cover your expenses if you suffer a loss. There are several different kinds of insurance. The chart on the facing page lists four common types.

THE COST OF COVERAGE

Insurance can protect you from a loss, but at the same time, it creates a steady drain on your income. Here are a few tips to help you keep your insurance costs at a level you can afford.

- Set priorities. Think about the kind of coverage you really need. For example, if you have a very old car, it may not be worth buying collision coverage (which covers the cost of damage from a car crash) because the value of the car is so low. Similarly, if you live in a very dry area, you probably don't need flood insurance.

- More risk means less cost. Many insurance policies have a deductible—a set amount that you must pay for any loss before your insurance coverage kicks in. In general, the higher your deductible, the lower your premiums. Choosing a policy with a higher deductible means you will have to pay more if you make a claim—but you will pay less in premiums. Unless you make a lot of claims, a policy with a high deductible will probably save you money in the long run.

- Shop around. Insurance rates vary from company to company. Get estimates from at least three companies before you choose a policy. An insurance agent may be able to help you find a policy that fits your budget.

Check the Net

Check the Net

Finding Insurance

Instead of going to an insurance agent, some people shop for insurance on the Internet. Some Web sites allow you to type in your information and get quotes from several insurance companies. Find a few sites like this and see how they work. Would you feel comfortable purchasing insurance this way?

Key Term: insurance quotes

TYPES OF INSURANCE

Type of insurance	What it covers	How you get it
Auto insurance	• Damage to your vehicle if you are involved in an accident • Damage you cause to other people in an accident • Some policies also cover damage to a vehicle from theft, vandalism, or natural disasters	Most states require drivers to have some minimum level of auto insurance. You can purchase a personal auto insurance policy directly from the insurance company. For more information, see Section 6.
Health insurance	• Coverage varies greatly among different insurance plans • Basic plans cover medical emergencies only • Full plans cover routine doctor visits, lab tests, and prescription drugs	Many employers offer health insurance plans for employees and their families. Typically, the employee must pay at least part of the cost of the premiums. For more information, see Section 7. Some employers have you purchase and pay your own health insurance.
Home insurance Renter's Insurance	• Damage to your home and its contents from theft, fire, flooding, etc. • Injuries sustained by visitors to your home	If you own your home, you can buy a homeowner's insurance policy to cover your house and its contents. If you rent, your landlord's insurance policy covers the building, but you should consider renters insurance to cover your personal property.
Life insurance	• Loss of income suffered by your family members if you die	You may obtain life insurance through your employer or buy your own. Needs vary from person to person. If no one depends on your income, you may need only enough life insurance to cover your funeral costs. Parents need more insurance to cover their children's care and education.

Looking into the Future

PICTURE THIS: YOU'VE JUST GRADUATED FROM SCHOOL and landed your first job. You have a source of income, a budget to control your expenses, an account for your savings, and insurance coverage. Your financial situation looks pretty good—right now. But ten years down the road, your situation may be completely different. You might be thinking about buying a home, or you might have young children to support. If you want to make your dreams for the future come true, you'll need to start investing now.

SAVINGS VS INVESTMENT

A savings account is a good place to keep your money if you want it to earn interest but still be available when you need it. The money in your bank account will be useful when major expenses come up—for example, if your car needs repairs or if you to decide to buy a couch for your living room.

The problem with keeping all your money in savings, though, is that your money won't grow much over the long term. When you make an investment, by contrast, your money is more likely to grow over time. You might not be able to use that money for several years, but in the end, your "nest egg" should be larger. There are three major reasons to invest:

To be prepared for emergencies.
Suppose one day you lose your job and find yourself without a source of income. Your investment fund can provide the money you need to live on until you get back on your feet again. Experts recommend having an emergency fund to carry you through six months of being unemployed.

To pay for future plans.
Saving for new luggage or a home theater system is a relatively short-term goal that you can meet through savings, but saving for your first home will take a lot longer. The money you invest today could become the down payment on a house in seven or eight years. Another reason to invest for the future is to save money for college—for yourself or for your children.

To support yourself when you retire.
Some day, you'll be ready to stop working. The question is, will you be able to afford to live without a paycheck? If you've invested wisely throughout your career, the money in your retirement fund should be enough to live on for the rest of your life.

KNOWING THE RISKS

Another difference between savings and investment is the amount of risk involved. When you put money into a savings account, it earns interest at a slow but steady rate. When you invest money, the value of your investment can swing up and down. If you buy stocks worth $1,000, you may find that a few weeks later, their value has dropped to $800. On the other hand, you may find that the value of the stock has increased and you now have $1,200.

You may wonder, "Why take chances? Why not just go with the safe interest rate?" The reason is that you can usually make more money by investing. If you just put money in a regular saving account, you won't lose any, but you won't gain much if interest rates are low.

Also, keeping all your money in the bank poses its own risk. Over time, the cost of living tends to increase because of inflation. This means that the money you keep in the bank will gradually lose its purchasing power. If the interest you earn doesn't keep up with inflation, you'll end up with a larger sum of money, but you won't be able to buy as much with it. To beat the inflation rate, you generally need some kind of investment that's better than an ordinary savings account.

DID YOU KNOW?

Diversification You can reduce your risk by diversifying— spreading your money out among different investments. That way, even if one investment does poorly, you'll lose only a portion of your money. Ideally, you'll build a collection of investments, known as a portfolio. You can balance your portfolio by choosing a mix of investments that fit your goals and timeline.

How Much Risk?

The shorter your timeline, the less risk you can afford to take. If you're saving up for a long-term goal, like retirement, you can afford to take some chances that might offer a bigger payoff in the long run. As you get closer to your goal, you'll need to revise your strategy and reduce the amount of risk you are exposed to.

KNOWING YOUR OPTIONS

Once you have a general idea what your goals are, you can start looking at ways to meet them. There are several types of investments, each with its own advantages and disadvantages.

Stocks. A stock is, essentially, a small portion of the ownership of a particular company. Companies sell stock in units called shares. If a company does well, the value of its shares goes up; if it does poorly, the value drops. If the company fails completely, the shares become worthless. This makes stocks one of the riskiest types of investment. However, they also have the potential for high gains.

Bonds. When you buy a bond, you are essentially lending money to the issuer, which may be the federal government, a local government, or a corporation. The issuer agrees to pay you back with interest by a certain date. United States savings bonds and Treasury securities are generally considered a very safe investment because they are backed by the government. Other types of bonds may be riskier.

CDs. A certificate of deposit is an agreement to deposit your money for a certain amount of time and receive a given rate of interest in return. Usually, the longer the term of the CD, the higher the rate of return. With a CD, you run little risk of losing your money, but you do tie it up for a specific length of time, as described earlier in this section.

Mutual funds. A mutual fund is a set of investments shared among many investors. Investors buy shares in the fund. The company that manages the fund takes the investors' money and distributes it among stocks, bonds, and other investments. Mutual funds are less risky than other investments because they are diversified and managed by experts.

Too Good to Be True?

Some investment opportunities sound too good to be true—because they are. Any scheme that promises you'll double your money overnight is almost certainly a fraud. Here are a few ways to spot a scam:

- Promises of big profits in a very short time

- Claims that there's no risk

- Pressure to "act now"

- Testimonials from people you don't know

- Advertisements received through e-mail

Insist on getting the details of any investment scheme in writing. Legitimate companies are happy to provide this information in a prospectus, and must do so by law. And if in doubt—don't invest. It's better to risk losing out on that "once-in-a-lifetime opportunity" than to risk losing everything on a crooked scheme.

SAVING FOR RETIREMENT

You may be thinking, "I'll be working the next 40 or 50 years. Why would I think about retirement?" No matter how old you are, it's never too soon to start thinking about saving for your retirement. The cost of living is only going to go up between now and the time you retire. After that, you may have more than 20 years to support yourself without the benefit of a paycheck. You'll probably have to replace the income you once earned with income from a variety of other sources.

Throughout your working life, you'll pay money into the Social Security fund. Once you reach retirement age, you'll receive monthly Social Security benefits. The money you get won't be enough to live on, however. You'll need to add to it with money you've invested at work or on your own.

Some companies maintain a retirement fund for their employees. Contributions to the fund may come from the employer, the employees, or both. Money in the fund is invested so that it grows over time. When an employee retires, he or she can collect money from the fund, which is called a *pension*.

Another type of retirement plan offered in many workplaces is a 401(k). Employees can have money taken out of their paychecks and put into a fund, where it may be invested in various ways. Workers don't pay taxes on the money they put into the fund until they begin withdrawing it. Usually, you can't take money out of your 401(k) until you retire. However, if you change jobs before then, you may be able to "roll over" the money into another retirement plan. That will prevent you from having to pay stiff penalties. The new plan could be a 401(k) held by your new employer or an individual retirement account (IRA).

A traditional IRA is similar to a 401(k): you invest pre-tax dollars and pay taxes on the money when you withdraw it. The difference is that instead of getting it through your workplace, you set it up yourself at a bank or other financial institution. A Roth IRA is like an IRA, but with a twist: you put in after-tax dollars, and your earnings from the fund are then tax-free.

QuickTip

Get in on the Ground Level

If your employer offers a 401(k), invest in it as soon as you can. The earlier you start, the longer your investment will have to grow. Also, many companies offer matching contributions: if you put money into the fund, your company will match your contribution with one of its own—say, 25 cents for every dollar you pay. It's like getting money for nothing! Another benefit is that the money you invest in a 401(k) comes out of your salary before taxes, so you'll pay less income tax too.

PUTTING IT ALL TOGETHER

YOUR MONEY AND YOUR LIFE

You've graduated from high school or college and started working full time. You have a steady income, along with some regular expenses. You want to make sure you have enough money for emergencies and also start planning to meet your future needs.

1. **START** by figuring out what your income is likely to be. Think of a job that you'd like to have. Be realistic—you can't plan on starting out at the top of your field. Pick an entry-level job that you could get fresh out of school. Find out what a person in this position typically makes after taxes. List your "new job" and income level here:

   Job Title:_____ **Income: $**_____

2. **ESTIMATE** your expenses. Make a list of the expenses you expect to have in a month, including rent, food, clothing, utilities, and entertainment. If the job you chose doesn't provide health insurance, be sure to include that on your list. You may also need to budget for other types of insurance, such as auto insurance if you plan to have a car. (If you do, also include gas and maintenance as expenses.)

3. **RESEARCH** the expected cost of each item on your list. For example, to find out what you may have to pay for rent, check the "Apartments for Rent" listings in your local newspaper. List your expenses below, along with the estimated cost for each one.

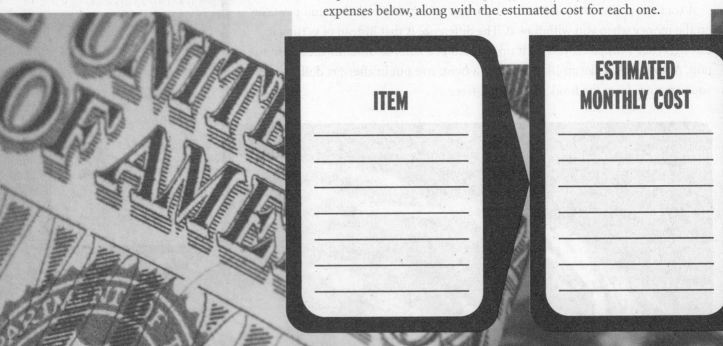

ITEM
_____
_____
_____
_____
_____
_____

ESTIMATED MONTHLY COST
_____
_____
_____
_____
_____
_____

4. **CONSIDER** other expenses that aren't on your list, such as personal grooming, pets, vacations, and gifts. Start by considering haircuts. If you usually get your hair cut every five weeks, that's ten times a year. How much would you spend on ten haircuts? How about services such as highlighting? Would you be willing to cut back? As for pets, how much would it cost to have a cat or dog? Could you afford to be a pet owner? If you were to take an annual vacation, where would you go? How much would it cost? How much would you spend on gifts for friends and family? Write your comments below, including ideas on how to save money in these areas. (For example, you might use your computer to make photo collages to give as special gifts.)

_____

_____

_____

_____

5. **RECORD** the additional estimated monthly expenses from #4 on the expense chart. Add these expenses and subtract the total from your expected income. The difference is the amount you should be able to save or invest each year. Write the amount here: _____ If your expected expenses are higher than your expected income, then you need to rethink your plans! Look for ways to cut your expenses, or consider training for a job that pays more.

6. Next, **CONSIDER** your financial goals. Write down three long-term goals, along with their estimated cost and timeline. Examples might be to have a $5,000 down payment to use toward a new hybrid car in five years or to travel to Australia in three years.

7. How much money will you need to put away per year to meet each goal? **FIND** the answer by dividing the total amount needed by the number of years between now and the goal. Don't panic if the number you get seems high—you don't have to start saving that amount the very first year. Your income will probably increase over time, and your savings will also grow as interest accumulates.

8. **WRITE OUT** a plan for reaching your financial goals while meeting your present needs. Remember that you may be able to save more money in future years, as your income grows. Be sure to include some money for savings that you can have available if an emergency comes up, as well as some in longer-term investments.

_____

_____

_____

_____

Long-Term Financial Goals

Goal 1:

_____

_____

_____

Amount: _____

Timeline: _____

_____

Goal 1:

_____

_____

_____

Amount: _____

Timeline: _____

_____

Goal 1:

_____

_____

_____

Amount: _____

Timeline: _____

_____

A Place to Call Home

New Digs

IT MAY BE HARD TO BELIEVE, but there's a good chance sometime soon you'll move into a new home. If college is in your future, a dorm could be your new home away from home. If you're planning to get a full-time job, then you may soon be looking for your first apartment. In either case, it's a big change. Being on your own for the first time definitely takes some getting used to.

DORM LIFE

Although some college students live off campus, many colleges and universities require first- and second-year students to stay in the dorms. The good news is that dorm living is an excellent way to meet new friends. The bad news is that your living space may be rather cramped. During high school, Tom's bedroom was the spacious basement of his family's home. He couldn't believe it when he first saw his 10-ft x 14-ft dorm room with bunk beds—and learned that he would be sharing it with a stranger! On top of that, they'd have to share the bathroom down the hall with dozens of other students.

Not all dorms are quite so confining. Some offer suites of rooms, each with a private bath (or a larger bathroom to be shared with another suite). Some schools give students the option of paying more for a single room.

Many dorms have common areas for socializing. Sometimes, there may be scheduled social activities, such as movie nights. Typically, each section of a first-year dorm has a resident adviser, or RA, who coordinates activities, helps students solve problems, and enforces dorm rules.

QuickTip

The Early Bird
Once you're accepted to a college or technical school, make your housing choice as soon as possible. Rooms are usually assigned on a first-come, first-served basis. Most students look for a newer dorm that is near their classes. If you set the housing application aside until later, you probably won't get your first choice.

DID YOU KNOW?

College Housing Community colleges don't operate dorms, but often have "student apartments" with one to four bedrooms on or near campus. The rent per person drops as the number of roommates increases. For students who commute more than 25 miles to school each day (1,000 miles per month!), this housing option is definitely worth checking out.

YOUR OWN PLACE

Apartments come in all sizes and shapes, furnished and unfurnished. Some of the possibilities include:

Studios or efficiencies (usually for one person). These tiny apartments cram everything you need into one room. They usually rent for less than apartments with separate bedrooms.

One-, two-, or three-bedroom apartments. A one-bedroom usually costs more than a studio. Unless you're making big bucks, you probably won't be able to afford a two-bedroom or a three-bedroom on your own. However, sharing one could cost you less than renting a tiny studio by yourself.

House shares. Renting a house with others can offer more freedom and a quieter setting than an apartment. However, it may come with extra responsibilities, such as maintaining the lawn or shoveling snow.

DID YOU KNOW?

Top Floor Top-floor apartments are more desirable (and more expensive) because there's no upstairs neighbor to make noise. By contrast, basement apartments (sometimes called "garden level") are usually cheaper because they have less light and no balcony or patio. On the plus side, they tend to stay cooler in hot weather.

Can You Handle It?

Maybe you've been dreaming about your first apartment—fixing it up, having friends over, and so on. What may not have made it into your dreams is the extra work it takes to have your own place. Whether you live alone or with roommates, you'll have a lot more to do than you did at home. You'll have to buy your own groceries, fix your own meals, keep the place clean—and pay the bills. So before you sign a lease on your first apartment, think long and hard about whether you're ready for the challenge.

Apartment Hunting

You expect your home to have the basics: areas for living and sleeping, kitchen facilities, and a bathroom. It may also have special features such as a dishwasher, a garbage disposal, a built-in microwave, a fireplace, a security system, garage parking, gym facilities, or a swimming pool. You can probably think of others. In general, the more of these extras you have, the more you will pay.

The location of the apartment will also affect your rent. For example, you can expect to pay more to live in a trendy area of a city. Housing in rural areas generally costs less, but make sure you weigh the pros and cons. What you save on rent could be spent at the gas pump.

Get a Sense of It

Once you've narrowed your search to a few places, look past the floor plan and the amenities and focus on what your senses tell you. Be aware of unpleasant odors—possibly from mold inside or the remnants of the last kitty who marked his territory. Walk around the neighborhood. Would you be disturbed by sirens from the firehouse on the next block or feel unsafe walking past alleyways? Trust your senses—and your instincts.

Learning the Lingo

Reading the ads for "apts for rent" can be challenging if you're unfamiliar with the abbreviations they contain. For instance, a "BR" is a bedroom, "2BA" means two bathrooms, and "LR w/fpl" means living room with fireplace. Most newspapers that run classified ads include a key somewhere that explains the abbreviations.

CAN YOU AFFORD IT?

Experts recommend that people spend no more than about 30 percent of their income on housing. That can be easier said than done, though, for young adults starting out near the bottom of the pay scale. To figure out how much you can afford to pay for an apartment, look at all the costs involved, including:

Rent. When you first move into an apartment, the landlord may require one or two months' rent in advance. In college towns, you may have to pay rent on a place for a full year—not just the nine months that you spend in school.

Utilities. The rent on some apartments includes utility costs, but more often it doesn't. You may have to pay for heat, electricity, water, and even garbage removal. Ask how much these bills typically run per month. Also, find out whether the utility companies require a deposit to have the service connected in your name.

Deposit. Most landlords require a security deposit to cover any damage you may cause to the apartment. You'll get the deposit back when you move out, as long everything in the apartment—refrigerator, oven, cabinet interiors, shower, and so on —is clean and shows only normal wear. To protect yourself from being asked to pay for damage you didn't cause, check the apartment for existing problems when you move in. Make a list with the landlord, and sign and date it.

Other services. Dorms and student apartments may provide cable TV, Internet access, and basic phone service, but you're on your own with these added expenses when you live elsewhere. If you're trying to cut expenses, consider which of these "extras" you can live without.

Check the Net

Insurance

For less than $200 per year, you can protect your belongings from theft, fire, and other perils by carrying renters insurance. Search the Web for more information on this type of insurance and find sample quotes for coverage based on where you live.

KeyTerm: renters insurance

TRIMMING THE EXTRAS

After crunching the numbers, you may conclude that you don't have the funds to live on your own yet—unless you want to eat ramen noodles every day. Before you give up, though, think about ways of trimming costs. For example, if you can't afford an apartment of your own, maybe you could share a place with one or more roommates. That way, all your expenses—rent, security deposit, and utilities—would be divided up.

Don't forget to look at your utility costs, too. You can beat the heating bill by keeping the thermostat no higher than 68°F and putting on a sweater and a pair of socks to keep warm. On hot days, use a fan to stay cool, and save the A/C for days when the heat is really intolerable. You can also cut your electric bills by using appliances less and making a conscious effort to turn things off when you're not using them.

Those "other services" are another place to cut costs. Maybe you don't need both a cell phone *and* a land line. Save money by making your phone calls in the evening and on weekends, when rates are lower (or, with some cell phone plans, free). Or use a prepaid phone card with a low per-minute rate for your long-distance calls. If you don't use the Internet much, maybe you can live without broadband access—or skip the Internet fees and log on for free at the library.

QuickTip

Cut the Cable?
Consider challenging yourself to a trial run without cable or satellite TV. You may be surprised at how little you miss the extra channels.

it's Your turn

If you were moving into an apartment, which of your regular expenses could you cut? Food? Clothing? Entertainment? On the lines below, list five ideas for reducing your day-to-day expenses.

1. _____
   _____
2. _____
   _____
3. _____
   _____
4. _____
   _____
5. _____
   _____

QuickTip

Don't Be Too Hasty

In some college towns, property management companies try to persuade students to commit to apartments nine or ten months before they'll occupy them. Don't take this bait—you may regret not waiting until later to lock in housing.

Subletting

Some landlords allow you to *sublet* a rental unit—that is, rent it out to someone else in your place. However, your name remains on the lease. If the replacement tenant causes damage or doesn't pay the rent, you are still held responsible. A better option, if possible, is to *assign* the lease, or transfer it to another person's name.

LEARN ABOUT LEASES

When you move into an apartment, you may have to sign a lease. A typical lease is shown on the facing page. When you sign a lease, you agree to rent the apartment for a certain period of time under a certain set of terms. The lease protects your rights as well as those of your landlord. For instance, it guarantees that the rent can't be raised during the term of the lease. Most leases cover the following points:

- The length of the lease (often one year).
- The monthly rent and when it's due.
- The penalty for paying rent late.
- The security deposit required.
- Which utilities are included.
- What types of alterations (such as hanging pictures and painting) are acceptable.
- Rules about quiet hours, guests, pets, parking, and laundry facilities.
- Who is responsible for maintenance and repairs.
- Can you sublet for the summer if it is a 12-month lease?

Before you sign a lease, ask a parent or another knowledgeable adult to review it for you. Don't be afraid to ask questions. You may be able to make minor changes, which you and the landlord should both initial.

What if you sign a lease on an apartment and after a living there for a short while you decide it's not the right place for you? Maybe it's too far from work. Or you find a place you like better. It could be that your roommates are driving you crazy. Too bad—the agreement you signed is a legal document. So the most important point to remember is never to sign a lease without giving it careful consideration. Make sure you have all the information you need to make sure the living arrangement is right for you.

A TYPICAL LEASE

LEASE AGREEMENT

This lease agreement, made this _____th day of _____, 20_____, between Chris Stephens, Landlord, and _____, Tenant(s).

The said landlord hereby agrees to rent the premises at ___402 E. ELM ST.___ to be used only as a residence. The effective date is _____ and this lease agreement shall terminate one year later. Tenant agrees to pay the landlord the sum of ___$525.00___ per month, payable in advance on the ___FIRST___ day of each month. If tenant fails to pay rent within five (5) days of the due date, an initial late charge of ___$50___ will apply, plus a charge of ___$25___ per day until paid in full.

Tenant agrees to pay a security deposit of ___$300___. Landlord shall have the right to retain the security deposit, or any portion thereof reasonably necessary to compensate Landlord for damages.

Tenant shall, at Tenant's expense, keep the property in a clean and healthy condition, and maintain the lawn, shrubbery, and plantings in a neat condition. The walls, ceilings, and woodwork will not be marred or defaced. Tenant shall not have the right to make changes to the property. Tenant shall keep no animals of any kind on the property.

Tenant will not house permanent guests on the premises or sublet said premises without landlord's written permission. Tenant will pay all utilities except water and sewer bills, which will be paid by Landlord.

Landlord shall, at Landlord's expense, maintain the roof, foundation, outside walls, heating and air conditioning, plumbing, electrical systems, and structural aspects of the property. Tenant shall allow Landlord or its designee to enter the property in the event of an emergency at any time or at all times upon reasonable notice for the purpose of inspecting the property or performing Landlord's obligations.

Making the

SUPPOSE YOU'RE LOOKING FOR AN APARTMENT or house to share with one of your coworkers. Each of you makes about $1,400 a month after taxes. How will you choose the best place to fit your needs?

START by thinking about what features you want most in an apartment. Here are some possible advantages an apartment could have. Rank these in order of what's most important to you.

_____ Safe neighborhood
_____ Convenient to work/school
_____ Laundry facilities
_____ Free parking
_____ On-site manager
_____ Secure building
_____ Quiet building
_____ Clean hallways
_____ Plenty of light
_____ Window coverings
_____ Pleasant view
_____ Pool or fitness center

NOW suppose you've managed to find two places you like reasonably well. Both are about a mile from your workplace and require a one-year lease. Compare the two ads and use the chart below to list the pros and cons of each choice.

4045 Westmont Rd., cozy 2BR townhouse w/new kit, beautiful décor, new blinds, c/a, W/D, free cable, no pets, immed occ. $695/mo

610 N. Oak St., spacious upper unit, 2BR, 2BA, fpl in LR, c/a, util included. $675/mo

Right Choice

	PROS	CONS
Westmont Road townhouse		
Oak Street apartment		

Which of these two options would you choose? Explain why.

_____

_____

_____

_____

_____

_____

_____

If you and your best friend head off to college together, consider starting out with different roommates instead of living together. Your circle of acquaintances will immediately double as you get to know your best friend's roommate and his or her friends.

Make Room for Roommates

HAVING ONE OR MORE ROOMMATES is a great way to cut living expenses. When you share housing costs, you can afford a bigger apartment in a safer, more convenient location. For some people, though, living with another person just isn't worth the trouble. It's a decision only you can make.

A GOOD FIT

While everyone wants a roommate who pays the rent on time and doesn't steal things, it's also helpful to find someone whose habits and personality fit well with yours. For example, what if you want someone to hang out with but your roommate is away most of the time? What if you study best with music in the background but your roommate needs absolute silence? Or what if you like to keep the thermostat down but your roommate likes the apartment toasty warm? The problem isn't that these people are "bad" roommates—it's that you're not a good fit for each other.

If you have the luxury of interviewing a potential roommate, try to get a feel for what it would be like to live with that person on a daily basis. Also, while it may seem impolite to ask about money, it's wise to make sure your potential roommate has the financial resources to afford his or her share of the rent and expenses.

BEST FRIENDS

Living with your best friend may seem like the greatest idea in the world, but people who have been there often advise against it. Why? For one thing, no matter how well you know each other, there are always things you don't discover until you move in together. If you end up driving each other nuts, it could ruin a good friendship. You may find yourself afraid of speaking up when things bother you for fear of upsetting your friend. You might also get annoyed if your friend starts to enjoy new friends and activities that don't involve you.

What about living with your sister or brother? That may actually have a better chance of success. After years of living together, you already know each other's habits and quirks, and you're probably not afraid to tell each other what's on your mind.

it's Your turn

Living with another person always involves give and take, but some issues can be deal-breakers. Check out the list below of qualities a roommate could have. Draw a line through any item you could not tolerate. Then rank the remaining items in order of their importance to you, with one being the most important.

_____ Respects my privacy

_____ Stays up late

_____ Is quiet

_____ Likes to cook

_____ Has same taste in music

_____ Hangs towels/leaves bathroom tidy

_____ Washes dishes after every meal

_____ Entertains frequently

_____ Respects my stuff

_____ Smokes

_____ Pays bills on time

_____ Relaxed attitude about cleaning

_____ Takes accurate phone messages

_____ Is a morning person

_____ Keeps his/her room neat

_____ Spends little time at home

Imagine that you're interviewing a potential roommate to share your two-bedroom apartment. Jot down at least three questions you would ask about the person's lifestyle and habits.

1. _____

_____

_____

2. _____

_____

_____

3. _____

_____

_____

GROUND RULES

When you embark on a new living arrangement, start out right by discussing the basics. Be honest about any pet peeves you have. It's better to hash the issues out up front than to get annoyed when a roommate crosses one of your boundaries. For instance, you might say, "I have this thing about my printer. The cartridges are so expensive that I don't like anybody else to use it." That would save you from being angry if you found your roommate printing a research paper. Make sure you cover the three issues that cause the most problems among roommates: guests, cleanliness, and food.

"Andy will be staying with us for..." It's fun to have company, but someone who's there every day isn't so much a guest as an extra roommate who doesn't pay rent. So while you may want to help out a friend by offering your place for a while, your roommate probably won't appreciate having the couch permanently occupied.

"Are these your dishes?" Nobody says your room or apartment has to be spotless. The important thing is for you and your roommate to agree on an acceptable standard of cleanliness and clutter. If one of you wants the garbage emptied twice a day and the other leaves dishes in the sink for a week, you may have a problem! If finding another roommate isn't an option, do your best to compromise and be tolerant.

QuickTip

Fair Share

Even if you don't normally share food with your roommate, have a heart—if homemade cookies arrive in the mail, or if you receive a box of chocolates, don't keep them all to yourself!

"Where's my bagel?" Some roommates share all the food they buy, while others prefer to distinguish "my food" from "your food"—a practice that works as long as one roommate doesn't take up three-fourths of the refrigerator. Even if you share food, you may sometimes want to set aside a special item, like a loose cinnamon raisin bagel or the salsa you bought to take to a party. In this case, tell your roommate or attach a note that says *reserved*.

PAYING THE BILLS

Suppose that you come home one day and find that you have no electricity. You check the circuit box: no problem there. So you call the power company. That's when you find out that the problem is your roommate, who never got around to paying the electric bill. You'd probably be pretty annoyed—and with good reason. If you want to avoid this situation, you need to work out a system with your roommate to make sure the bills get paid.

Your biggest bill each month will be the rent. You'll need an agreement for how to divide this up. For example, suppose you're sharing a place that costs $1,000 a month with one roommate. First you need to consider whether you should split the rent 50-50 or not. If one bedroom is much bigger than the other or has its own attached bathroom, it may not be fair to split the rent evenly. Then you need to decide how you will pay the rent. Will one person write a check for the full amount, and receive a check for the roommate's share? Or will you both make out separate checks to the landlord?

The same applies to other bills. You need to agree upon a payment system. If the phone, for example, is in your name, then you'll have to pay the phone company each month and get your roommate to pay you back. If you both use the phone about the same amount, you might agree to split the bill down the middle. However, if your roommate spends three hours a week on the phone with relatives in Japan, you'll probably want to break down the bill so that your roommate pays for those international calls.

QuickTip

Allow Time for Delays

Don't wait until the day a bill is due to drop it in the mail. If the mail is delayed your payment could arrive late. To avoid a late charge, send in your payment five to seven days in advance.

What's the Rush?

Paying bills on time is critical for several reasons:

1. You avoid late fees.

2. You don't risk having your service cut off.

3. You won't receive a black mark on your credit record due to late payments.

4. You don't risk being refused service when you move again.

QuickTip

Budget Decorating

WHEN YOU MOVE INTO A PLACE OF YOUR OWN, you'll want to add some special touches to make it feel like home. Your greatest challenge, next to a limited budget, will probably be that you can't make major changes to a place you don't own. Some landlords will let you paint the walls, but most won't. Whatever you do, don't just go ahead without asking—you might violate your lease. You can always focus on things that you can take with you when you move.

As for having a measly amount to spend, that can actually work to your advantage. You're more likely to be creative and a little daring with things that didn't cost much.

FINDING FURNITURE

Unless you move into a fully furnished place, you'll need to acquire some basic furniture—a bed, chair, and table at the very minimum. Few people can afford brand new furniture when they start out; most furnish their first home with used or borrowed items.

You may be able to find used furniture just by asking around. Friends and relatives may be happy to give you their unwanted items for free. You can also watch for garage sales, newspaper ads, and signs posted on bulletin boards. Departing college seniors can be a real bonanza; they're often willing to unload furniture at rock-bottom prices so they won't have to move it.

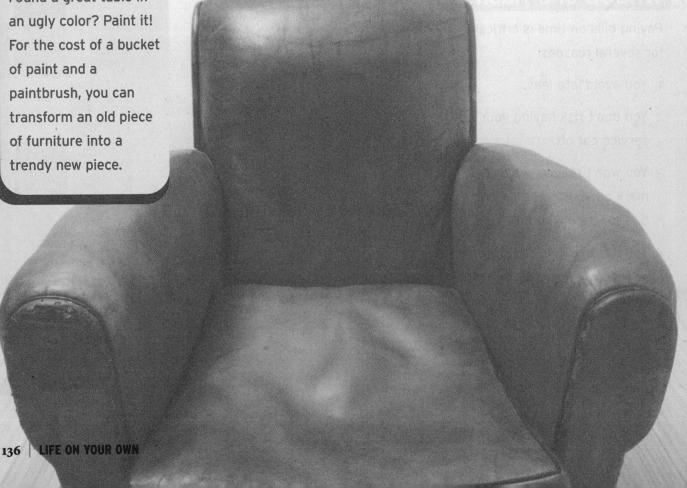

QuickTip

Dorm Rules

Check to find out what is and isn't allowed in your dorm room. Many colleges ban items such as electric grills, immersion heaters, incense, and candles. If you do have electrical items make sure they are turned off or unplugged when not in use.

DORM DECOR

Decorating a dorm room poses special challenges. In many cases, you can't even rearrange the furniture—it's fixed in place. Here are some helpful tips, some of which will also work for a studio or other small apartment:

- Contact your roommate before move-in day to figure out who's bringing what. You might each need your own computer, but you can share a TV.

- If you're renting a truck to move into a dorm room, you're probably taking too much stuff. Take only the essentials!

- Try using an area rug to warm up a cold tile floor. Be sure to measure the room size before you buy it.

- Consider investing in a mini fridge and microwave, if these items are allowed. You may even be able to buy used ones from departing students for reasonable prices.

- Decorate bare walls with posters, maps, photos, and other art works. If you're not allowed to put nails in the walls, hang pictures with poster putty or masking tape.

- Choose easy-to-clean items. A dry-clean-only comforter isn't a good choice if your bed doubles as the sofa. Don't bring anything that will break easily—or has sentimental value.

QuickTip

Picture Perfect

Not allowed to put nails or picture hangers in the walls? Try this decorators' trick: prop a picture or mirror against the wall on top of a dresser, mantel, or shelf.

DECORATING KNOW-HOW

Although there are no hard-and-fast rules about how to arrange your space, there are certain basic strategies that can help you. The most important principle to keep in mind is that your home should fit your needs. Whether you're arranging furniture, hanging art, or installing lights, try to set everything up so that it works with the way you'll be using the space.

Set up "zones."

Arrange furniture to create areas for different activities. A computer desk and file cabinet in one corner could make a mini office. A futon, chair, and entertainment center could be your main area for relaxation. Draw possible arrangements to scale on graph paper to judge how pieces will fit.

Use color. Colors can

create a mood or atmosphere, and tie a room together. For instance, if your rug has yellow in it, you might pick up this color in pillows, blinds, or an art object.

Create a focal point.

Make a room interesting by emphasizing a feature such as a fireplace, window, or an interesting architectural artifact (old gates have become very collectible).

Keep things in proportion. A set of

delicate wicker chairs wouldn't look right around a heavy oak dining table. Try to choose furnishings that are similar in size and weight and in proportion to one another.

Group similar items together. Baskets, pot-

tery, or candles of varying sizes and shapes can be grouped into attractive collections. Scattered about the room, they don't have the same visual impact.

Use light effectively.

Arrange lamps so you have enough light in every area. If your home is dark, you can use mirrors to reflect light and make the space look bigger and brighter. Make the most of natural light.

Introduce touches of nature. Add some

plants, natural fibers, or a tabletop fountain to bring a soothing influence to a room.

IMPROVISE

Before you go out and buy something you need, see if something you already have could do the job. Use your imagination to see old things in new ways. The classic example is to create bookshelves from planks of wood set on piles of bricks. You can also place an old door across two file cabinets to create a desk. An old crate, hidden under some nice fabric, makes a fine end table, and a couple of sturdy cardboard boxes hidden under fabric can be used as a coffee table.

If you want to create a window treatment but don't want to go to the trouble of buying or sewing curtains, drape a length of fabric across the top of a window. Or here's a way to add interest to a sunny windowsill: fill clear glass bottles with water tinted with food coloring and line them up along the sill.

Check the Net

Do It Yourself

Doing things yourself—painting, sewing, refinishing furniture, and even upholstering—is a great way to stretch your decorating budget. Go online to learn more about home projects you can tackle on your own.

KeyTerms: home decorating projects, do-it-yourself decorating

QuickTip

Get Closer

There's no rule that says that furniture has to be pushed against the walls. Pulling chairs and sofas closer together can make a space look more inviting and certainly makes conversation easier.

QuickTip

Wipe It Up!

If you spill anything, wipe it up right away. You'll feel pretty embarrassed if you end up walking around on crutches because you slipped in your own kitchen.

Mail Call

Stay on top of the daily mail so it doesn't pile up. Discard the junk mail and figure out what you want to do with the rest. Magazines might go on the coffee table and bills in a basket until it's time to pay them. Toss newspapers in the recycle bin as soon as you've read them—or after they've sat unread for three days.

Taking Care of Your Place

ONCE THE FURNITURE IS IN PLACE and the pictures are all on the walls, you may think your work is finished. If only that were true! The fact is, keeping your home looking decent is an ongoing job. Even the most gorgeous apartment can look like a real dump if there's dust on the furniture, dishes in the sink, and clothes scattered everywhere.

It doesn't take a lot of effort to keep your apartment in reasonably good shape. The trick is to clean as you go. If you don't clean the toilet for weeks at a time, it turns into a job too horrible to face—but if you give it a quick brush and flush once a week, it's a snap.

DAILY DUTIES

It takes only 20 to 30 minutes a day to keep the mess at bay. Start by making your bed in the morning. You may think that there's no point to this, since you'll just pull it apart again at night, but your room just *feels* cleaner when the covers are pulled up. While you're in the bedroom, put away yesterday's clothes. Hang or fold the ones you can wear again, and place the dirty ones in a clothes hamper until it's time to do laundry.

Keep the kitchen tidy, too. Wash dishes as soon as you use them, or load them into the dishwasher, if you have one. Wipe down the stove, sink, and counters, too. This removes stray food particles that could attract ants and other pests. Since your kitchen sponge sees a lot of use, replace it frequently, wash it in the dishwasher with the dishes once a week, or sterilize it with bleach. Wash your dishcloths and towels regularly as well. Finally, check the kitchen garbage, and empty it as soon as it gets full. Full means up to the rim of the container—not piled so high that it's in danger of falling onto the floor!

REGULAR MAINTENANCE

On top of these daily tasks, there are other chores that you'll need to do regularly. How regularly depends on your lifestyle. For example, if you cook every night, your kitchen will need a thorough cleaning a lot more often than if you eat out most of the time. If you have pets—the furry kind, at least—you'll need to sweep or vacuum more often. And of course, the more people sharing your apartment, the more mess you'll all make.

Tasks like sweeping, dusting, changing the sheets, or cleaning the bathroom are probably once-a-week jobs, although you may be able to get away with doing some of them less often. You can spread these tasks out over the week or tackle them all at once when you have a few hours free. A couple of times a month—or whenever they start to look dirty—tackle things like kitchen floors, upholstered furniture, or the refrigerator. A few chores can wait even longer. Those might include washing windows, wiping woodwork, and dusting ceiling fan blades.

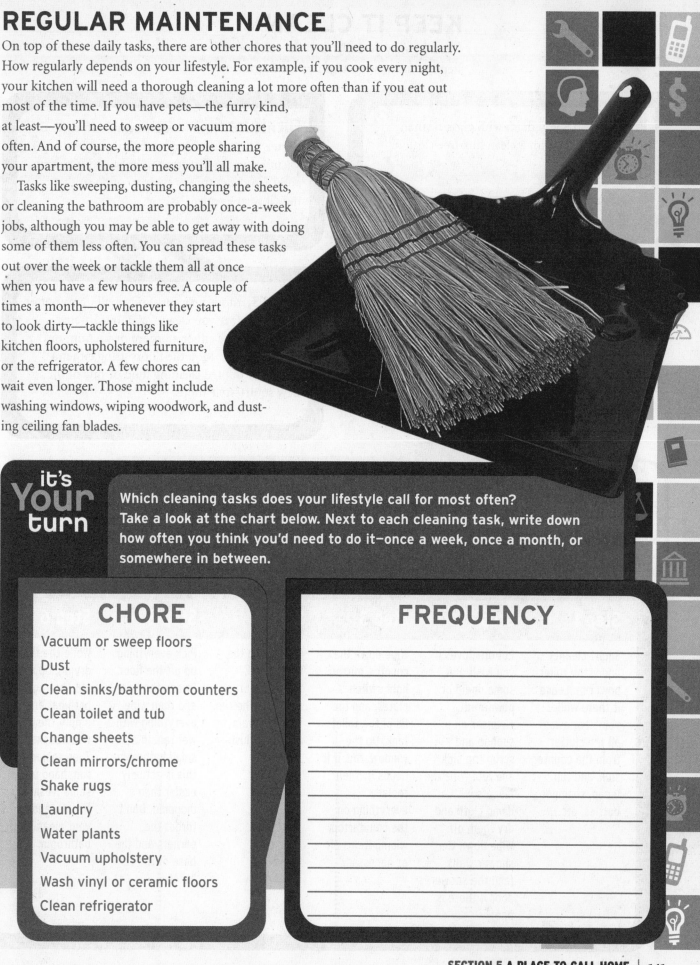

it's Your turn

Which cleaning tasks does your lifestyle call for most often? Take a look at the chart below. Next to each cleaning task, write down how often you think you'd need to do it—once a week, once a month, or somewhere in between.

CHORE	FREQUENCY
Vacuum or sweep floors	
Dust	
Clean sinks/bathroom counters	
Clean toilet and tub	
Change sheets	
Clean mirrors/chrome	
Shake rugs	
Laundry	
Water plants	
Vacuum upholstery	
Wash vinyl or ceramic floors	
Clean refrigerator	

KEEP IT CLEAN

Cleaning may be dull, but it doesn't have to be complicated. Just use these simple steps to clean every item in your home.

Windows. Spray them with glass cleaner, then wipe them with a clean lint-free cloth or a paper towel.

Furniture. Remove dust with a soft cloth or duster. Use a dusting spray first if you wish. Vacuum up the dirt from upholstered furniture, and turn the cushions every so often so that they'll wear evenly.

Walls and cabinets. Wipe away spots and fingerprints with a sponge or cloth.

Floors. Move furniture and small items out of the way before you clean. Vacuum carpeted floors, and use either a broom or vacuum on smooth floors. Mop tile floors using either a bucket of diluted cleaning fluid or one of the new squirt-style mops.

How-To

Clean Your Bathroom The bathroom is most people's least favorite room to clean. Breaking the job down into steps can make it easier. Make this routine a weekly habit, and you should never be ashamed of the way your bathroom looks.

Step 1	Step 2	Step 3	Step 4	Step 5	Step 6
Squirt cleaner under the toilet bowl rim. Leave it there while you clear away all the clutter from the counter, sink, and tub (soap, shampoo bottles, etc.).	Put on gloves if you wish. Put some liquid or powdered cleanser on a sponge and scrub the sink and tub. Wipe the faucets with a damp cloth and dry them off. Wipe down the shower walls (and the shower door if there is one).	Wipe down the counter, mirror, light switch plates, and the lid of the toilet tank. Do the window, too, if it needs it. Then replace everything on the countertop, wiping items off as necessary.	Go back to the toilet bowl. Swish the brush up under the rim, into the drain and then flush.	Pick everything up off the floor. Sweep the floor and then wipe everything with a wet rag. In a small bathroom, this is actually easier than mopping. Don't forget the corners and the base of the toilet.	While the floor is drying, go shake out the rug or bathmat and empty the wastebasket. Then replace the rug, hang up some fresh towels, and enjoy your clean bathroom.

SAFE AT HOME

One bonus of keeping your home free of clutter is that you'll be less likely to trip over something and hurt yourself. Unfortunately, that won't help you if you fall off a chair that you were climbing on to reach the top shelf of your closet. So for safety's sake, invest in a sturdy stepstool for reaching high places. Also, keep all staircases clear and well lit—these are one of the most likely areas for falls. Keep nonskid mats under your rugs so that they won't slide, and avoid stretching electrical cords across places where people walk.

Speaking of electrical cords, you've probably heard before that overloading your outlets can start a fire. So if you need to plug more than two or three items into one outlet, use a power strip. And be extra careful with matches, candles, or anything else that burns. Just in case a fire does start, make sure your home has smoke detectors—at least one on every floor— and a fire extinguisher (keep it in the same spot for ease in grabbing it if needed).

QuickTip

Spring Forward... to Safety

How can you remember to check the batteries in your smoke detectors? Make it part of your "Spring Forward, Fall Back" routine. As you go around your home changing the clocks, check the smoke detectors too. If one of them needs a new battery, replace it immediately. Otherwise you could go a full six months without the protection that the smoke detector provides.

Intruder Alert

To keep intruders out of your home, keep doors and windows locked, especially at night. Keep an outdoor light on, if possible—burglars try to enter where they won't be noticed. If you're going to be away, don't advertise the fact: have someone take in your mail for you and consider investing in a timer to switch on a light in the evening.

What Could Go Wrong?

THE FIRST NIGHT YOU GO TO SLEEP in your very own place, it may feel like a dream come true. But you'll get a rude awakening the first time you wake up to discover that there's no heat or that the kitchen drain is blocked. Dealing with these kinds of minor emergencies comes with the territory, so be prepared.

For most problems, the first thing to do is call the landlord or building manager. Keep this person's number handy, along with numbers for the electric company, gas company, and so on. Also, as soon as you move in, find out where your circuit box is, as well as the shut-off valves for water, power, and gas. Finally, arm yourself with the following information on how to handle specific crises:

The power goes out. First, check to see if it's only one circuit that's out, or the whole apartment. If you were vacuuming or using a small appliance, unplug it. Then check fuses or circuit breakers. If a breaker's been tripped, you can reset it. If it's a fuse, you'll need to replace it. If the whole apartment goes dark, grab a flashlight so you can investigate. If the entire neighborhood is affected, you'll want to call the power company. Meanwhile, don't open the refrigerator or freezer.

The toilet overflows. First, stop the flow of water by turning off the shut-off valve, usually found behind the toilet. Use towels to soak up the water. Remove the tank lid and press the stopper closed at the bottom of the tank. Bale about half the water from the toilet bowl, then set a plunger over the hole. Pump it rapidly about 10 times and remove it. If that doesn't fix the clog, call the landlord or a plumber.

You smell gas. A gas leak can result in a deadly explosion, so don't light any matches or turn on anything electrical—including lights—to avoid sparks. If the odor is strong, don't even use the phone. Open doors and windows for ventilation, leave the area and call the gas company from someplace else.

The drain is clogged. You can also use a plunger on a sink clog. Stuff a rag in the small overflow opening of a bathroom sink before trying to plunge it. If the plunger doesn't do the trick, call the landlord.

You're locked out. Consider leaving a key with a trusted neighbor in case this problem comes up. (Don't hide a spare key anywhere near the door—burglars know where to look.) If no one else can let you in, call the landlord. If your key is really lost—not just locked inside— you'll probably have to pay the landlord to have the locks changed. Even if you have a spare key, losing the old one means someone else could find it—and use it.

SAFETY SUPPLIES

When things go wrong in the home, it's good to know that you have the right tools and equipment to deal with the problem. When you move into a place of your own, make a point of stocking up with the basic supplies that will help you in an emergency. Here's what you should have on hand:

- first aid kit
- basic tool kit
- fire extinquisher
- flashlight
- plunger
- tape measure
- light bulbs
- batteries
- candles and matches

QuickTip

It's Not Your Problem

Don't worry that you're being a pain by bugging the landlord about problems in your rental unit! Little problems can turn into big ones if they're not fixed—like a leaky roof that leads to major mold problems or fallen ceilings. You can try to solve minor problems yourself, such as a slow-running drain or ants invading the kitchen, but if you can't fix it, call the landlord.

QuickTip

Don't Risk It

You may be tempted to leave the dishwasher or washing machine running when you go out, but you'd be unwise to do so. If a washing machine overflows, you want to be home to stop the flooding.

On the Move

IF YOU'VE NEVER LIVED ON YOUR OWN BEFORE, you probably don't own huge amounts of stuff. This makes moving a lot simpler, since you can use a car to carry your belongings to your new home. But the next time you move will probably be a different story. By then, you may have furniture, dishes, audio systems—much more than you can carry in a couple of car trips.

The idea of packing everything you own into boxes and moving it somewhere else—even if it's only across town—can seem overwhelming. The trick is to use your management skills and plan in advance.

How-To

Packing It In Packing up everything you own is a daunting task. These tips will help you.

Step 1

Gather the packing supplies you'll need: sturdy boxes, tape, bubble wrap, newsprint, garbage bags, and markers.

Step 2

Begin your packing with the items you use least often. Label each box with the type of items it contains and the room it should go in—for example, "Pots and pans (kitchen)" or number them and keep a list. Put lighter items in larger boxes and heavier ones in smaller boxes. Avoid loading more than 50 pounds in any box.

Step 3

Pack fragile items in separate boxes. Wrap each item carefully in bubble wrap, tissue paper, or blank newsprint. You can also use towels and blankets. Clearly label these boxes "FRAGILE."

Step 4

Pack books in small boxes so they won't be too heavy. Set them in upright and pack them as tightly as possible.

Step 5

Pack your most needed items last—dishes, bedding, and so on. Label these boxes "Load last" so that they'll be the last things onto the moving van. That way you'll be able to get them out right away.

Step 5

Pack a "trip kit" of essential items that should go with you in your car, rather than in the van. It should include important documents, your checkbook, cash and other valuables, medications, toiletries, toilet paper, light bulbs, paper products (plates, napkins, towels, and silverware) and anything you'll need on your trip.

GETTING READY

If you leave everything until the last minute before a move, you'll never be ready in time. Start preparing well in advance. The following checklist shows some things you'll need to do before moving and how much time you should leave for each one.

Time before move	Things to do
Six weeks	• Start selling, giving away, or throwing out items you don't want to take with you.
One month	• Make an inventory of what you're moving to help you keep track. • Fill out forms at the post office to have your mail forwarded. • Begin gathering packing supplies. • Reserve a rental truck if you'll be using one.
Three weeks	• Make any necessary travel arrangements. • Begin packing items you don't use often. • Get copies of medical records and other important documents.
Two weeks	• Ask friends and family members to help with your move. • Start using up the food in your fridge and freezer. • Notify people and businesses of your change of address. • Cancel utilities that are in your name, as well as cable TV, Internet service, and renters insurance. Set up these services for your new home. • Transfer all prescriptions to a drugstore in your new hometown. • Start cleaning your current rental unit by removing pictures from the walls and spackling nail holes. • Start your serious packing.
One week	• If you'll be changing banks after you move, close your account and transfer the money to your new bank. (Make sure you have no outstanding checks on your old account.) • Pack your "trip kit."
One day	• Pack any remaining items except what you'll need overnight. • Clean your rental unit thoroughly so you'll get your security deposit back.

QuickTip

Truck Rentals

The busiest times for truck rental companies are the beginning and end of the school year. If you plan to move during peak season, make sure you reserve a truck as early as possible.

Who Needs to Know?

Who needs to know that you're moving? In addition to friends and family, you'll need to notify:

• doctors and dentists
• utility companies
• subscriptions
• banks and credit card companies
• insurance companies
• the IRS
• clubs and organizations
• office of voter registration

QuickTip

First Things First

If you're planning to paint the walls in your new apartment, do it before you unpack. Otherwise you'll just have to pack everything away again before you can paint the room.

Check the Net

A Moving Experience

The Internet has all kinds of useful resources for people planning a move. You can create personalized checklists and packing lists, change your address online, and calculate the costs of moving services. Go online to find out what sites would be most helpful to you when you move.

KeyTerms: moving checklist, moving calculator

MOVING DAY

On moving day, you'll have a lot to do, so you'll probably want to make an early start. Begin by packing up your last remaining items, such as the sheets you slept in the night before and the dishes you ate breakfast from. Next, you'll need to pick up your rental truck, if you're using one. Along with your helpers, start loading items into the truck. Try to take the big boxes and pieces of furniture first— you can tuck smaller boxes in around them. Supervise the whole process to make sure that people handle your fragile items with care and that your "load last" boxes are the last onto the truck.

Once everything is loaded, do a "sweep" of the apartment to make sure nothing's been left behind. Be sure to check inside closets and cupboards. Double-check your inventory list to make sure you have everything, and make sure your "trip kit" is in the car. Last, now that the apartment is empty, do a little last-minute cleaning to make sure everything is in good enough shape for the new tenants to move in. Your security deposit may depend on it!

Once you arrive at your new home, you'll have to go through the whole process in reverse—unloading the essential items first, then the rest of your belongings. As soon as you arrive, check to make sure the utilities in your new apartment are connected. You may also need to clean up the new apartment before you start putting stuff away. You'll be moving in for a few weeks as you unpack your knick-knacks, hang pictures, and so on. A good plan is to get at least one room set up, with all the furniture and large accessories in place, on the first day. That way there will be one place in the apartment that feels like home right away.

Weeding Out

SINCE MOVING INTO his apartment, Frank's gathered a lot of new stuff—furniture, accessories, dishes, books, and lots of electronics. Now, he's been offered a job in another state and will be moving 400 miles away. Frank realizes that moving all this stuff is going to be a big task. He'll have to hire a truck, and get people to help him load it. And who will help him at the other end? On the other hand, he could just get rid of some things, but then he'd have to replace them once he gets to his new home.

YOUR IDEAS

1. What factors should Frank weigh as he decides what to do about his move?

_____

_____

_____

_____

_____

2. If Frank decides against moving everything, which items should he get rid of? Which should he keep? Why?

_____

_____

_____

_____

_____

3. How could Frank avoid losing too much money if he discards and later replaces some of his belongings?

_____

_____

_____

_____

_____

SETTING UP HOUSEKEEPING

Finding and setting up your first home is a complicated business. Do a "trial run" to see just what this process involves. Start by searching classified ads and Web sites to find a place where you think you'd like to live. Clip out or print out a description of the apartment and use it to answer the questions that follow.

Check the Net

Check the Net

Clean Up Your Act

There's a wealth of housekeeping shortcuts and tips on the Web. You can learn how to save time, save money, or even make your own nontoxic cleaners. Go online to dig up useful tips for keeping your home clean.

Key Terms: cleaning tips, housekeeping tips

1. DESCRIBE the apartment and explain why you chose it.

_____

_____

_____

2. NEXT, figure out whether you can afford this apartment. On the lines below, list the monthly rent and your best estimates of the other expenses you would be likely to have.

Rent	$_____
Heat/AC	$_____
Electricity	$_____
Water	$_____
Phone	$_____
Internet	$_____
Cable	$_____
Other	$_____
	$_____
	$_____
	$_____
Total	$_____

Assume that you want your housing expenses to be no more than 30 percent of your total income. How much would you need to make per month to afford this apartment?

$_____

3. Would it be possible to cut these costs by sharing the apartment with a roommate? **EXPLAIN** why or why not.

_____

_____

_____

4. LIST the furnishings and other items you would need to outfit this apartment.

_____   _____

_____   _____

_____   _____

_____   _____

_____   _____

5. USE store fliers and catalogs to figure out the approximate cost of each item you listed above. Next to each item, write down its estimated cost. Then add up the total. How much would it cost to buy all these items new?

$_____

6. IDENTIFY the three most expensive items on the list. List one way you might try to acquire each of these items for less than it would cost to buy at a store.

1) _____
_____

2) _____
_____

3) _____
_____

7. FINALLY, pick one room and describe how you would furnish and decorate it. If you have a floor plan of the unit, explain how you would arrange the furniture to make good use of the space. On a separate sheet of paper, draw pictures of furnishings and accessories you would use.

_____
_____
_____
_____
_____
_____
_____
_____

QuickTip

Take a Little Bit of Home

Whether you're moving into a local dorm or across the nation, take your favorite mug, family picture, or some other piece of home in your "trip kit." It will give you a sense of family and the essence of home as you transition into a new life.

Going Places

Getting There

HOW DO YOU GET WHERE YOU WANT TO GO—school, work, out with friends, shopping? Maybe you take the bus to school and catch a ride home with a friend after team practice or a meeting. Perhaps your mom lets you borrow her car to go to the movies or to the mall. Have you thought about how your transportation needs might change after graduation? If you attend college or start a full-time job, how are you going to get there?

Having your own car is probably your first choice, but it may also be the most expensive one. Before you go into debt or spend any hard-earned savings, consider your other transportation options. There may be more than you think.

FARE DEALS

If you'll be living in or near a city, check out the mass transit system. It might offer some options you haven't thought of. For example, James rides his bike to work in the morning, but rides the bus home if it's dark or rainy after work. His bicycle rides for free on a handy rack.

Taking mass transit can have some distinct advantages over paying for your own vehicle. You might even meet new friends on the commute to and from school or work!

Despite its benefits, public transportation does have some drawbacks. The main disadvantage is the lack of flexibility. When you take a bus, train, or subway, you don't get to set the schedule; the transit service does. There's also a potential for delays and cancellations. And some days your bus or train may be so crowded that you have to stand.

Cost. Public transportation almost always costs less than paying for gas, tolls, parking, insurance, and maintenance. Buying a youth/student fare will save you money. So will a monthly pass.

Time. Taking the train or bus gives you time to catch up on your reading, homework, or even sleep! Some passengers pass the time "people watching."

Traffic. When people use public transportation, there are fewer vehicles out there. Fewer parking spaces are needed. That's good news for the environment.

Stress. Using mass transit means that you're leaving the driving—and the hassle— to someone else.

QuickTip

Mass Transit Schedules

Search the Internet for information about the mass transit available in your area. Determine whether the service seems economical.

KeyTerms: mass transit, bus schedule, train schedule

Pool Rules

Consider these questions when setting up a carpool:

- Who will drive? Will one person drive, or will you take turns? If there's one driver, how much will everybody chip in for expenses?

- Where will you meet? Will you be picked up at home or meet at a central place?

- What time will you leave? What if someone oversleeps or has to work overtime?

- What happens when the driver is on vacation?

it's Your turn

Answer these questions to assess your transportation needs and options.

1. Where do I go most often? How far away are these places?

   School: _____

   Work: _____

   Friends: _____

   Shopping: _____

   Social activities: _____

   Other: _____

2. Is mass transit available in my area? What kind? _____

3. Does the public transportation serve the places I need to go? _____

4. Would the schedule work for me? _____

5. Are the stations and pickup points convenient for me? _____

6. How much would mass transit cost per month? _____

7. What other transportation options are available? _____

   _____

   _____

Review your answers. What can you conclude about your transportation needs and options? _____

_____

COULD YOU CARPOOL?

Carpooling can be a great option for transportation. If the idea appeals to you, check with people at school or work to find out who lives near you and has a similar schedule. Carpools can work very well, provided everyone involved understands and follows the ground rules. Having the same taste in music can help too!

Your Own Wheels

IF YOU DON'T HAVE ACCESS TO MASS TRANSIT—or even if you do—you may still want your own vehicle. Just make sure that you consider all the expenses involved. Josh traded in his old car for one that was just a couple of years old. It made him *feel* good to drive it. The payment was about $100 higher than before but he figured he could afford it if he picked up a few more hours at work. Six months down the road, Josh regretted his decision. He had to sell the car and lost money in the process.

WHAT IT REALLY COSTS

Millions of people have been in Josh's situation. His auto expenses were so high that he couldn't afford to go out with his friends or buy new clothes. Making his loan payment wasn't the real headache; it was the insurance and other costs that were eating up his paycheck.

Before *you* commit to a vehicle purchase, make sure you're looking at the whole picture. Consider these expenses:

Insurance premiums. How much will you pay in auto insurance premiums? Car insurance is essential and can be very expensive. Young drivers pay a higher rate, even if they have a clean driving record. Accidents can be financially, as well as physically, painful.

Tolls and parking. Will you travel on a toll road or use a toll bridge? Even $1 in tolls each way to work or school will add $40 a month to your driving expenses. Will you have to pay for parking? A parking permit at some colleges and apartment complexes can add up to hundreds of dollars a year, as can daily rates in some parking lots.

Routine maintenance. Plan on spending about $200 a year on maintenance; less if you learn how to do some tasks yourself. You may face bills for routine work on brakes and tires, too.

Fill-ups. How many miles will you average each week? If gas prices are high, you'll need to allow a tidy sum for filling the gas tank. You'll also want a vehicle that isn't a gas guzzler.

Loan payments. Obviously the more you borrow, the bigger your monthly payments will be. Low financing rates may sweeten the deal, but you still have to make payments for many, many months.

Repairs. If you're lucky, your vehicle won't need repairs, but don't count on it. If you buy a new vehicle, most repairs will be covered by the warranty for a few years. If you have a used vehicle, however, be prepared to pay.

Shopping for a Loan

Take time to shop around for a car loan; it's a relationship you'll have for a long time. Your goal is generally to find the lowest interest rate. Keep in mind, though, that the amount you pay for the loan depends not only on the interest rate but also on the length of the loan. Sometimes a shorter loan at a higher interest rate costs less in the long run than a longer loan at a lower rate. The lender should be able to "run" the numbers so you can compare terms.

ADDING IT ALL UP

It's easy to be fooled by ads that promise "Yours for just $299 a month." Car ownership is *always* more expensive than the ads suggest. Here's a fairly conservative example of costs:

COSTS OF VEHICLE OWNERSHIP

Category	Cost	Monthly Payment	Yearly Expense
Auto loan	$10,000 + 5 percent interest (3-year loan)	$300	$3,600
Fuel	$20 per week	$80+	$960+
Tolls	$2.50 per day (5 days per week)	$50	$600
Insurance	$600 for 6-month policy	$100	$1,200
Maintenance	$20 every 3 months + $80 every 6 months	$20	$240
Repairs	$300 every 6 months	$50	$600
Totals		$600	$7,200

HOW WILL YOU PAY?

If you've been able to save for a vehicle of your own, congratulations! You will save a ton of money. Most people need to get a loan from a bank or credit union, or from the dealership. The length of a standard car loan may be 36, 48, or 60 months. A loan has two parts:

DID YOU KNOW?

Cosigning Because of your age and limited credit history, most lenders will require you to have a *cosigner*—another person to sign the loan papers with you. If someone declines to be your cosigner, don't be offended. The cosigner is legally responsible for the payments if you don't make them. Some people may not be willing to accept that risk.

Down payment. With most loans, you make a down payment, or a portion of the purchase price up front in cash. A typical minimum down payment is 10 percent of the purchase price. If you can afford a larger down payment, go for it. You'll borrow less and will pay less in finance charges.

Monthly bills. The amount of your monthly payment will depend on the loan amount, the number of months, and the interest rate. No matter how long the loan period, your monthly payments will stay the same. After the loan is paid in full, you'll receive the *title*, a legal document that shows who owns the vehicle.

Accepting a Gift

WOULDN'T IT BE GREAT IF somebody wanted to *give* you a car? That's what happened to Katherine. Her Aunt Marie could no longer drive due to failing eyesight and wanted to give Katherine her 10-year-old car. Katherine was allowed to drive her family's SUV when she needed transportation, but the freedom of having her own car would be great, she thought. Then she started to think about it. Aunt Marie had mentioned the car had new tires, but needed a little transmission work. Katherine wondered how much that might cost. She had put money away for college and was reluctant to dip into that account. Was accepting the gift a wise move, or was it something she might regret later?

YOUR IDEAS

1. What if the transmission work was estimated to cost $100? What would you do if you were Katherine? What if the mechanic estimated $600 in repairs?

_____
_____
_____
_____
_____

2. What other expenses should Katherine calculate? List at least four.

_____
_____
_____
_____
_____

3. If you were Katherine, would you accept the car? Why or why not? What other factors might influence your decision?

_____
_____
_____
_____

Wheeling & Dealing

NOW THAT YOU HAVE A CLEAR PICTURE of some of the costs of owning a car, you can proceed accordingly. If you still want to buy a vehicle you need to decide what kind is right for you. Fortunately, you have a wide variety of makes, models, options, and price ranges to choose from.

RESEARCH PROJECT

Buying a car or truck is a much bigger deal than buying a computer or a treadmill, so be prepared to devote some time to the process. Don't rush to buy the first thing that you see. Treat the process as a research project.

One way to compare different makes and models is to use the Internet. Most dealers have Web sites where you can learn about the standard features and options available in vehicles in your price range. On these sites, you can often "build" a vehicle that matches your specifications by stating your preferences. Once you've identified a vehicle that meets your criteria, you might be able to get a price quote.

As you compare vehicles, be sure to look at performance, fuel economy, and safety features. Check other online sources as well as car buyers' magazines for objective information about quality and reliability. When thinking about optional features, consider the cost versus the value. That sunroof or rear spoiler might look awesome, but is it really worth the extra cash?

it's Your turn

Do you know what you *want* in a vehicle? How about what you *need*? Answer the following questions to help determine what type of vehicle would be a good choice and which features would fulfill your needs.

1. Where will I do most of my driving? Do I plan to take long road trips? _____

2. How many miles do I expect to drive each week? _____

3. What road and traffic conditions will I normally drive in? _____

4. Will I have passengers often? How many? _____

5. Will I need extra cargo room (for bike, skis, or Saint Bernard)? _____

What type of vehicle would best suit your needs—compact car, full-size sedan, SUV, truck, van, other? Why? _____

_____

USED OR NEW?

Will you buy a new vehicle or a used one? Although a shiny new car or SUV might look tempting, the high sticker price could place most new models out of your financial reach. Choosing a used vehicle instead can be a sound and affordable decision. You might be able to get an "almost new" vehicle—one that's only a year or two old—for 20 to 30 percent less than the same vehicle purchased new. That's because new cars *depreciate*, or decrease in value, as soon as they're driven off the dealer's lot.

Deciding on a used car might allow you to purchase a higher quality vehicle. For example, you might be able to buy a two-year-old, well-built, reliable vehicle with some luxury features for the same price as a new, but less well-made, vehicle with no extras. Some used vehicles are still covered by the manufacturer's factory warranty. And some dealers sell used cars that include warranties.

LOAN OR LEASE?

If you want a *new* vehicle, you might consider leasing, an option that is almost like renting. This is how it works: You pay a monthly fee in exchange for exclusive use of the vehicle for a certain period of time, typically three years. When the time's up, you have to return the vehicle unless you opt to pay a buy-out fee.

So what makes leasing attractive? Monthly lease payments are almost always lower than loan payments. Before signing a leasing arrangement, just make sure that you understand all the terms and conditions. If you'll be driving more than 12,000 to 15,000 miles per year, leasing is not for you. You'll be charged for every mile you drive past the designated mileage limit. Another drawback to leasing is that you don't have a tangible asset to show for the money you've paid. You have no trade-in to use as a down payment when it's time to buy your next vehicle.

QuickTip

By the Book
How can you tell if the asking price for a used vehicle is fair? The best way is to check the vehicle's *book value*— the estimated value of a specific make, model, and year. The book value is based on the vehicle's condition, mileage, included options, and other factors. Book values can be found in the Kelley *Blue Book* and on the Internet.

> "YOU MIGHT BE ABLE TO GET AN "ALMOST NEW" VEHICLE—ONE THAT'S ONLY A YEAR OR TWO OLD—FOR 20 TO 30 PERCENT LESS THAN THE SAME VEHICLE PURCHASED NEW."

Comparison Shopping

FIND INFORMATION ON THREE NEW OR USED VEHICLES that interest you. Complete the chart below to help you compare features.

ORGANIZE THE INFO

Vehicle Features	Vehicle #1	Vehicle #2	Vehicle #3
2-door/4-door			
Transmission (automatic/manual)			
Odometer reading (miles traveled)			
Fuel economy (miles per gallon)			
A/C (yes/no)			
AM/FM (yes/no) CD (yes/no)			
Reliability rating			
Other options (list)			
Price			

WHICH of the three vehicles do you find most appealing? Why?

_____

_____

_____

_____

_____

FINDING YOUR DREAM CAR

After you've done the research and narrowed down your options, you're ready to shop! If you're planning to spend your money on a new vehicle, you'll need to visit dealers. If you want a used car, you can check with dealers and also with private owners. On most dealer Web sites, you can search the inventory to find a vehicle that meets your specifications. For used cars sold by individuals, check classified ads in the newspaper.

When you find a car that you're interested in, take the time to evaluate it carefully. Here's the process to follow:

1

Window sticker. When shopping at a dealership, be sure to read the window sticker carefully. It will list standard equipment, along with optional features installed on that particular vehicle. Check the list to ensure that you're getting the equipment that you want but not paying extra for options that you don't want.

2

Test drive. Driving the vehicle will help you decide if it's comfortable, operates properly, and handles well. Make sure that you have enough headroom and legroom and that all the controls are within easy reach. Notice the acceleration, braking, and shifting. Listen for noises, rattles, or squeaks that could signal problems. Make sure there's no blue smoke from the exhaust— a sign that the car is burning oil.

3

Inspection. If you're buying a used vehicle, it's essential to do a thorough inspection. This is especially true if you buy from a private seller because you won't receive a warranty. It's worth the cost to have an auto mechanic examine the vehicle. With a new vehicle, you'll receive a warranty that will pay for repairs.

4

Warranty. If you purchase a new car, it'll come with a manufacturer's warranty. Some used cars sold by dealers also come with limited warranties. Read the warranty to make sure that you understand what's covered and for how long.

Used-Car Checklist

Before buying a used car, use the following checklist to make sure that the vehicle is in good condition and that you're getting a good value for your money.

UNDER THE HOOD

☑ **Fluid leaks.** Do you see any fluid leaks under the hood or under the vehicle? They could indicate the need for costly repairs.

☑ **Engine.** When you start the vehicle, do you hear any loud or strange noises? While the car is running, check all gauges and look for warning lights on the dashboard.

☑ **Service record.** Ask for records of maintenance performed on the car, such as oil changes and tune-ups. A well-maintained vehicle is likely to have fewer problems down the road.

INTERIOR

☑ **Odometer.** How many miles has the car been driven? Check the odometer on the dashboard. A vehicle with high mileage is more likely to need major repairs soon.

☑ **Upholstery.** Is the fabric in reasonable condition? It doesn't have to be perfect, but you may not want a car with major rips or stains on the upholstery.

☑ **Windows and doors.** Do all the windows and doors open easily? A window that doesn't open is a problem, especially if you don't have air conditioning. Do the doors lock properly?

☑ **Safety systems.** Do the safety belts function properly? Is the vehicle equipped with air bags? Antilock brake system?

☑ **Comfort and entertainment.** Do the heating and cooling systems work effectively? How about the radio and CD or tape player? Remember you can have one installed if you want.

EXTERIOR

☑ **Paint.** Is the paint in good shape? Be wary of new or mismatched paint—it may indicate that the vehicle has been damaged.

☑ **Tires.** Is there plenty of tread left on the tires? Look for uneven tire wear, which may signal alignment problems.

☑ **Rust.** Do you see rusted-out areas along the bottom or sides of the car? It's best not to purchase a vehicle with major rust problems.

☑ **Lights.** Do the headlights, taillights, turn signals, and brake lights work properly?

☑ **Tailpipe.** What color is the tailpipe? Light gray indicates proper combustion.

LET'S MAKE A DEAL!

When you buy cereal at the supermarket, you expect to pay the price marked on the shelf. The same is not true when purchasing a vehicle. New or used, buy or lease—there's almost always room for negotiation. At a dealership, the sticker price attached to the vehicle is the dealer's *initial* asking price. Most dealerships expect you to pay less than the sticker price. Similarly, the price for a used car in a classified ad is usually negotiable, especially if the ad states "OBO" next to the price. That means "or best offer."

Make sure that you've done your homework before you start negotiating the price of a vehicle. Check *Consumer Reports*, the Kelley *Blue Book*, *NADA Guides*, or other sources to get the information you need to negotiate the best price. When purchasing a new vehicle, find out the *invoice price*—the price the dealer paid for the car. Your negotiating room is the difference between the invoice price and the sticker price. It's a good idea to decide ahead of time what price you're willing to pay.

DID YOU KNOW?

Resale Values You may be puzzled as you investigate vehicles' book values. Why do some 1999 models, for example, cost so much more than others? Their resale value, also known as residual value, may be higher because they have a positive repair rate and are more reliable and popular.

DID YOU KNOW?

Lemon Laws In all 50 states, lemon laws protect consumers who buy cars that have major problems. A "lemon" is identified as a vehicle with a defect that hasn't been fixed after four attempts or a vehicle that has been unusable for 30 days because of defects. With lemon laws, a dealer usually must refund the purchase price or replace the vehicle.

QuickTip

Hidden History? How can you be sure that a used vehicle is all that it's cracked up to be? For about $25, you can purchase a vehicle history report. This document, which is obtained using the vehicle identification number (VIN), will tell you if the vehicle has been involved in a major accident or has experienced flood or fire damage. It will tell you if it was used as a rental car. Vehicle history reports can be purchased on the Internet and elsewhere.

How-To

Here Comes the Hassle Although you might feel awkward about negotiating the price of a car, you'll regret it if you don't. Negotiating can save you hundreds of dollars, maybe more. For starters, don't try to go it alone. Take along a friend or relative who's been through the process before. Then follow these steps to negotiate the best deal:

Step 1	Step 2	Step 3	Step 4	Step 5
Start with the invoice price. Although most salespeople will attempt to negotiate down from the sticker price, it works in your favor to negotiate up from the dealer's invoice price.	Avoid talk about financing. When negotiating a fair price, don't let the salesperson focus on monthly payments or lease options. This will only muddle the negotiations. Determine the price of the car first, and then discuss financing.	Leave out the trade-in. If you intend to trade in your current vehicle, don't let the trade-in value enter into your negotiations. Settle on a price for the vehicle you want to purchase first, and then ask the dealer for an offer on your trade-in. Don't be surprised if the offer is low. Unless it has mechanical problems, you may be better off advertising and selling it on your own.	Ignore rebates and incentives. Auto manufacturers sometimes offer a rebate, which is cash back on the price of the vehicle, or other incentives, such as low-interest financing. Although you'll want to take advantage of these special offers, leave them out of the negotiation process. Rebates and incentives come directly from the manufacturer and don't affect the dealer's profit.	When in doubt, walk out. The salesperson may want to seem like your new best friend, but don't worry about offending him or her. If you can't reach an agreement on price, or if you feel bullied or intimidated, leave the dealership. You may have to visit several dealers before you find one that meets your needs and your price.

Used Car Superstores

If you dread the idea of negotiating, you might want to visit a used car superstore. A somewhat new phenomenon, used car superstores offer a large stock of vehicles at prices that are fixed and non-negotiable. Customers can use a touch-screen computer to search for a vehicle that matches their criteria. When they find one, the computer prints out an information sheet and directs them to the location on the lot where they can find and inspect the vehicle.

Indispensable Insurance

WHEN YOU BUY A VEHICLE it will probably be your most valuable possession. It will also be your most dangerous one. Motor vehicle accidents are the leading cause of death and disability in the United States. You must carry auto insurance so you're covered in the event of an accident. Several standard types of coverage are available.

Collision. If you're involved in an auto accident, collision coverage pays to repair damage to *your* vehicle.

Comprehensive. This coverage pays for damage to your vehicle that's not related to a collision. Examples include theft, vandalism, flood, fire, and damage from a falling tree limb.

Liability. This coverage pays for damages that your vehicle causes to someone else's vehicle or property. Bodily injury liability coverage pays for medical expenses related to injuries suffered by someone else.

Personal injury. If you're involved in a collision, personal injury protection covers the cost of medical expenses for injuries to you and your passengers.

Uninsured/underinsured motorists. This pays for damage or injury to you, your passengers, or your vehicle if you're involved in a collision caused by a driver who has no insurance or insufficient insurance.

How do you decide how much insurance to get and what types of coverage you need? The most important type of coverage is liability, which is a legal requirement in most states. Liability insurance would cover claims against you if you were to cause an accident that resulted in injuries or damage to other people or their vehicles. Liability coverage is essential because medical costs are often extremely high.

The Ratings Game

Auto insurance rates are based on statistics. Your age, gender, marital status, driving record, where you live, and type of vehicle you drive all affect your insurance rates. For example, younger drivers are considered a higher risk for accidents than older drivers, and married drivers are a lower risk than unmarried drivers. Insurers look at accident rates and car thefts in given geographic areas, often determined by zip code. If you move to a different town or even a few blocks away, your rate could go up or down.

QuickTip

Collision and comprehensive coverage can be important but aren't legal requirements. If you take out a loan for a new vehicle, however, they may be required by the lender. If you buy a used vehicle, especially an older one, collision and comprehensive coverage may not be worth the extra cost. This type of coverage pays for only what the vehicle is worth. For an older car, the repair costs may be higher than the value of the vehicle. An insurance agent can help you choose the appropriate amount and types of coverage.

Safety First

WHEN YOU GET BEHIND THE WHEEL OF A CAR, you take on a huge responsibility. You're responsible not only for your own safety but also for that of your passengers and other people sharing the road with you. While driving, always be alert and aware of your surroundings, including weather, road conditions, and other vehicles. Following all traffic rules helps everyone stay safe. As a bonus, good driving habits can improve the fuel efficiency of your vehicle and give it a longer life.

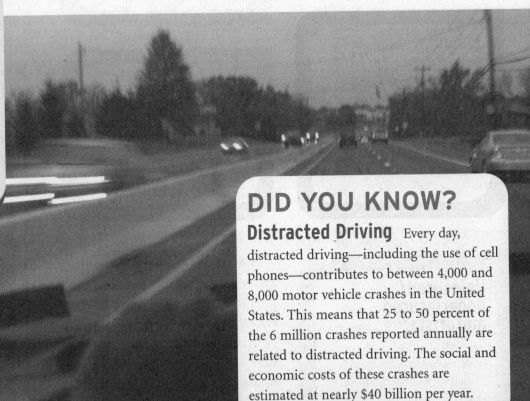

DID YOU KNOW?

Distracted Driving Every day, distracted driving—including the use of cell phones—contributes to between 4,000 and 8,000 motor vehicle crashes in the United States. This means that 25 to 50 percent of the 6 million crashes reported annually are related to distracted driving. The social and economic costs of these crashes are estimated at nearly $40 billion per year.

DRIVING DO'S & DON'TS

Following these suggestions will help to protect you and others:

DO...

- Always wear your safety belt and insist that passengers buckle up too.
- Buckle up young children in car seats in the back seat. (Check state laws for car seat ages.)
- Choose a radio station or CD *before* you hit the road, and keep music volume at a moderate level. You need to be able to hear emergency vehicles.
- Review maps or driving directions *before* getting behind the wheel. Pull over as needed.
- Keep your eyes on the road, and focus on the task of driving.

DON'T...

- Drive when you're tired.
- Allow road rage to cloud your judgment.
- Eat while driving.
- Comb your hair or do other personal grooming behind the wheel.
- Let conversations with passengers distract you.
- Use a cell phone while you're driving.
- Drive while under the influence of alcohol or other drugs.

Just in Case...

Keep these items in the glove compartment or trunk of your vehicle:

- cell phone and charger
- owner's manual
- pencil and pad of paper
- flashlight
- umbrella
- windshield-washer fluid and wiping rag
- ice scraper, snow brush, snow shovel, and bag of salt.
- warning triangles, reflectors, or flares
- jack and lug wrench (for changing a flat tire)
- jumper cables (for starting a dead battery)
- fire extinguisher
- blanket and heavy gloves
- first aid kit
- bottled water

Car Troubles

YOU'RE DRIVING ALONG WHEN YOU HEAR A LOUD POP and your vehicle begins to shake. You've got a flat tire! Or maybe the engine suddenly sputters and dies on the highway. You look down at the gas gauge and realize that the needle is on "Empty." What should you do? The first step is not to panic. If you experience car problems while on the road, follow these guidelines:

Where are you? Know your location. Look for street signs, mile markers, or exit numbers. Be aware of landmarks, such as restaurants, stores, or a cell phone tower.

Pull off the road. Move the car as far off the road as you can while remaining on level ground. If you can't get off the road, get out of the car and walk to a safe location. Be extremely cautious of oncoming traffic.

Be visible. Let other drivers know that you have a problem by turning on the emergency flashers. Raise the hood, and put out warning triangles if possible.

Stay put. Get back in your car and stay there until help arrives. Keep doors locked and windows cracked slightly for fresh air. If someone stops to help, ask the person to call the police for you. You may be relieved to have help, but don't open your car door or window for a stranger.

Call for help. If you have a cell phone, use it to call a friend or relative, or call 911 in an emergency.

Provide details. Give the person your location, a description of your car, its license plate number, and the phone number where you can be reached.

Receipt, please. If your car requires towing, you may have to pay for it up front. Ask for a receipt because you'll need it for reimbursement from your insurance company or auto club. (For a few dollars, towing is a wise addition to your auto insurance policy.)

TLC for Your Vehicle

HOW CAN YOU HELP ENSURE THAT YOUR CAR will run smoothly, last a long time, and not cost you a bundle in expensive repairs? Maintenance is the key. Check your owner's manual for the vehicle maintenance schedule. If you purchase a used car and don't receive the owner's manual, contact the automaker and ask for one. Follow the manufacturer's recommendations for maintenance.

For complex tasks, find a reliable mechanic or service center. Ask for recommendations from friends or relatives. Before using a shop with major repairs, check its rating with the Better Business Bureau. For routine maintenance, you can save a little money with coupons or by doing the work yourself. Some routine maintenance checks that you might tackle include:

Motor oil. It's important to maintain the oil at the proper level for a smooth-running engine. Check the oil level regularly. Have the oil changed at recommended intervals—typically every 3,000 miles.

Windshield washer fluid. Check the level on a regular basis, and add more fluid when needed.

Tire pressure. If your tires don't have enough air, they'll wear out faster and you won't get optimum gas mileage. Improper pressure can also be dangerous and result in an accident. Look in your owner's manual for the proper tire pressure. Once a month, or whenever a tire looks low, use a tire pressure gauge and add air if needed.

Lights. With the help of a friend, make sure that your headlights, tail lights, brake lights, and turn signals are functioning properly.

Whether you perform your own vehicle maintenance or leave it to a pro, it's a good idea to keep a written record of work that's been performed. Keeping track of oil changes and other maintenance makes it easier to know when your car is due for its next checkup. Plus, when you sell the vehicle, the new owner will be assured that it was well maintained.

PUTTING IT ALL TOGETHER

BUYING A CAR

Next month, you'll begin commuting to a full-time job and taking classes at night. You need reliable transportation to get you to both places. Mass transit isn't going to work for you, so you've decided that your only option is to buy a car. You want to investigate both new and used vehicles to see what's available. You've saved $3,000 to use as a down payment. After reviewing your budget, you feel that you can afford to spend no more than $450 a month on auto-related expenses.

1. **START YOUR RESEARCH** by looking for new and used vehicles on the Internet and in your local newspaper. Keep in mind the general price range you can afford.

2. **NOTE WHICH FEATURES AND OPTIONS** are most and least important to you:

ESSENTIAL FEATURES/OPTIONS

_____
_____
_____
_____
_____
_____

LEAST IMPORTANT FEATURES/OPTIONS

_____
_____
_____
_____
_____
_____

3. **BASED ON YOUR RESEARCH**, list the year, make, model, and price of three vehicles that might fit your needs and price range. Include at least one new car and one used car.

Vehicle #1:

_____
_____
_____

Vehicle #2:

_____
_____
_____

Vehicle #3:

_____
_____
_____

4. FOR EACH USED VEHICLE listed above, use online or library sources to find the car's book value. Is the asking price in the appropriate range according to the book value?

Book Value   In Right Range?

Vehicle #1: _____ _____

Vehicle #2: _____ _____

Vehicle #3: _____ _____

5. FOR EACH NEW VEHICLE listed above, use online or library sources to find the dealer's invoice price. Also check for rebates or incentives.

6. USING AN ONLINE LOAN CALCULATOR, figure out your monthly payment for each vehicle based on a 5 percent loan for five years. (Don't forget to subtract the amount of the down payment from the price of each vehicle.)

MONTHLY PAYMENTS

Vehicle #1:   Vehicle #2:   Vehicle #3:

_____ _____ _____

7. ASSUME THAT YOU'LL BE DRIVING 250 miles per week (city driving) and that gas costs $2 per gallon. Based on the fuel economy of each vehicle, how much will you spend per week at the gas pump?

FUEL COSTS

Vehicle #1:   Vehicle #2:   Vehicle #3:

_____ _____ _____

8. CHECK WITH AN AUTO INSURANCE COMPANY—either online or by phone—to get a rate quote for each vehicle based on full coverage.

Which vehicle is the least expensive to insure? _____

Which vehicle is the most expensive to insure? _____

9. BASED ON YOUR RESEARCH and cost estimates, which vehicle would you purchase?

_____

10. PROVIDE THE RATIONALE for your choice of vehicle:

_____

Get into the Habit

ONE OF THE EXCITING THINGS about being on your own is that there are no set rules. No one is going to tell you what to eat or how late you can stay out. If you decide to sit around eating ice cream from the carton and watching television, no one is going to stop you—no one, that is, except you. As you take charge of your life, you take charge of your health, too. Do you want to enjoy optimum health for years to come? It's easy enough to do. You just need to make health a habit.

Health habits are just like other habits—once you make them a part of your life, you follow them almost without thinking. When you exercise regularly, it becomes part of your everyday routine. When you make a practice of eating right, you simply do it. Just as you start each day with a shower, you take other actions throughout the day that help to promote good health and prevent disease. So skip the bad habits, learn the good ones, and make them part of a healthy lifestyle.

> **SKIP THE BAD HABITS, LEARN THE GOOD ONES, AND MAKE THEM PART OF A HEALTHY LIFESTYLE.**

it's Your turn

How many good health habits do you already have? Think of five things you do on a regular basis that benefit your health. List them in the first column. Then list five habits that might be harmful to your health. For each bad habit, think of a good habit that you could replace it with.

My healthy habits	My harmful habits	Better habits I could develop

Adjust Your Attitude

QuickTip

Count the Positives
A great way to maintain a positive attitude is to "count the positives in your life." Make it a habit each morning to think of at least three things you have to be grateful about. Don't use the same things every day; think about new sources of pleasure in your life. Remind yourself of all the good stuff in your life!

YOUR EMOTIONAL HEALTH contributes to your overall health in significant ways. Clear thinking and a can-do attitude help you cope with the challenges that life throws your way every day. Here are a few examples of what it means to be emotionally healthy and how it can affect your daily life.

You accept yourself and others. You're out on a bike ride with a friend who's going a lot faster than you are. Instead of being angry at your friend for beating you—or at yourself for not being able to keep up—just call out, "Hey, can you slow down?" Don't get embarrassed just because you can't excel at everything.

You learn from your mistakes. You tease your sister about her weight. You think you're just kidding around, but she gets upset and storms off. Instead of thinking, "She just can't take a joke," you realize that your remarks hit a nerve. You make up your mind not to tease her about her weight again, even in fun.

You have a positive attitude. Suppose that you're nervous about a job interview. Instead of thinking, "I'll never get this job—I'm too inexperienced," remind yourself of all the skills you bring to the job and all the reasons you're a great person to work with. Then when you walk into that interview, you can hold your head high and let yourself shine.

You can deal with your emotions. After going out for three weeks with someone you really thought was "the one," you get dumped. Instead of holing up in your room for days feeling miserable, you turn to your friends for consolation. Complaining to them helps you feel better and reminds you that your life isn't over.

You can handle stress. You've got a major report due, you're moving, and on top of everything else, your car broke down. Instead of getting so stressed out that you can't focus on anything, you force yourself to take time out to relax. When you're calm again, you can consider all the things you need to do and figure out how to tackle them one at a time.

LIKING YOURSELF

Suppose that you just met someone for the first time—yourself. What would strike you about that person? Would you think, "He's a good listener," or "She has a great sense of humor"? Would you recognize a special talent or a friendly attitude? In short, do you think you're the kind of person you'd enjoy being with?

Self-esteem—liking and respecting yourself—is a key part of emotional health. It helps you cope with problems by giving you the confidence to believe that you can solve them. You make friends more easily when you approach people with the belief that they'll like you. And when you disagree with other people, self-esteem gives you the courage to stand up for what you believe.

DON'T SWEAT IT

Think about something that gets you really stressed out. It could be speaking in public, being at a party with people you don't know, or just having too much to do. Stress is a normal part of life. The trick is to control your stress instead of letting it control you. Here are some ways to avoid getting overwhelmed:

- **Plan ahead.** If you have a big project that's due in a month, break it up into smaller tasks that you can take on one at a time. Spread those tasks out over the course of the month, so you'll never have more than you can handle.

- **Learn to say no.** Don't take on additional commitments when you're already stretched thin. Wait until that big project is out of the way before you agree to anything else that will take up a lot of your time.

- **Get active.** Doing something physical can help you work off tension and take your mind off your problems.

- **Talk it through.** Talk about your problems to a family member, a friend, or a professional counselor. Another point of view may help you.

- **Don't push yourself.** Sometimes you may not have time or energy to do as good a job as you'd like. Give yourself permission to be good enough.

When to Say No

MARIA FEELS TRAPPED. She just started a volunteer job at the homeless shelter. She feels good about the work she's doing there, even though she has to stay late some nights. She also works as a volunteer at the nature center two Saturdays a month. Her boss at the video store where she works on weekdays has started to complain that she's late to work and isn't giving customers her full attention. Now her parents want her to look after her two younger brothers for the weekend while they go away. She'd love to spend some time with the boys, but then she'd have to reschedule her hours at the nature center. Just thinking about it makes her feel exhausted.

YOUR IDEAS

1. What do you think Maria should eliminate from her busy schedule? Why?

_____
_____
_____
_____
_____

2. What would be the best way for her to tell the person she can't handle this responsibility right now?

_____
_____
_____
_____
_____

3. Do you think Maria has balance in her life? Explain.

_____
_____
_____
_____
_____

Are You a People Person?

GOOD EMOTIONAL HEALTH contributes to good social health—the way you relate to other people. When you finish school and enter the workplace, you'll develop new kinds of relationships. You'll spend most days with coworkers. If you share an apartment, you'll spend some of your time with one or more roommates. The way you relate to these people will affect your social health.

MAKING NEW FRIENDS

One of the hardest things about leaving school is not seeing the people you've become friends with over the years. Sure, you can still keep in touch, but it's not the same as spending time together every day. And what if you move away when you go to college or start working? How do you find new friends in a place where you don't know anyone?

One way to meet new people is to join some kind of group. You could sign up for a photography class, join a health club, or volunteer for a cause you believe in. Just by being part of a group, you'll meet other people who share an interest with you.

You can also try to turn casual acquaintances, such as coworkers, into friends. Bring up personal interests, such as hobbies or pets, as a way to get to know each other better. If you'd like to spend time with someone you meet at work, suggest getting together after work or on a weekend.

How did you meet your best friends? Use the chart below to list your three closest friends, the way you met them, and the reasons you like them.

Name of Friend	How We Met	Why We Get Along

What generalizations can you draw from your chart about the kinds of people you like the most and how you can meet more people like them?

Set ground rules.

Agree ahead of time about things like who will do which chores and how late it's okay to have people over. Then stick to your side of the agreement.

Respect each other's privacy.

Recognize that your roommate's room is a private place, just as yours is. Don't enter without knocking, and don't snoop when your roommate's not around. And don't "borrow" things without asking!

RELATING TO ROOMMATES

At first you may think that living with a roommate is completely different from sharing a home with people you've known all your life. In fact, though, you already know a lot about how to get along with a roommate. Mostly, it boils down to common courtesy.

Be flexible. Be prepared to change some of your rules if they cause friction. Say you've set aside week-nights from 7 to 9 to turn off the television so you can both study, but then your roommate's favorite show is moved to 7 o'clock on Tuesdays. A simple solution would be to change study time to 8 to 10 on Tuesdays.

Take care of shared spaces. Don't leave a mess in the kitchen for your roommate to step over or clean up. Also, don't tie up the bathroom for hours—your roommate needs to use it too.

QuickTip

A Can-Do Attitude

Employers and coworkers value a positive attitude. Show enthusiasm for your work and be willing to take initiative. When times are tough, make an effort to stay upbeat. You'll help others, and you'll develop a reputation as a can-do person who can accept a challenge.

WORKING TOGETHER

When you work full time, you'll probably spend more time with your coworkers than with anyone else in your life. Working relationships are different from other relationships. You don't choose your coworkers in the way that you choose your friends, but you must find a way of working with them—even if they're very different from you, and even if you don't particularly like some of them.

When you're new to a job, you need to earn your coworkers' respect. You can do that by showing that you're responsible and can be trusted. If you say you'll do something, do it. If you can't complete a task in the time allotted, tell your supervisor right away. It's natural to worry about getting in trouble, but it'll be worse if you wait until the deadline to let people know that you're having trouble finishing on time.

You'll be more popular with coworkers if you make them feel appreciated. If your boss compliments you on a job well done, make sure you give credit to everybody who helped you. Remember to thank your coworkers when they do something for you and compliment them when they've done a good job. Little touches like this are like the grease that keeps the machinery of the workplace running smoothly.

Fit for Life

YOU'VE SEEN THAT EMOTIONAL AND SOCIAL HEALTH are closely linked. Now it's time to take a closer look at physical health. The three parts of health are like a tripod, with each leg helping to support the others. To be truly healthy, you need all three legs on your "health tripod" to be strong.

Let's look at what physical fitness means, and then you can think about what you need to do to achieve it. When you're physically fit, you're strong enough and flexible enough to do the things you want to do, and to keep doing them without getting tired. Here's what you want to strive for:

Strength. You need strength every time you use your muscles to lift, push, pull, kick, or throw. Various types of exercise can help you build strength in different muscle groups. For example, pull-ups and push-ups can strengthen the arm muscles, while running and biking strengthen leg muscles. With the proper equipment and training, you can also lift weights to increase the strength of various muscle groups.

Flexibility. You need flexibility to move your joints through their full range of motion. Flexibility allows you to bend, kneel, stretch, turn, reach, and throw. When you're flexible you're less likely to strain muscles during exercise. Activities that involve stretching or bending, such as gymnastics, martial arts, and yoga, help you develop flexibility.

Body Composition

One measure of physical fitness is body composition—the ratio between fat tissue and lean muscle tissue in your body. Being in shape involves having a high proportion of lean tissue and not too much fat. A fitness instructor or a physician can measure your body composition using specialized equipment. You can improve your body composition by shedding excess fat through exercise and sensible eating, and by developing muscles with strength-building exercises.

Endurance. You need endurance to maintain high levels of activity without getting tired. Your muscles need endurance to keep moving over an extended period of time. And your heart and lungs need endurance to keep supplying your body with oxygen during periods of activity. Many of the activities that improve strength also build muscle endurance. Sustained exercise, such as running or cycling, helps the heart and lungs build endurance.

GET IN SHAPE, STAY IN SHAPE

How do you get in shape and stay that way? You need a little discipline and a few good habits. Here are some suggestions:

Plenty of zzz's.

Teens and young adults are notorious for trying to get by on too little sleep. If you're pressed for time and tempted to skimp on sleep, remember that sleep is your body's way of restoring itself. Without enough sleep, you may feel tired and irritable, and may be easily distracted. Most people need about eight hours of sleep a night.

Eat right.

Food is your body's fuel. It gives you energy and keeps body systems running properly. Eat a variety of healthful foods so that you get the nutrients you need. Good nutrition can also help you maintain a healthy weight and reduce your risk of disease. You'll learn more about good nutrition in Section 8, Eating Well.

Why weight?

Managing your weight doesn't mean that you should strive to look like a pencil-thin model or an athlete. It means maintaining a weight that's healthy for you—and that will depend on your age, build, gender, and genes. When you're at the right weight for you, you look better, feel better, and have the energy you need. How do you manage your weight? By eating right and getting enough exercise.

QuickTip

Sleep until Noon?

Are you one of those people who tries to catch up on sleep on the weekends? Sleep experts say that it's best to go to bed and get up at about the same time every day of the week. Sleeping in at the weekend can actually do more harm than good. So try to set a reasonable bedtime for yourself and stick to it—even on the weekend.

Drug free.

Drugs damage your mind and your body and have no place in a healthy lifestyle. Don't let anyone tempt you into using drugs—even legally available substances such as alcohol and tobacco can do long-term damage. By steering clear of drugs, you'll avoid a long list of potential health and relationship problems.

DID YOU KNOW?

Sleep on It

A German study suggests that sleep is essential for creativity and problem solving. Scientists gave a simple math test to three groups of volunteers. One group had slept for eight hours before taking the test; the other groups didn't sleep before they took the test. The participants who had slept for eight hours were three times more likely to solve the test problems than those in the other two groups.

Move it.

Your body is made for movement—it needs activity. Plan regular sessions at a health club, or join a sports team, or go for a run several mornings a week. There's a lot more on this topic to come.

GET MOVING!

Being active doesn't necessarily mean a strenuous workout. You can benefit from almost any activity that gets your body moving. Look for everyday opportunities for activity. Park at the far side of the lot so you'll have to walk farther. Treat your dog to a long walk. And forget about elevators and escalators—use the stairs!

Aim to be active for at least 60 minutes a day. You don't have to do it all in one session; smaller blocks of activity spread throughout the day provide the same benefits. Actually, you may be getting more than an hour of activity from things you already do. If you need to add more activity to your daily routine, here are a few ideas:

- When you do errands, walk or ride your bike instead of driving.
- Do yard work, such as mowing lawns, raking leaves, or gardening.
- Walk to the mailbox to send letters, or to the library to return books.
- Clean your room or scrub the kitchen floor.
- Do sit-ups or leg lifts while you watch television.
- Find a pilates or yoga video that you like and follow it.

it's Your turn

Write down five things you do regularly that contribute to the 60 minutes of activity that you need each day. Then if you need additional activity, list as many as five simple changes you could make in your daily habits.

REGULAR ACTIVITIES

1. _____
2. _____
3. _____
4. _____
5. _____

ADDITIONAL ACTIVITIES

1. _____
2. _____
3. _____
4. _____
5. _____

Work Out Your Social Life

If you can't find the time for exercise *and* a social life, try combining the two. If your friends already participate in physical activities, ask if you can join them. If your friends tend to be couch potatoes, help them and yourself by being more active. For example, if you like to get together on a weekend, suggest that you all go hiking or rent canoes instead of shopping. In the evening, you might all go out dancing instead of to a movie. There are lots of ways to make exercise fun, especially when you do it with friends.

Joining

IF YOU WANT TO GET IN SHAPE, your first thought might be to join a gym, health club, spa, or fitness center. Whatever name they are given, these facilities usually offer members a variety of workout options, including classes, weight rooms, a lap pool, and other equipment. Before you rush to sign a contract, though, ask yourself whether a gym membership is right for you.

FIRST, here are some of the pros and cons to consider:

PROS
- Gyms provide a variety of activities, equipment, and expert instruction under one roof.
- You can exercise without being concerned about the weather.
- Having a class to attend regularly can be a source of motivation.
- A gym is worthwhile if you live in an area where it might not be safe to jog or engage in other outdoor activities.

CONS
- Belonging to a gym is no guarantee that you'll actually go there. You have to be able to motivate yourself.
- Memberships can be expensive. If you attend only once or twice a month, it may not be worth the cost.
- Traveling to a gym may be less convenient than working out at home.
- Spending an hour or two at a gym each week isn't a substitute for daily physical activity.

a Gym

IF YOU THINK a gym may be a good choice for you, the next thing to consider is what features are most important to you. Are you interested in classes? Swimming? Kickboxing? Weight machines? Use the checklist below to find out if the gym you're considering measures up in the areas that you care about most.

1. What kinds of exercise equipment are available? _____
_____

2. Are there several machines of each type, so that you won't have to wait in line for one? YES / NO

3. Does the gym have a wooden spring floor in the room where classes are held? (Jumping around on carpet and hardwood floors can put stress on the back and legs.) YES / NO

4. Is the pool large enough for swimming laps (at least 25 yards)? YES / NO

5. Are the changing rooms well maintained? YES / NO

6. Are lockers provided? YES / NO

7. How crowded are the classes and other facilities? _____

8. What qualifications do the instructors have? _____
_____

9. What hours is the gym open? _____

10. Do staff members seem friendly and attentive? YES / NO

11. What is your overall impression of the facility? _____
_____
_____

ONCE YOU FIND a gym that meets your standards, there's one more factor to consider: money. Health clubs have different ways of charging members so it pays to shop around to find the best deal. Keep these tips in mind:

- Avoid signing a contract that requires you to remain a member for several years. If you move or change jobs, you may be stuck paying for a gym that's no longer convenient. A short-term membership may be a better deal, even if it costs more per month.

- Find out whether it's possible to have the unused portion of your payment refunded if you have to cancel your membership.

- Ask about special offers. Some clubs offer trial memberships, giving you a chance to try the facilities for free before you decide to join. You may also be able to get a discount for joining as a group with family members or coworkers.

- Read the contract carefully before you sign. Make sure that what you're agreeing to matches what you were promised.

BE A SPORT

If you're looking for a way to make your fitness routine more exciting, playing a sport may be just what the doctor (or the coach) ordered. You can play some sports on your own and others as part of a team or league. Each sport offers its own fitness benefits and each requires different kinds of equipment. To get started in tennis, for example, you need sneakers, a racquet, balls, and access to a court. Swimming is even simpler, all you need is swimwear and a pool.

Besides providing fitness benefits, sports can improve emotional and social health. Developing your skill at a sport is a way to boost your self-esteem, and like other forms of exercise, sports activities can reduce stress and help you relax. Joining a league gives you a chance to socialize, have fun, and get fit at the same time. Many individual sports can also be performed with others as social activities.

it's Your turn

Write down three sports that interest you. Do some research to find out where in your community you could play these sports and what clothing and equipment you would need to get started.

SPORT

_____
_____
_____

WHERE I COULD PLAY

_____
_____
_____

CLOTHING & EQUIPMENT NEEDED

_____
_____
_____

Which of these sports interests you the most? _____
Why? _____
_____

DID YOU KNOW?

Team Mates If you're looking to make new friends, taking part in a team or league sport is a great way to do it. You meet people who are interested in the same sport as you. More important, you learn about their personalities when you see how they handle competition and perform as part of a team.

PLAYING IT SAFE

All sports have certain risks. The most obvious one is injury. When you're running, jumping, throwing, or kicking for an hour or more at a time, there's a chance that you could get hurt. Common sports injuries include sprains (injuries to joints), strains (injuries to muscles or tendons), and muscle cramps. To avoid sports injuries, follow these steps:

Warm up at least five minutes before you work out. A low-intensity activity gets your muscles moving.

Know your limits. Don't try to compete beyond your ability level.

Wear the right **safety equipment**. Make sure that safety equipment is in good condition and fits properly.

Cool down after exercise. Spend at least five minutes engaging in less intense activity.

Have a sports **physical** before playing a sport for the first time.

Drink enough water before, during, and after exercise. It's easy to get dehydrated.

Stop if you feel pain. Continuing to play may aggravate the injury.

How-To

Develop an Exercise Plan. If you choose activities you enjoy, it will help you stick to your program. Here are some steps to follow when developing your personal plan.

Step 1

Determine your fitness goals. Are you trying to build upper body strength? Trying to build endurance? Choose activities that will help you reach your goals.

Step 2

Evaluate your schedule. Figure out when you can fit physical activity into your schedule, and choose activities that you can do at those times of day.

Step 3

Consider your personal tastes. Do you prefer to work out alone, with a partner, or with a group? Do you like to have a routine and stick to it, or do you need variety to keep you motivated?

Step 4

Keep yourself motivated. What really encourages you to exercise? Maybe you want to run a marathon or just look good at the pool. If you start to lose motivation, remind yourself of your goals.

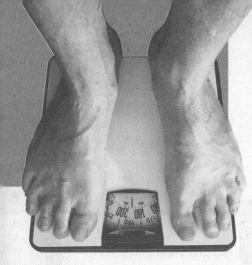

Watching Your Weight

ONE BENEFIT OF STAYING ACTIVE is that it helps you control your weight. Most people care about what their weight because it affects their appearance, but there are more important reasons why weight matters. When you're at a healthy weight, you're less likely to develop heart disease, diabetes, or other so-called lifestyle disease. You also have an easier time staying active because you have less weight to carry around.

A healthy weight is different for everyone so don't make the mistake of thinking that you need to be the same weight as your friend. A person with a large frame and a muscular build will weigh more than someone the same height who is slightly built, yet both could be at a healthy weight. That's why weight guidelines are given in ranges.

So what's the right weight for you? The most accurate way to figure it out is to measure your body composition, but for that you need to see a doctor who has special equipment for the job. A quicker way to is to calculate your Body Mass Index (BMI). The BMI uses weight in relation to height and age to determine whether your weight is appropriate. In general, a healthy BMI for adults is between 18 and 25. The charts below explain BMI ranges in more detail.

To calculate your BMI, divide your weight in pounds by your height in inches. Divide again by your height in inches. Multiply by 703. The result is your BMI. Find the point on the chart where your age and your BMI intersect. This will tell you if you are in an appropriate weight range.

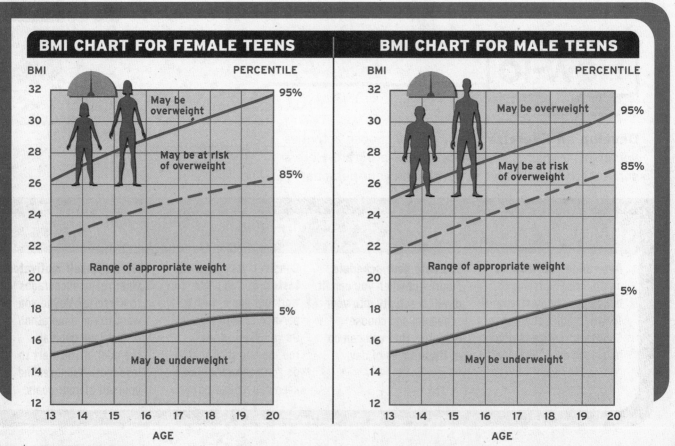

BODY IMAGE

SOME PEOPLE—women and girls especially—claim that they're fat when there's absolutely nothing wrong with their weight. Similarly, you may know guys who've become convinced that they are too thin and not muscular enough. They may spend hours at the gym trying to "bulk up."

Why do some people have a negative body image? Because they compare themselves to fashion models, athletes, or celebrities. Don't fall for it. Trying to look like someone else is unrealistic. You inherit your body shape, and while it's fine to make the most of it, you also need to accept that there are some things you simply can't alter. So instead of trying to lose or gain weight so that you can look like someone else, focus on maintaining a healthy weight for you.

LOSING WEIGHT SAFELY

If you want to lose weight, talk to a doctor first. He or she can help you figure out what weight is healthy for you and how you can reach it. No one weight-loss plan is right for everyone; you need to choose a plan that will work with your body and your lifestyle. Just keep a few general guidelines in mind:

There are no shortcuts. No matter which plan you follow, the only way you'll lose weight is by using up more calories than you take in. That means you have to eat less and exercise more—there's no way around it.

Choose a plan you can stick to. Many people choose extreme measures, such as half-starving themselves or working out for three hours a day. They soon give up. It's better to develop a plan that can become part of your normal lifestyle.

Lose pounds gradually. Dropping 1 to 2 pounds per week is a safe and attainable goal.

Treat yourself. If you give up all your favorite foods, you'll feel frustrated and may give up on your weight-loss plan. Allow yourself an occasional treat.

DID YOU KNOW?

Good Role Model? According to one estimate, the average female fashion model weighs 23 percent less than the average American woman.

Be more active. Increasing your activity level can boost your metabolism so that you use more energy—even when you're not exercising.

CALORIES DO COUNT

A calorie is a measure of the energy supplied by food and of the energy your body uses in physical activity. If you take in more calories than you use up, you gain weight. If you use more than you consume, you lose weight. It's that simple. But how can you tell how many calories you take in and how many you use?

In general, high-fat foods have more calories than foods that contain mostly protein or carbohydrates. However, even low-fat foods can be surprisingly high in calories. If you want to find out how many calories are in the foods you eat, read the labels on the packages or check a reliable reference source that lists calorie counts. The chart below shows how many calories are found in some common foods.

Check the Net

Check the Net

Calorie Counters

You can look up the number of calories in almost any food and the number burned by almost any activity you can think of. Search the Internet for more information about calorie counts.

Key Terms: calorie counter, nutrient data

CALORIES COUNT

Food	Amount	Calories
Apple, raw	1 medium	70
Carrot, raw	1 medium	25
Chicken, roasted	1 drumstick	110
Chicken, fried	1 drumstick	195
Chocolate-chip cookie	1 medium	80
Ice cream, vanilla	Small scoop	145
Peanut butter	2 tablespoons	190
White bread	1 slice	65

If you want to avoid gaining weight, you have to be active enough to burn off all the calories in the food you eat. Your body is always using energy, even when you're asleep, but it uses a lot more when you're moving around. This chart shows how many calories you burn per hour doing various activities. (These numbers are for someone who weighs about 150 pounds. A smaller person would use fewer calories and a larger person would use more.)

CHECK YOUR ACTIVITY LEVEL

Activity	Calories Used Per Hour	Activity	Calories Used Per Hour	Activity	Calories Used Per Hour
Bicycling (on a flat surface)	440	Gardening	325	Sleeping	45
Cleaning, light	240	Mowing the lawn (non-riding mower)	325	Walking briskly	300
Dancing	370	Office work	240	Watching TV	70

YOU CAN BE TOO THIN

Some teens become underweight while their bodies are developing. Their weight usually returns to normal when they reach their adult size and shape. In most cases, though, being underweight is a sign that a person isn't getting enough food. People who are underweight don't have enough stored fat to provide them with an energy reserve. This can lead to lots of health problems, including illness, muscle weakness, dry skin and hair, and a short attention span.

If your Body Mass Index is less than 18.5 percent, consult a doctor to find out whether you need to gain weight. If you do, then you'll have to make some careful choices. Of course, you could gain weight by eating lots of ice cream or by giving up exercise, but it's pretty obvious that this approach isn't going to do much for your overall health. You need to find ways to boost your calorie intake with nutritious foods.

One way to gain weight is to eat bigger portions. Another option is to have more between-meal snacks. Choose nutritious, but high-calorie foods, like dried fruit, nuts, or granola. If you still can't get enough calories in your diet, ask your doctor about a liquid supplement to add more calories along with plenty of nutrients.

Don't Go There

Some people try to gain muscle mass by taking supplements like androstenedione ("andro" for short) and creatine. Studies have found, though, that these supplements have serious health risks. Two studies found that males who took andro while on a strength-training program didn't get any stronger or gain any more muscle than males who followed the same program without using andro. What they did increase was the level of harmful cholesterol in their blood. Creatine, by contrast, has been found to improve performance in sports that require brief bursts of strength, but it may also cause muscle cramps and kidney problems.

Eating Disorders

SUPPOSE YOU KNOW SOMEONE WHO'S UNDERWEIGHT, but instead of trying to gain weight, he or she's trying to lose more. The person eats almost nothing and exercises all the time, and shrugs off comments about being too thin. You would probably suspect an eating disorder—a dangerous way of dealing with food.

Millions of Americans suffer from eating disorders, and about 90 percent of them are female. Most people develop them during their teen years or in early adulthood. The chart below compares three common eating disorders.

DISORDER	SYMPTOMS	HEALTH RISKS
Anorexia nervosa	• extreme, irrational fear of weight gain • drastic reduction in food intake • unhealthy weight loss • distorted self-image (seeing themselves as fat when they're seriously underweight)	• malnutrition • weakness and fatigue • interruption of menstrual cycles • damage to skin and hair • low blood pressure • loss of bone density • irregular heart rate • slowed metabolism • low body temperature • damage to internal organs • loss of hair
Bulimia nervosa	• eating binges (consuming huge amounts of food in a short time) • purging (trying to rid the body of excess food by vomiting or using laxatives) • frequent dieting • obsession with weight	• dehydration • stomach pain • irregular heartbeat • wearing away of tooth enamel from repeated vomiting • sore gums/tooth loss • swelling of the face • increased blood pressure • damage to heart, kidneys, and digestive tract • loss of hair
Binge eating	• uncontrollable overeating • extreme weight gain • feelings of shame or guilt • depression	• obesity • high blood pressure • high cholesterol • gallbladder disease • heart disease • diabetes

Helping Out a Friend

"UGH, I'M SO FAT!" COMPLAINED Marcie, examining herself in the locker room mirror. "I have got to lose more weight."

Alison glanced over at her friend as she rummaged through her gym bag. "What are you talking about? You look fine."

Marcie made a face. "Thanks for trying to be nice, Alison, but let's face it, I look terrible. I'm going to make sure I do a whole bunch of extra sit-ups."

"Come on, Marcie, stop it," said Alison. "I mean, you're healthy, right? You're in good shape—you work out almost every day. What are you so worried about?"

"Swimsuit season is coming up, that's what I'm so worried about," Marcie answered, turning her body to see her reflection from the side. "It's easy for you to say it's no big deal— you're skinny. But I'm going to look like a whale in a two-piece."

Alison bit her lip. She still didn't think there was anything wrong with Marcie's weight.

YOUR IDEAS

1. Why might Marcie be convinced she is overweight if she isn't?

_____
_____
_____
_____
_____
_____
_____

2. If you were in Alison's situation, what might you do to help Marcie? Who could you turn to for advice?

_____
_____
_____
_____
_____
_____
_____
_____

HOW EATING DISORDERS HAPPEN

No one knows exactly why eating disorders develop, but some patterns have been established. People with eating disorders often have low self-esteem and feel that they are not in control of their lives. They strive to be perfect and may suffer from anxiety or depression. Social and family problems sometimes contribute. Teens whose family members have problems with weight may be at a higher risk for eating disorders. So may people who have been abused, either physically or sexually.

GETTING HELP

Eating disorders aren't just serious; they can be deadly. Getting professional help is vital. There's no quick fix. It usually takes a team of medical professionals to treat an eating disorder effectively. First, a doctor must treat the physical problems caused by the disorder. A therapist addresses the mental and emotional problems that led to the disorder, and a nutritionist helps the person develop healthy eating patterns.

With treatment, about 60 percent of people with eating disorders recover completely. They're able to eat normally, maintain a healthy weight, and live a full life. Some even say that the process of overcoming an eating disorder made them stronger. However, others aren't so fortunate. Some make only a partial recovery and remain overly concerned with food and weight throughout their lives. Others show no improvement at all, even with treatment.

The recovery process can take a long time. Most people improve gradually over a period of three to five years, often with setbacks along the way. People who think that treatment isn't working for them may need to give themselves more time to heal.

DID YOU KNOW?

The Statistics Up to 20 percent of people with an eating disorder who don't receive treatment die as a result of the disorder. For people who do receive treatment, the death rate drops to 2 or 3 percent.

Know the Risks

YOU'VE JUST SEEN HOW SOME PEOPLE use food in unhealthy ways. That doesn't make food a health hazard—in fact, you can't survive without food. But there are some things people put into their bodies that they definitely *don't* need. Using alcohol, tobacco, illegal drugs, and some prescription drugs can lead you on a path that you definitely don't want to take.

DRINKING IS NOT A GAME

Picture this: it's your 21st birthday. Your friends take you to a bar to celebrate. You figure now that it's legal, you might as well have a couple of drinks. So you have a couple, and then a couple more...and the next thing you know, you're feeling very drunk and very sick.

Until you're 21, the law is simple: you're not allowed to drink, period. But when you reach that magic age, you don't automatically know how to drink responsibly. It doesn't take much alcohol to impair your judgment to the point that you might do something you'll regret the next day.

Does this mean you shouldn't drink at all? That's an option. Millions of people choose not to, or to drink only on special occasions. You may worry about standing out from the crowd if your friends drink, but if they're real friends they won't give you a hard time. In fact, if you agree to be a designated driver, they'll probably be thrilled!

If you do choose to drink when you're old enough, you have to know your limits. Alcohol affects people in different ways. Until you have a good idea of how it affects you, be very careful. Most important, don't drive after drinking. It could cost you a lot more than just your license.

UP IN SMOKE

You probably know someone who smokes, and maybe you're a smoker yourself. Even though it's illegal to sell tobacco to anyone under 18, about 90 percent of tobacco users start before they're 18. It's no secret that smoking is bad for you. There's plenty of evidence that links tobacco to cancer, heart disease, and a whole list of other problems. So why do people continue to smoke? The reason is that the nicotine in tobacco is an incredibly addictive drug.

Most teen smokers say they'd like to quit but can't. Some tobacco users find that nicotine-replacement products, such as gum or patches containing nicotine, can help them kick the habit. These products work best along with other types of treatment that help former smokers avoid situations that trigger the urge to light up.

DID YOU KNOW?

Better Buys If a pack of cigarettes costs about $4, then smoking a pack a day costs $1460 per year. With that amount of money, you could buy:

- 97 CDs at $15 each
- 208 movie tickets at $7 each
- 146 pizzas at $10 each
- An awesome vacation like a weeklong cruise.

STEERING CLEAR OF DRUGS

Marijuana. Cocaine. Heroin. You know what they are, and you know they're dangerous. But it's not enough just to know that drugs can hurt you—you need to understand what leads people into drug use.

The National Institute on Drug Abuse describes characteristics that drug users often have in common, along with factors that seem to make people less likely to use drugs. These include:

- **FAMILY.** People whose parents are drug users are more likely to use drugs themselves. On the other hand, people who have close relationships with their families and whose parents set clear limits for them are less likely to become drug users.
- **FRIENDS.** Teens are more likely to use drugs when their friends do.
- **COMMUNITY.** Poverty seems to increase the risk of drug use, while strong ties to community and religious groups reduce it.
- **SCHOOL.** Teens who like school and get good grades are less likely to use drugs.
- **AVAILABILITY.** Not surprisingly, people are more likely to use drugs if it's easy to get them.

It's not hard to turn these facts to your advantage. Avoid people who use drugs and avoid the places where drugs are available. If you're at a party and you see people using drugs, simply leave and find something else to do. Concentrate on your ties to friends, family, school, and community. When you believe that your future is worth something, you won't be willing to risk it.

Safety First

YOU FOLLOW ALL THE RULES—you eat right, exercise regularly, stay away from drugs—but then you get into a car and you don't bother to fasten your safety belt. What's wrong with this picture? If you want to stay healthy, you also have to stay safe. Staying safe means being aware of possible danger and knowing how to protect yourself. Wherever you go, you need to learn about the dangers you'll face. You have to adapt in order to stay safe. The most important rule is: be aware.

HOME ALONE

Make your residence as secure as possible by keeping doors and windows locked, both when you're at home and when you're not. A locked door won't keep an intruder out if the key is right there, however, so don't hide a key outside. You might think it'll be safe enough on top of the doorframe or under the doormat, but those are the first places a thief will look.

Don't open the door to anyone you don't know. If someone knocks or rings your bell, check to see who it is by looking through a peephole or opening the door while keeping the safety chain fastened. If a stranger asks to use your phone, offer to make the call yourself instead.

Keep a list of emergency phone numbers, such as the police and the fire department, near the phone. You don't want to have to scramble for them in a crisis. If your phone has a speed dial feature, program these emergency numbers in ahead of time.

QuickTip

Campus Phones

Many college campuses have special phones that you can use to alert campus security officials. If your school uses a system like this, make sure you recognize these phones and know how to use them.

it's Your turn

Do you feel safe in your home, or do you have concerns about safety and security? Conduct a security check. Identify five possible threats to your security. For each one, figure out what action you could take to remove the threat.

THREATS TO SECURITY

1. _____
2. _____
3. _____
4. _____
5. _____

HOW TO STAY SAFE

1. _____
2. _____
3. _____
4. _____
5. _____

SAFE SURFING

Thanks to the Internet, you have a wealth of information and entertainment literally at your fingertips. However, Web surfing does have its hazards. If you aren't careful, you could fall victim to anything from annoying spam to Internet predators. You may have heard these tips before, but it doesn't hurt to review them:

- Don't give out personal information by e-mail. It could easily fall into the wrong hands. This includes your Social Security number, credit card numbers, and e-mail passwords.
- If you send any personal information to a Web site, first check the site's privacy policy to find out how your information could be used.
- If you buy things online with a credit card, make sure the site is secure.
- Have antivirus software on your computer and update it regularly.
- Be careful in chat rooms. Recognize that you may encounter predators who prey on people in your age group. Don't give out your name, address, or any other information that could allow someone to track you down. If you decide to meet an Internet contact in person, arrange to meet in a public place, preferably accompanied by a friend.

STREET SMARTS

Staying safe when you're out isn't the same as protecting yourself at home. You can't just lock out anyone who might pose a threat. You can take precautions, though. As always, you should be aware of your surroundings and trust your instincts. If you notice anyone who seems to be acting suspiciously, or if you feel threatened for any reason, don't hesitate to get out of the area.

In general, you're safer in places where more people can see you. Criminals don't want witnesses. Busy streets are safer than deserted lots, and well-lighted sidewalks are safer than dark alleys. You're also safer with a group than on your own. And of course, the old rule "Don't get in a car with a stranger" is just as true now as it was when you were little.

Have you considered taking a self-defense class? It would help prepare you to defend yourself if necessary. In the event of an attack, you'd learn to make as much noise as possible to attract attention. Even if no one ran to your rescue, the fear of being caught would probably cause the attacker to flee.

Check the Net

Check the Net

Drug Slipping

Some predators take advantage of their victims by slipping certain drugs into their drink. This makes it harder for the victim to fight off an attack or remember it clearly afterwards. Check the Internet to learn more about this danger and how to prevent it.

KeyTerms: drug slipping, date rape drugs

SETTING LIMITS

As a single adult, you'll probably be dating. Along with all the other things you'll worry about, such as what to wear and whether you'll like each other, you should give some thought to your safety. In particular, you should take steps to avoid date rape and sexual assault.

Although most victims of sexual assault are female, that doesn't mean that only women need to worry about it. Men and women share the responsibility for preventing unwanted sexual activity. The most important thing they can do is communicate their expectations clearly.

When a person doesn't want to have sexual relations, he or she has an obligation to say so clearly and firmly—and the partner has an obligation to respect that message. Ideally, this conversation should happen *before* any sexual contact has taken place, while both people are thinking clearly. Both men and women can also help prevent date rape by avoiding drugs and alcohol, which can interfere with their judgment.

SURVIVING SEXUAL ASSAULT

If you are assaulted sexually, do whatever it takes to survive. You can try to escape or you might scream or shout to attract attention. If you decide to fight back, aim for vulnerable spots such as the eyes or the groin. However, if your attacker has a weapon, you may have no choice but to give in. Concentrate on keeping yourself alive, and get help afterwards as soon as you can. A date rape hotline or a hospital emergency room can help you. Try not to bathe or change your clothes before being examined; you may remove physical traces that could help prosecute your attacker. Most of all, remember that the attack was *not* your fault. Feelings of shame, guilt, or fear are common. Many victims of sexual assault benefit from professional counseling.

> "WHEN A PERSON DOESN'T WANT TO HAVE SEXUAL RELATIONS, HE OR SHE HAS AN OBLIGATION TO SAY SO ... AND THE PARTNER HAS AN OBLIGATION TO RESPECT THAT MESSAGE."

The Great Outdoors

Keep these general tips in mind for any kind of outdoor activity.

- **Know your limits.** Don't try to take on the expert trails when you're still a beginner. If you can't swim, stay away from water. Better yet, take lessons.

- **Know the rules.** A sign that says "No Swimming" or "Danger—Thin Ice" is there for a reason.

- **Take the right supplies.** Wear appropriate clothing to protect you from the sun, heat, or cold. Use life jackets for boating, and take drinking water for any outdoor activity.

- **Talk about your plans.** Make sure someone knows where you're going and when you'll be back. If possible, take a cell phone to use in an emergency.

AN ACCIDENT WAITING TO HAPPEN?

Every year, millions of Americans are injured in the very place they should be safest—their home. Most accidents that occur in the home could have been prevented. You can make your home safer by being aware of the most common types of home accidents and taking some basic steps to prevent them.

Falls. Falls are the number one cause of injuries and deaths in the home. One obvious way to prevent falls is to clear the floor of stuff that people could trip over. Rugs can trip people up too, so use tape or nonskid mats to hold them in place. Finally, get a sturdy step-ladder for reaching things on high shelves—don't stand on a rickety chair.

Cuts. People can cut themselves on knives or other household tools. Store kitchen knives in such a way that the first thing you grab is the handle, not the blade. Follow commonsense precautions when you use power tools: wear the right equipment to protect your eyes, hands, and feet.

Fires and electrical shocks. Make sure that all electrical appliances are in good condition and that your electric outlets aren't overloaded. Keep space heaters away from curtains or anything else that could catch fire. Never leave a heater unattended—or anything that burns, such as candles or cigarettes. And in case a fire does occur, make sure you have smoke alarms in every area of your home.

Poisoning. While most home poisonings involve young children, poisonous fumes can pose a threat to anyone. Use products that give off fumes—such as ammonia, bleach, or paint—in well-ventilated areas only. Follow the same rule with fuel-burning appliances. If your home uses gas heat and if you smell gas, get out right away and call the gas company from the nearest phone.

Fighting Off Disease

GOOD HEALTH CALLS FOR A TWO-TIERED APPROACH. You need to take steps to promote health and, at the same time, you need to do your part to prevent disease. You've now heard about many different ways to promote health. Next we're going to look at the preventive measures you can take to keep yourself from getting sick.

As you know, many diseases are caused by tiny microorganisms such as viruses and bacteria that can spread from person to person. A few strategies—most of them matters of common sense—can help you avoid these germs and the illnesses they cause.

One simple rule is to avoid people who are sick so that their germs won't spread to you. This isn't always possible, though, so you need to do the next best thing: wash your hands often. This is the single most effective way to prevent disease. Why? Because you pick up germs on your hands and then, when you touch your eyes, nose, or mouth, you give them an opportunity to enter your body. You can also stop germs from spreading by not sharing dishes, utensils, combs, brushes, and other personal items—especially with someone who's sick.

You can prevent foodborne illness—sickness resulting from eating contaminated food—by handling food with care. In the kitchen, make sure all utensils and surfaces are clean. Keep raw meat and fish away from other foods at all times. Use hot, soapy water to wash cutting boards, knives, and any other items that come into contact with raw meat and fish before using them again. Cook food thoroughly to kill bacteria. And remember the general rule about temperatures: "Keep hot foods hot and cold foods cold."

DID YOU KNOW?
Stay Out of the Sun

A disease that is *not* caused by a germ, but that is easily prevented, is skin cancer. To reduce your risk of contracting this disease, avoid excessive exposure to the sun and use a sunscreen or sunblock.

Check the Net

Online Health Information

The Internet offers a wealth of useful information about diseases. Many doctors now direct their patients to specific Web sites to learn more about a particular condition. Become familiar with sites that offer reliable advice. Look for sites that end in ".gov" and ".edu."

Key Terms: health promotion, disease prevention

QuickTip

Wash Your Hands

Wash your hands well with soap and hot water before and after you prepare food, before you eat, after you use the bathroom, and after handling a pet. When someone you live with is sick, wash your hands after handling items the person has used.

FREEDOM FROM STDs

Some diseases, such as colds and flu, spread very easily. You can catch a cold simply by shaking hands with an infected person. But there are certain diseases that spread in one very specific way: through sexual activity. Sexually transmitted diseases, or STDs, have other defining characteristics:

- Some have no symptoms. Chlamydia, the most common STD, produces no symptoms in 50 percent of males and 75 percent of females. As a result, it often goes untreated until it progresses to the point where it can cause serious complications.
- Some have no cure. The herpes virus, for example, remains in the body of an infected person for life. Though it produces no symptoms most of the time, it can flare up periodically to cause painful sores on the mouth or on the genitals.
- Some can cause infertility. Gonorrhea, if left untreated, can leave both males and females permanently unable to have children.
- Some can be deadly. Syphilis, an STD caused by bacteria, can damage nearly ever system of the body. Without treatment, it can cause paralysis, blindness, mental illness, and death. The STD that scares people the most is AIDS (acquired immunodeficiency syndrome), which is incurable and fatal.
- All can be passed on to a person's sexual partners. In addition, some of them can be transmitted from a pregnant woman to her child.

WAYS TO PROTECT YOURSELF

The only way to guarantee that you won't get an STD is not to engage in sexual activity. However, for people who are sexually active, there are ways to reduce the risk. One is to limit the number of partners. Another is to avoid high-risk partners. These include people who've had many partners themselves and people who inject illegal drugs, since HIV and other STDs can spread through infected needles. Using condoms also provides some protection. Condoms aren't foolproof, but they can reduce the spread of some STDs by as much as 85 percent.

If you ever suspect you may have been exposed to an STD, see a doctor right away. There are tests for most common STDs, including HIV. Don't let embarrassment stop you. Adopting a "wait and see" approach doesn't make sense with STDs. If you're infected, you need to find out so that you can be treated before serious problems develop.

MYTHS & REALITY

A lot of people have mistaken beliefs about STDs and how they spread. The chart below lists some common myths and facts about STDs.

MYTH	FACT
You can tell if someone has an STD.	Since many STDs have no symptoms at first, it's often impossible to tell whether a person has one—or even whether you have one yourself.
STDs only happen to people who have lots of sexual partners.	It only takes one sex act with one infected partner to get an STD. However, the more partners a person has, the greater the risk that one of them will be infected.
You won't get AIDS unless you're gay.	Anyone who has sex with an infected person, or whose blood comes in contact with the blood of an infected person, can become infected with HIV (the virus that causes AIDS).
You can't get an STD if you don't have intercourse.	STDs can be spread through other types of sexual contact. However, activities such as hugging and kissing pose little to no risk.
Using birth control pills protects you from STDs.	The pill and most other methods of birth control do not protect against STDs.
It's impossible to get an STD if you use a condom.	Condoms can reduce the spread of STDs, but they're not 100 percent effective. If they break or slip, viruses or bacteria can get through.

As an adult, you will be making your own choices about whether to be sexually active. Be aware of the dangers and take responsibility for your actions. Remember that taking chances doesn't just affect you—it puts a partner at risk, as well.

Navigating the Health Care System

NO MATTER HOW CAREFUL YOU ARE, you're still likely to get sick once in a while. In some cases, you might need to see a doctor. The doctor you see or the hospital you choose may be determined by the health insurance you have. Health insurance plans vary widely in what they cost and what they cover.

People who have full-time jobs often get coverage through their employers. This keeps their costs down in two ways. First, the employer may pay part of the employee's insurance costs. Second, insurers may offer better rates to companies and other large groups than they do to individuals. If your employer offers a health insurance plan, make sure you study it carefully and understand what it covers—*before* you need medical attention.

HOW HEALTH INSURANCE WORKS

In its most basic form, health insurance works like this: an individual pays a regular fee, called a premium, to the insurance company. In exchange, the company agrees to pay for a portion of the person's health care costs. This is a good deal for most people because, although they have to pay a premium even if they require no health care, they don't run the risk of huge bills if they need expensive tests or surgery. It's good for the insurance company, too, because the total amount that it takes in from premiums is more than the total it pays out for care.

Medical advances have led to increased health care costs, however. As a result, insurance companies have introduced various strategies to reduce their expenses. Many offer managed care plans, which keep costs down by limiting the fees that doctors can charge. Most managed care plans require participants to choose their doctors from a specified list of physicians known as the plan's "network." Participants must also contribute more of their own money toward their health care costs.

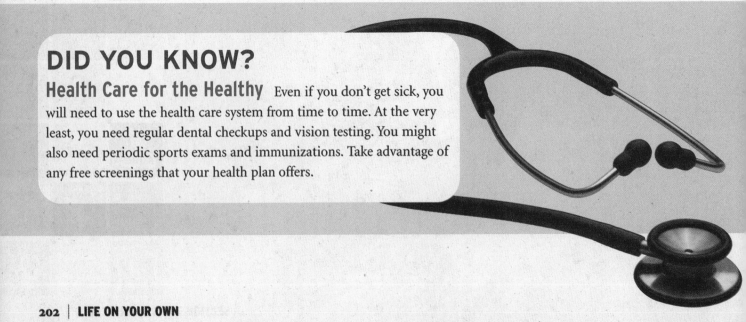

DID YOU KNOW?

Health Care for the Healthy Even if you don't get sick, you will need to use the health care system from time to time. At the very least, you need regular dental checkups and vision testing. You might also need periodic sports exams and immunizations. Take advantage of any free screenings that your health plan offers.

OUT-OF-POCKET COSTS

The term "out-of-pocket costs" refers to the total amount you pay for health care. Several things contribute to these costs:

1. The premiums, or the fees you pay on a regular basis to the insurance company.

2. The coinsurance, or the portion of costs that you pay yourself. In most cases, the insurance company will pay for only a portion of your actual health care costs. If the company pays for 80 percent, for example, then the remaining 20 percent comes out of your pocket. In some cases, your share of the bill comes in the form of a co-payment, a flat fee that you pay every time you receive a medical service. For example, you may pay $20 every time you visit your doctor.

3. The deductible, or the amount that you must pay up front. Most plans require you to pay a certain amount before the company will begin to pay for your care. For example, if your plan has a $500 deductible, then your insurance company will begin to cover your costs only after you've paid the first $500. Some plans have a deductible of $2,000 or more.

These different costs can vary considerably from plan to plan. If your employer offers a choice of plans, take time to compare them carefully. Suppose, for example, that you have a choice of two plans. One has a $100 monthly premium, a $1,000 yearly deductible, and 20 percent coinsurance. The other has a $200 monthly premium, a $500 deductible, and 10 percent coinsurance. Which plan will cost you less out of pocket? Well, if your medical expenses were $5000 in a given year, here's how the two plans would stack up:

COMPARING HEALTH PLANS

Plan 1		Plan 2	
Premiums: $100 x 12 =	$1200	Premiums: $200 x 12 =	$2400
Deductible:	$1000	Deductible:	$500
Coinsurance: ($5000 total cost - $1000 deductible) x .20 =	$800	Coinsurance: ($5000 total cost - $500 deductible) x .10 =	$450
Total out of pocket cost:	$3000	**Total out of pocket cost:**	$3350

In this case, Plan 1 costs less. However if your medical expenses had been higher, the extra cost of coinsurance would have made Plan 1 more expensive. Figuring out which plan will be the best deal for you depends partly on being able to predict how much health care you're likely to need each year.

PUTTING IT ALL TOGETHER

GO FOR THE GOALS

Almost everything you do affects your health in some way. What you eat, how long you sleep, how you spend your time, who you spend your time with, how you relate to your family— these are just a few of your daily activities that can affect your health in positive or negative ways. Use what you've learned in this section to figure out which habits contribute to your health, which harm it, and what changes you need to make.

1. **START BY BRAINSTORMING.** Write down as many habits that affect your health as you can think of. Remember to cover all aspects of your health—physical, emotional, and social. Include everything from your diet to your love life—nothing is off limits. If you can't think of anything, go through a typical day in your head, starting with what you do when you get up in the morning. Every time you run across something that affects your health, write it down.

2. **LOOK AT YOUR LIST** and try to sort out the healthy habits from the unhealthy ones. Use the lines below to list any habits you think may be harming your health.

_____

_____

_____

_____

_____

_____

_____

3. **LOOK AT THE UNHEALTHY HABITS** you listed above. Which ones do you think are most harmful? Try to put them in order, labeling the most harmful habit on your list with the number "1" (because it's your number one health problem) and moving down from there.

4. **LOOK AT THE TOP FIVE HARMFUL HABITS** on your list and try to come up with a basic solution for each one. For example, if your number one problem was "I spend most of my day sitting down," your solution could be "Increase my activity level." Write down your top five health goals here.

1. _____

2. _____

3. _____

4. _____

5. _____

5. BRAINSTORM SOME MORE. For each health goal listed on page 204, write down all the strategies you can think of for reaching that goal. For now, don't worry about sorting out the good ideas from the bad ones—just name as many as you can. Remember that a single strategy can apply to more than one health goal.

HEALTH GOAL	POSSIBLE STRATEGIES

6. EVALUATE EACH IDEA you came up with based on the information in this section. Also, consider how well each of them applies to you personally. Cross off ideas that are unrealistic or that probably won't work with your lifestyle. Try to narrow your total list down to four or five main points.

7. ORGANIZE THESE POINTS into a plan for improving your health. Try to set specific short-term goals to help you reach your long-term goals. For example, if one of your goals is to exercise for at least an hour every day, then a short-term goal could be "Increase my exercise to one hour every other day within two weeks." Come up with benchmarks to help you measure your progress, and think of ways to reward yourself when you meet them.

Eating Well

Helping Yourself

YOU COME HOME LATE AND YOU'RE STARVING. You look in the fridge and find some wilted lettuce, some takeout leftovers from last week, and some stale bread. You can't turn this into dinner! You'll just have to order pizza again or settle for some microwave popcorn. Somewhere in the back of you head, a little voice is hinting that you really should get more serious about food. And the good news is that it's easy. Today, more than ever, supermarket shelves are packed with foods that make it simple to eat well no matter how hectic your life is.

THE GOOD STUFF

Once you're on your own, you can eat whatever you want, whether it's chocolate chip cookies for lunch or bacon cheeseburgers on a daily basis. But you also know that eating that way isn't really good for you. To feel your best, you need to eat a variety of foods—and that doesn't mean three different kinds of chips!

Sure, a few cookies won't hurt, but you can't meet all your body's needs that way. A balanced approach—a little of this, a little of that—is the best way to make sure you get all the nutrients you need. So even if you don't know much about nutrition, you probably won't go wrong if you select an assortment of foods in the cafeteria line—say, a bowl of chili and a spinach salad or some fresh melon, with a whole wheat roll to round out the meal. This combination of foods will give you a variety of nutrients to keep you going through the day. And *then* you can have a cookie to top it off.

QuickTip

Check Your Options
Living on your own doesn't mean you have to prepare *all* your food. Some colleges offer partial meal plans to students living in off-campus apartments, allowing them to eat in the cafeterias. Employees of hospitals and large companies can often buy nutritious, tasty meals at work for much less than they'd spend on fast food.

Cholesterol

The bad thing about saturated fats and trans fats is that they raise the level of cholesterol in your blood. Cholesterol is a white, waxy substance produced mostly in your liver. It helps your body transport and digest fat, but too much of it can lead to heart disease, high blood pressure, and other health problems. You can have a simple blood test to see whether your cholesterol levels are healthy.

DID YOU KNOW?

H$_2$O for Health

Water is a nutrient, too. It helps moves food through your digestive system and waste out of your body. Water is found in every cell in your body, as well as in your blood. Make sure you drink plenty! Have a tall glass while you study, watch TV, or sit at the computer.

NUTRITION IN A NUTSHELL

Here's a quick rundown of the basic nutrients your body needs:

Carbohydrates, or "carbs," are your main source of energy. Simple carbs, or sugars, are found in fruits, milk, and some grain products, as well as in anything that contains added sugar. Complex carbs, or starches, occur in grains, beans, potatoes, and some other veggies. Many of these foods are also high in fiber, which aids digestion and helps keep your heart healthy.

Your body uses **protein** to build and repair its tissues. Protein can come from animal products, such as meat, fish, and eggs, or from plant foods, such as beans, grains, and tofu. If you get all your protein from plant sources, you need to eat a variety of them.

Fats help transport other nutrients and regulate growth. Stored fat provides an energy reserve for your body and helps keep you warm. Too much fat in your diet can be bad for your heart, though. The worst offenders are saturated fats (found mostly in animal products) and trans fats (found in products such as margarine or vegetable shortening).

Vitamins do various important jobs in the body. They help you process other nutrients and fight diseases of the eyes, skin, and bones. Examples of vitamins include vitamin A (found in yellow and dark green vegetables), vitamin C (found in oranges, tomatoes, and other fruits), and vitamin E (found in vegetable oils, nuts, and some vegetables).

Minerals also serve several purposes. Calcium, found in dairy products and some vegetables, maintains strong bones and teeth. Iron, found in red meat, dried fruits, and dark green, leafy veggies, is vital for healthy blood. Your body also uses other minerals, such as zinc, iodine, phosphorus, and magnesium. In general, you need only small amounts of minerals to meet your body's needs.

CALORIE COUNTING

As you know, food is a source of calories as well as nutrients. Calories are a measure of the energy your body gets from carbs, fats, and proteins. The more calories there are in a food, the more energy your body can extract from it to fuel its basic processes and all the other activities you do in a day.

For energy, then, you *need* calories. But here's the catch: any calories your body doesn't use get stored as fat. This means that if you take in more calories that you use, you gain weight. That translates into a pound of weight gain for every 3500 calories your body doesn't use. It sounds like a lot of calories, but actually, if you were to eat just 500 calories more than you burn each day—about the amount in a jumbo-size muffin—you'd gain a pound a week!

So how many calories do *you* need? The number depends on a lot of different factors. Your age, gender, activity level, general health—even the climate you live in—all play a part. You probably know some guys who seem to eat all the time without ever gaining a pound. Just wait, though—in 20 years they won't be able to eat that way without packing on the pounds. They'll either have to reduce their food intake or bump up their activity level to stay in shape.

At this stage of your life, you may or may not need to "count" calories. It may be enough to let your clothes tell you if you've consumed too many calories. If your waistband feels tighter than usual, take that as a cue to watch your food intake more closely that week. Skip dessert, have salad instead of fries, and don't eat junk food between meals.

DID YOU KNOW?

Bigger Than Ever

According to government figures, about 31 percent of American adults are seriously overweight. Equally serious is the fact that more and more youngsters are classified as obese.

Drinks Count, Too

When you think about the nutrients and calories you consume, don't forget to consider your beverages. A cup of low-fat milk gives you lots of nutrients for just 100 calories. The same is not true of soft drinks. When you drink juice, make sure it's juice that provides some vitamins and not a flavored fruit drink. When you order a smoothie, pay attention to what's in it. Choose one that tastes good and is good for you because it probably contains at least 400 calories!

EXPLORE more

Energy Bars

PEOPLE WHO ARE VERY PHYSICALLY ACTIVE—or who often have to eat on the run—may try to fill in their diets with energy bars. An energy bar is designed to pack all the calories and nutrients of a small meal into something that can fit in your pocket. But just how healthy are they?

Check out the nutrition information on several energy bars. Use the chart below to compare the levels of calories and various nutrients in each bar.

	BAR #1	BAR #2	BAR #3
Brand name			
Calories			
Total Fat			
Saturated Fat			
Trans Fat			
Polyunsaturated Fat			
Monounsaturated Fat			
Cholesterol			
Sodium			
Potassium			
Total Carbohydrates			
Dietary Fiber			
Sugars			
Protein			
Vitamins and Minerals			

Based on your findings, which energy bar do you think is the healthiest? Why?

_____
_____
_____
_____

Do you think that energy bars in general make good meal substitutes? Why or why not?

_____
_____
_____
_____

Do you think that they make a good between-meal snack? Why or why not?

_____
_____
_____
_____

FINDING FOOD FACTS

Does it sometimes seem like every time you turn around, someone is offering new advice about what to eat? One day you read that you need lots of high-fiber carbs; the next day, you hear that carbs are bad and you should focus on protein and fat. How do you know what to believe?

You can follow the same rules for evaluating food facts that you'd use for any other kind of information. Look for reliable sources, such as government agencies, educational institutions, and well-known health organizations such as the American Heart Association and the American Medical Association. The more sources you have for a particular fact, the more faith you can put in it. Information that comes from companies trying to make a buck (for example, by selling a dietary supplement) probably isn't trustworthy, and you shouldn't buy it—or the product—unless you find a reliable source to back it up.

Don't trust information that seems to contradict common sense. You already know the basics about how to eat right: eat a varied diet with plenty of fruits and vegetables, and don't overload on sweets and fatty foods. Be open-minded about reliable new findings, however. Not so long ago, Americans were advised to limit the number of eggs they consumed each week, a recommendation that no longer stands.

Do You Need Supplements?

The best way to get all the nutrients you need is to eat a variety of healthy foods. If you think you need dietary supplements, ask your doctor. Supplements can be helpful for pregnant women and for people who are on certain medications, following special diets, or recovering from illness. Most people who buy supplements, though, are wasting their money because they don't really need them.

Check the Net

Dietary Guidelines

For more details on how to eat right, check the Dietary Guidelines for Americans, published every five years by the U.S. Department of Agriculture. The guidelines offer broad advice on how to eat a healthy diet. Go online to learn more about the most recent set of guidelines.

KeyTerm: Dietary Guidelines for Americans

QuickTip

Plan Ahead

WHEN YOU HAVE TO DO YOUR OWN COOKING, you may be tempted to eat most of your meals out or to get by on snack foods like microwave popcorn. This has real drawbacks, though. Eating out can put a serious dent in your budget, and relying on fast food—or eating a bag of pretzels and calling it dinner—is definitely not the best way to fuel your body. Sooner or later, you're going to have to start fixing real food in your own kitchen—and that takes a little planning.

Planning meals ahead of time has several advantages. It helps you make sure that you eat a variety of foods and aren't relying too much on junk food. It can also save time and money, especially if you plan several meals in advance.

Here's how Elana planned for her meals: She spotted an ad for chicken breasts on sale for $1.49 per pound at her favorite supermarket. She planned to simmer them on the range and then use the meat for meals for the next few days: chicken salad, chicken and noodles, and a favorite chicken and rice casserole. Before shopping, Elana checked the recipes and added mayonnaise, noodles, and celery to her list. If she still had leftover chicken, Elana would simply pop it in a freezer bag to use later.

FOOD FOR THOUGHT

When it comes to food, there is much to consider. Here are some food thoughts:

Food preferences.
Pick foods you like. There's no point making steamed broccoli because it's good for you if you know you won't eat more than a bite. When you cook for family or friends, keep their tastes in mind, too.

Skills.
If you don't have much cooking experience, start with simple, basic recipes, then work your way up to more complex ones. Combining some packaged foods with fresh ingredients is a good shortcut.

Money.
Consider not just the cost of ingredients but how long they'll stay fresh. Fresh spinach may be cheaper (and tastier) than frozen, but if you aren't going to use it within a week, it could spoil and end up in the garbage.

Supplies and equipment.
Before getting started, check that you have all the ingredients and tools you need. Otherwise you could find yourself with a bowl of cake batter and no pan to pour it into.

Time.
When you're pressed for time, plan simple meals that you can either eat on the go or prepare ahead of time and heat in the microwave. Tony likes to make a pot of soup or his mom's famous taco bake casserole on Sunday afternoons. That gives him meals for the next few days.

QuickTip

Don't Shop on Empty
Don't shop for food when you're hungry. It's a lot harder to stick to your list when everything you see makes your mouth water.

Boa or Grazer?

Some people eat like boa constrictors—consuming a large meal and then spending hours digesting. Others prefer to "graze," eating five or six small meals throughout the day. Either approach is okay, as long as it works for your lifestyle. If a snack helps you make it through the morning, plan for it. Take along some fruit, string cheese, or graham crackers. Otherwise you may end up in front of a vending machine for chips or candy when your hunger pangs hit.

Shopping Smarts

So you've planned out a week's worth of menus and you've made a list of the ingredients you'll need. Now it's time to go shopping. You have plenty of choices for buying groceries, so where you shop will depend on what's convenient for you—and what you can afford.

Supermarkets. Most supermarkets offer tens of thousands of items. Many also include bakeries and delis. Pay special attention to the discounted products.

Discount stores. Watch for deals on food when you're shopping at a discount store or even the drug store. Check food expiration dates—don't purchase food with expired dates just to save money.

Convenience stores. Often open all night, these stores are usually smaller than supermarkets. They offer fewer choices, and their prices tend to be higher.

Specialty stores. These stores focus on certain ethnic foods or on special foods, such as organic produce or gourmet products.

Food co-ops. A group of consumers band together to purchase food at whole-sale prices, then share the work of running the store. Many co-ops are open only to members.

Farmer's markets. A great source of really fresh produce, they may offer lower prices because you're usually buying directly from the farmers. However, they have only foods that are in season.

it's Your turn

Imagine that you're stocking the kitchen of your first apartment. Put a check mark next to products you'd want to keep on hand. Add other foods and seasonings that aren't listed.

_____ Tuna

_____ Margarine/butter

_____ Canned pasta

_____ Spaghetti sauce

_____ Macaroni and cheese

_____ Soup

_____ Cereal

_____ Granola bars

_____ Sugar/sweetener

_____ Coffee

_____ Mustard

_____ Ketchup

_____ Salt

_____ Cooking spray

_____

_____

_____

_____

TAKE YOUR PICK

No matter where you shop, you'll want to get the best value for your food dollars.
The chart below offers tips for picking out the best, freshest foods.

Fresh fruits and vegetables	• Look for a healthy color with no spots or bruises. • Very soft fruit may be overripe. Buy it only if you'll eat it right away. • Fruits and vegetables are cheaper when they're in season. • Pre-packaged bags of vegetables (e.g., mini carrots and pre-washed salads) offer convenience, but often at a higher cost.
Meat, poultry, fish and eggs	• Beef should be bright red, lamb light to dark pink, and pork grayish-pink. Brownish meats probably aren't fresh. • Lean cuts of meat, such as loin or round, are healthiest. Some cuts may have visible fat around the edges (which can be trimmed away) or marbling (white streaks in the center). Game meats (bison and ostrich) have very little fat. • Poultry should be plump, with a pinkish color. • Fresh fish shouldn't have a fishy odor and should feel firm to the touch. • Check eggs for cracks. You don't want to pay for the broken ones! • Wrap meats, poultry, and fish in separate bags to avoid leakage on other purchases.
Grain products (pasta, bread, cereal, rice)	• Whole grain products—such as whole wheat bread and cereal—are the healthiest choices. • Products marked "enriched" have had part of the grain removed and the lost nutrients added back in. • "Fortified" grain products contain added nutrients.
Dairy (milk, cheese, yogurt)	• Check labels for fat content. • With ice cream and yogurt, "low-fat" may not mean low-calorie because of added sugar. Check the "calories per serving."
Canned and packaged foods	• Check labels for sodium, sugar, and fat content. • Don't buy canned goods that are dented, bulging, rusty, or out of date. • Avoid packaged items that have been opened or damaged.
Frozen foods	• Select these products last so they'll stay cold. • Avoid soft or soggy packages, as well as those that are stained or covered with ice.

BUDGET SHOPPING

Buying food is no different from buying other items: you want to be a wise consumer. Just remember that eating right is a key to your health and to your appearance so don't try to scrape along on a bare-bones food budget. If you focus on nutrient-rich dishes, you can squeeze the most possible nutrition out of every dollar you spend on food.

Look for bargains.

Most supermarkets list weekly specials in flyers or newspaper inserts. The same information is usually available online. Save money by stocking up on canned or packaged goods when they're on sale. Take advantage of savings on meats by freezing what you can't use right away.

Know your brands.

Brand-name products—the ones you see advertised on TV and in magazines—often cost more because of hefty advertising expenses. Give "store brands" a chance before deciding to pay more for a national brand. Often, they're just as flavorful as name brands.

Compare unit prices.

Buying items in larger containers seems like it would save money—but that's not always true. Check the unit price (the cost per quart, pound, ounce, etc.). If your store doesn't provide unit prices, carry a calculator so you can figure them out yourself. And don't buy the economy size if it's more than you'd ever use. Who needs a half-gallon of barbecue sauce?

Clip coupons.

You can find coupons for name-brand products in the Sunday newspaper, in magazines, and on various Web sites. Coupons can offer real savings if you shop at a store that offers double coupons.

Carry a card.

Frequent shopper cards give you discounts on certain items when you shop at a specific store. You can get the cards for free just by filling out a form, so there's no reason not to have one for every store where you shop!

DID YOU KNOW?

Round the Edges Most nutrient-rich foods, such as meat, produce, and dairy products, are found around the outer edges of a typical supermarket. By sticking close to the perimeter and spending less time in the center aisles where packaged foods are displayed, you'll find fresh foods that are healthier and often cheaper.

What's Cooking?

IF YOUR COOKING EXPERIENCE IS LIMITED to heating soup or canned ravioli, the idea of cooking a "real" meal may be intimidating. The trick is to start small. One shortcut is to buy prepared foods at the store. Then all you have to do is zap them in the microwave. The downside is that frozen meals can be rather expensive and after a while you'll probably grow tired of eating food that comes in a plastic tray.

Another shortcut is to use a combination of fresh ingredients and prepared ones. For example, you can assemble a pizza at home using a prepared crust, sauce from a jar, and your own combination of peppers, onions, mushrooms, and so on. When you choose recipes, start with simple ones that just have a few ingredients. You can graduate to more complex recipes when you have more experience.

STOCKING YOUR KITCHEN

Before you can start cooking for yourself, you'll need a few pieces of equipment. Although there are tons of fancy cookware and gadgets out there, you don't really need most of them. Start with the basics, and as you do more cooking, you can decide which gadgets will be most useful for you. Use the list on this page as a guide.

Measuring cups and spoons	Mixing bowls	Cake pan	Coffee pot
Paring knife	Mixing spoon	Pie plate	Microwave
Bread knife	Slotted spoon	Cookie sheet	Crock pot
Chef's knife	Ladle	Casserole dish	Pot holders
Carving knife	Colander	Toaster	Trivet
Cutting board	Saucepans	Blender	
	Skillet	Electric mixer	

it's Your turn

Study the list of kitchen tools. List the ten items you would find most useful in your kitchen.

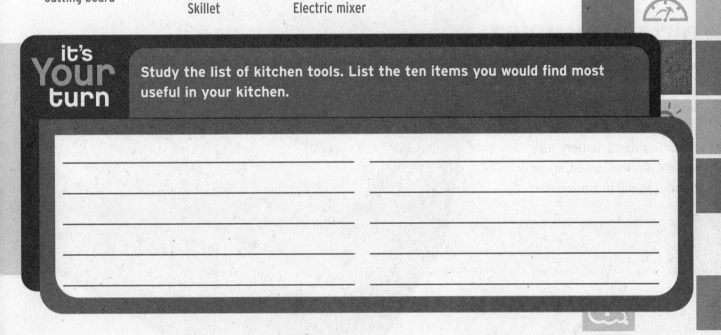

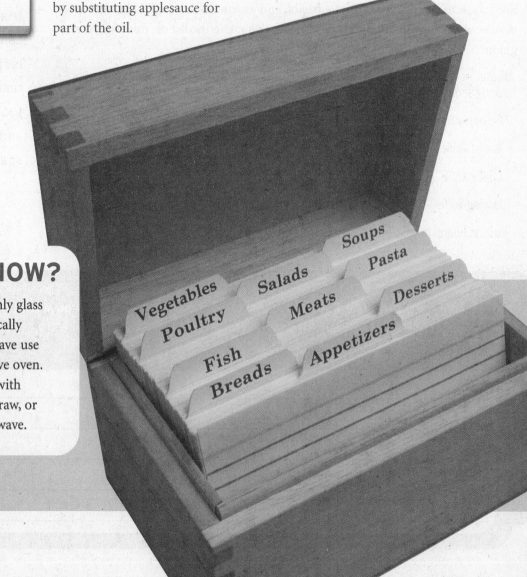

Check the Net

Check the Net

Recipe Files

Many Internet sites are excellent sources of recipes. Choose a particular dish you'd like to learn to make and search the Internet for recipes. Try to find at least three recipes for the same dish and compare them.

KeyTerm: recipes

COOKING BY THE BOOK

Some meals are so simple, you don't need a recipe. For example, you can roast a chicken, bake a potato, steam some veggies, and have a complete meal. Eating the same things can get dull, though, so you may want to move on to tackle other dishes. You can find recipes in cookbooks, magazines, and newspapers, and on the Internet. You can also ask friends and relatives if they'll share their favorites.

When you choose a recipe, you'll have to consider several factors. First of all, what's in it? Do you like all the flavors, and are all the ingredients going to be available? Think about how long it will take to make and how complicated it looks. If the recipe takes two hours and has six different steps, you probably don't want to tackle it on a weeknight after a busy day. Also, think about nutrition. If a dish is high in fat, you can balance it with a salad or steamed vegetables.

When you try a new recipe, read it through carefully from start to finish. Identify all the steps and the order they should be done. Make sure you under-stand the instructions and have all that you need. The first time through, follow the recipe exactly. As you become more experienced, you can start modifying recipes to make them tastier or healthier. For instance, in many breads and cakes, you can cut the fat by substituting applesauce for part of the oil.

DID YOU KNOW?

Microwave Safe Only glass cookware or items specifically labeled as safe for microwave use should go into a microwave oven. Never put metal, pottery with metallic finishes, wood, straw, or aluminum foil in a microwave.

How-To

Plan a Potluck Eating alone night after night can be a bummer so why not invite some company over for a home cooked meal? A potluck offers you and your guests a nice variety of foods you wouldn't have on your own, plus a fun social event. Pick a day, possibly on the weekend, when you'll have a little extra time to prepare. Your potluck might be such a success that your guests will decide to take turns hosting the event on a monthly, or even more frequent, basis.

Step 1

Decide on a main course. As the host, that's typically what you'll provide. Maybe you'll bake a frozen vegetable lasagna or a turkey breast. Or you could make homemade pizza dough and ask guests to bring the cheese and other toppings.

Step 2

Invite a few friends, classmates, coworkers, or neighbors. Let them choose between bringing a salad, vegetable, or dessert. Somebody might want to bring an appetizer, such as cheese and crackers, or a dip with celery and carrot sticks. A friend who's particularly busy that week might opt for bringing beverages or bread. If one guest is allergic to a food such as milk or nuts, remember to advise the others.

Step 3

Give your kitchen a good cleaning. Nobody feels comfortable eating in a place that doesn't look sanitary. Set the table or set out plates, napkins, and silverware.

Step 4

Time the main course so it's ready to be served about 30 minutes after guests arrive. That will give people a little time to relax and mingle. Set out food and let your friends help themselves. Relax and enjoy the delicious meal. Let guests help you with the cleanup.

Cooking School

If you're interested in tackling some more serious cooking, consider taking a class. Cooking classes may be offered through colleges, hospitals, community programs, or kitchen stores. The best part can be sampling the prepared dishes at the end of class! If you can't find time for a class, maybe you can ask an experienced cook, such as a friend or relative, to demonstrate how to make some of your favorites.

Handling Meats

If juices from raw meat, fish, or poultry come into contact with other foods, they can spread harmful bacteria. Prevent this by keeping meat, poultry, and seafood separate from other foods. When cutting meats, use a plastic cutting board with no cracks that could harbor bacteria. Wash the cutting board and anything that comes into contact with the meat (such as the countertop, dishes, utensils, or hands) with hot, soapy water before using it again.

DID YOU KNOW?

Foodborne Illness Government health officials estimate that 76 million Americans suffer from foodborne illness each year. When people suspect they have the "24-hour flu" or food poisoning, they often think back to the last meal they ate. The truth is that some types of foodborne illness don't show symptoms for several days.

BETTER SAFE THAN SORRY

This may have happened to you: a few hours after a meal, you start to feel just awful. It may start with a headache, nausea, or cramps, and then you end up spending a great deal of time in the bathroom. Unpleasant as this is, it's not the worst that could possibly happen—severe cases of foodborne illness (also known as food poisoning) can land you in the hospital or even result in death.

To make sure your own cooking doesn't make you (or anyone else) sick, follow some basic precautions. Cleaning, cooking, and storing food properly will usually kill the bacteria that cause foodborne illness. Wash fruits and vegetables thoroughly, especially if you're going to eat them raw.

The foods most likely to go bad are meat, fish, poultry, eggs, and dairy products. Make sure that you handle them with special care. Never store these foods at room temperature—that's an ideal climate for bacteria to grow. Never buy them if they're past their expiration date. Refrigerate meats promptly, but only for a day or two; if you won't be using them right away, freeze them. When you cook meat, cook it thoroughly, and keep it hot until it's time to eat. And of course, use common sense with any food. If it looks or smells wrong, throw it out. Never use an egg with a cracked shell. It's better to waste a little money than to make yourself sick.

PUTTING IT AWAY

Storing food safely is just as important as preparing it properly. Use the fridge for anything that needs to stay cold, and keep the temperature inside between 32°F and 40°F. The inner shelves and drawers are the coldest parts of the refrigerator, so use them for foods that spoil easily, and save the space inside the door for items like soft drink bottles and jelly jars. Keep your fridge clean by wiping up any spills as soon as you notice them. Also, clean it out regularly and throw out anything that's gone bad—or anything that's been in there so long you can't remember what it is.

Keep your freezer at 0°F or below. You'll store your ice cream, frozen veggies, and microwave meals there. It's also a good place to store perishable foods for long periods of time. Most things will keep up to a year in the freezer, although dairy products should be tossed after six months. Whenever you freeze something, label it with the date and the contents so you'll know when it's too old to use.

Lots of food items, like canned or packaged goods, don't need to be kept cold. They can go into dry storage in a pantry or cabinet. Avoid storing dry foods too close to a heat source or in any spot that could get damp. Don't even think about storing food under the sink. Kept in a cool, dry place; unopened packages should stay good for a long time. Potatoes and onions can also go in dry storage, but don't keep them in the same container—they'll go bad faster that way.

QuickTip

First In, First Out

When you put your groceries away, place the new items behind the old ones. That way, you'll use the older tomato sauce or canned corn first.

QuickTip

Save Those Leftovers

To keep leftovers from spoiling, refrigerate or freeze them immediately after the meal. Put them in a sealed container or cover them with foil or plastic wrap to keep them from drying out in the refrigerator.

QuickTip

Eat Early, Save Money

Take advantage of the early-bird specials offered by some restaurants. By eating before a specified time, you might be able to have a great meal for much less than it would cost later in the evening.

Eating Out

NO MATTER HOW GOOD A COOK YOU ARE, you probably won't eat every meal at home. You may eat out when you're with friends, traveling, celebrating a special occasion, or when you simply need a break. It's fun to treat yourself to a meal out from time to time, but eating out too often can take a toll on your wallet and your waistline.

FREE LUNCH? NOT QUITE

Eating a meal out is almost always more expensive than cooking for yourself. However, there are ways to keep the cost down. The most obvious is to choose lower-priced restaurants or those that offer good specials. Buffets tend to be cheaper than sit-down restaurants where you order from a menu. You can comparison shop for restaurants as you would for anything else you buy. Check out prices ahead of time by looking at menus posted in windows or near the entrance to a restaurant. Restaurants that are part of a chain have Web sites with menus too.

At many restaurants, a typical entrée is likely to be more than you really want to eat. Rather than letting the food—and the money you spent on it—go to waste, take your leftovers home if you'll be able to refrigerate them promptly. You may be able to stretch out your one restaurant meal into two or three! An alternative is to ask the server how big a portion is before you order. If it's large, you might want to split an entrée with a friend or simply order a salad, soup, or appetizer as your main course.

DID YOU KNOW?

Overpriced Drinks

Drinks are one of the biggest profit-makers for most restaurants. A soft drink or two can add several dollars to your bill. If you want to save money when eating out, stick to water—but not "designer" water.

Out to Lunch

HOW MUCH DOES IT REALLY COST to buy your lunch every day instead of making it yourself? Do a simple comparison to find out.

START by collecting take-out menus from places where you might eat lunch during the week. Choose a meal for each day and calculate its total cost, including beverage, tax and tip (if applicable). On the chart below, enter what you would have ordered each day and its cost.

NOW calculate the cost of making the same lunches at home for a week. Estimate the costs of bread, sandwich fillings, drinks, and so on. If you don't think you could make exactly the same foods at home, choose other foods that are similar. Add up the total cost of the ingredients for each day's lunch. List the brown-bag lunches and their costs on the chart.

	Restaurant Lunch	Cost	Brown-Bag Lunch	Cost
Monday				
Tuesday				
Wednesday				
Thursday				
Friday				
	TOTAL COST		**TOTAL COST**	

Compare the totals at the bottom of the chart.
How much do you save per week by packing your lunch? _____

If you packed your own lunch every week for a year, how much would you save?

_____

What else could you do with this amount of money? _____

_____

WHAT TO ORDER

Do you tend to order the same thing when you eat out? Maybe you always order the cheeseburger and fries without really thinking about all the fat that's packed onto your lunch tray. Eat this way all the time, though, and you'll eventually notice the extra fat that's packed onto you. So before following your regular routine, think twice. If you still want the burger, try ordering it by itself (hold the fries and drink) and balancing it out with a lighter meal in the evening. Or, if you had a large breakfast, maybe a salad is in order for lunch. Just remember that choosing the salad bar is no guarantee that you'll be eating light. It's what you put on your salad plate that counts. A big scoop of potato salad, two ladles of thick dressing, and cheese and bacon bits on your salad is not exactly low-cal!

Usually, it's pretty easy to tell which menu choices are healthiest. For example, a meal with lots of fresh veggies or fruit is sure to be healthier than one heavy on meat and cheese. Fried foods, rich sauces or toppings, and sweet drinks are all red flags as far as calories are concerned. If you can't pass on dessert, fresh fruit or low-fat frozen yogurt can satisfy your sweet tooth for a modest number of calories.

Sometimes, when you're eating out, it's hard to tell just how much you're really eating. Portions have gotten a lot bigger over the years—a single plate can contain enough for two or three people. If you want to avoid "portion creep," learn to judge how much food you really need and pack up the leftovers.

QuickTip

Please May I Have Less

Sometimes, a special request to the server can "lighten up" a meal for you. For example, you can ask to have dressings or toppings on the side, or add extra nutrients to your meal by requesting extra veggies instead of French fries.

Packing on the Pounds

TAYLOR HAS GAINED WEIGHT—ten pounds since high school graduation last spring. She's heard of the "freshman fifteen," but she's not happy that some of her favorite clothes don't fit. Worse still, she doesn't have as much energy as she used to. Taylor realizes the problem is the way she's been eating since she moved into the dorm. What with classes, her job, and her social life, she's often in a hurry. She survives on dorm food and fast food between classes in the student union. Most evenings Taylor and her roommate unwind by ordering pizza with some other girls on the dorm floor at about 10 p.m. They save a little money by keeping soft drinks in their mini-fridge to have with the pizza.

YOUR IDEAS

1. How could Taylor make healthier choices when eating in the dorm or the student union?

_____
_____
_____
_____
_____

2. What foods could Taylor and her roommate keep on hand in their room?

_____
_____
_____
_____
_____

3. Would you recommend that they skip the late-night snacks in the dorm? How could they enjoy socializing without the take-out pizza?

_____
_____
_____
_____
_____

PUTTING IT ALL TOGETHER

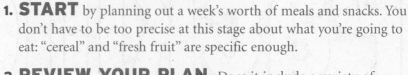

READY, SET...COOK!

You've just moved into your very own apartment, with your very own kitchen—and your own, completely empty refrigerator. You'll need to start from scratch to stock your new kitchen with the food and other supplies you'll need to prepare meals. Grab a pencil and some paper, and get ready to make some lists.

1. **START** by planning out a week's worth of meals and snacks. You don't have to be too precise at this stage about what you're going to eat: "cereal" and "fresh fruit" are specific enough.

2. **REVIEW YOUR PLAN.** Does it include a variety of foods that provide all the basic nutrients your body needs? Does it provide the right number of calories for someone of your age and activity level? Most importantly, have you chosen foods that you like and will actually eat? If you answer "no" to any of these questions, go back and revise your food plan to make it fit your needs better.

3. **FIGURE OUT** which foods you'll need recipes for. Use cookbooks, the Internet, and the recipe files of friends and family members to find these recipes. List the name of each dish and where you found the recipe:

Food: _____ Source: _____

Food: _____ Source: _____

Food: _____ Source: _____

Food: _____ Source: _____

Food: _____ Source: _____

4. What kitchen equipment and tools will you need to prepare the foods on your list? You can assume that your kitchen has a sink, stove, refrigerator, and oven. **LIST** everything else you'll need on the lines below.

_____
_____
_____
_____
_____
_____
_____
_____
_____
_____
_____

5. **MAKE** a grocery list based on your meal plan and recipe choices. Include all the ingredients you'll need for the recipes, as well as other foods you'll need during the week.

6. Now it's time to **SHOP!** Use store flyers, coupons, and ads to check the prices of the items on your grocery list. You can also visit stores or go online to check their prices. Next to each item on your list, write down both the lowest price and the highest price that you found for the item.

7. **TOTAL UP** the lowest prices and the highest prices on your list. How much could you save on your entire week's supply of groceries by being a cost-conscious shopper?

What to buy

Looking Your Best

What to Wear?

HAVE YOU EVER STOOD IN FRONT OF YOUR CLOSET

thinking, "I don't have a thing to wear!"? It may seem silly, especially if your closet is filled with clothes, but it's normal to feel that none of your clothes is quite right for your mood or for the occasion. After all, your clothes say a lot about you. For example, suppose you're sitting on a bus next to someone dressed in khaki pants, a button-down shirt, and loafers. You'd probably have a different view of that person than you would of the person seated in front of you wearing ripped jeans, a T-shirt, and sandals. Not necessarily better or worse—but definitely different!

When you're choosing what to wear, you have several things to think about. Appropriate clothing choices depend on several factors:

QuickTip

Just Ask
When you're headed into an unfamiliar situation, you may be unsure about how to dress. Don't be afraid to ask advice from someone who has already been there or had a similar experience. If you'll be part of a group, ask others what they plan to wear.

The weather.
The most important job your clothes have is to protect you from the elements. In hot weather, you'll probably choose light, cool clothes, while in cold weather, you'll want multiple layers of warm clothes.

The occasion.
Naturally, you wouldn't wear the same outfit to a job interview that you'd choose for a picnic at the park. In both cases, you'd try to pick clothes that would be suitable for the setting and for the activities you'd be doing.

Your personality.
Your clothes can make a statement about you in lots of different ways. For example, if you are an outgoing, fun-loving person, you might choose flashy, trendy clothes. A shy, serious person, on the other hand, might choose quieter, less noticeable styles and colors.

Your mood.
When you're feeling good about yourself, you might be more likely to choose bright colors or eye-catching styles that make you stand out. On the other hand, when you're feeling insecure, you might hide yourself in dark, baggy clothes.

Your Clothing Needs

IF YOU LOOK IN YOUR CLOSET, you'll probably see a lot of clothes that fit your lifestyle as a student. Depending on where you go to school—and what you do when you're not at school—there might be blue jeans and T-shirts or somewhat dressier shirts, slacks, or skirts. Perhaps you have some trendier clothes that you wear when you go out and some nice outfits for special occasions. In other words, you have clothes that are right for the things you normally do.

This works fine as long as you do the same things all the time, but what if a new situation comes up and you realize that nothing you own is right for the occasion? You may end up making a frantic trip to the mall to find something to wear—and possibly settling for something that's less than ideal. If you want to avoid having this problem, plan ahead! Figure out what your wardrobe needs will be, not just right now, but for several months down the line. Then you can take your time and find just what you need.

it's Your turn

What special events are you likely to attend in the next six months? A job interview? A school dance? A family wedding? List these events below, and then describe the kind of clothes you think you'll need for each one.

EVENT AND DATE

1. _____
2. _____
3. _____
4. _____
5. _____

WHAT TO WEAR

1. _____
2. _____
3. _____
4. _____
5. _____

WHAT'S THE OCCASION?

In order to decide what clothes you'll need, you must think about the situations you'll be dressing for. For example, if you will be starting a new job in the next few months, you might need different clothes from those you usually wear to school. Some office jobs call for corporate dress—suits or jackets and ties for men, and suits or business dresses for women. On the other hand, many offices have adopted "business casual" wear, which might include casual pants or skirts and collared shirts or sweaters. If you're looking for a job, pay attention to what people are wearing when you go on interviews. Use their clothes as your guide.

You may also need clothes for special occasions, such as weddings, funerals, or your own graduation. For an informal party such as a baby or wedding shower, a casual skirt or nice pants and a top should be fine. For weddings, graduations, and other formal events, you'll need dressier clothes, although these events tend to be less formal than they used to be. Funerals are a special case. It's no longer necessary to dress all in black, but bright colors aren't appropriate.

Guest Garb

In general, the later in the day that a wedding or special party occurs, the dressier it is meant to be. If an invitation says black tie, that means formal—tuxes for men, long or short dresses for women. It used to be a no-no for guests to wear white or black to a wedding. Now it's okay, as long as female guests in white don't look bridal. That honor is reserved for the bride!

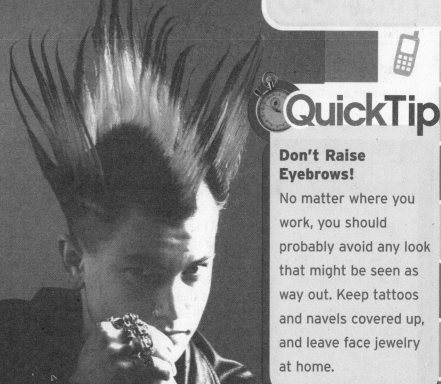

QuickTip

Don't Raise Eyebrows!

No matter where you work, you should probably avoid any look that might be seen as way out. Keep tattoos and navels covered up, and leave face jewelry at home.

QuickTip

Space Savers

When you're squeezed for closet space, get creative. Stash out-of-season clothes and shoes in boxes under your bed or in luggage that you're not using. You might even store them in an old chest that can double as a coffee table.

CHECK YOUR CLOSET

Once you know what situations you need to dress for, take a look at the clothes you have. Do you already own something that would be appropriate? Before you say no, try to look at your clothes in a new light. It's easy to fall into a rut, always putting the same outfits together. Think outside the box and consider some different combinations. Maybe your old yellow shirt would look great with your new pants. An old blouse might dress up well with a new necklace or scarf.

If you've looked at everything you own and you still see holes in your wardrobe, try to figure out what items you could buy to create more outfits. You can stretch your clothing budget by picking versatile items that can be combined with the clothes you already have. You might, for example, choose a tweed jacket that will go with your jeans or your khaki pants, and with several shirts that you already own. Don't forget to consider shoes and accessories, too. Sneakers won't cut it for formal wear!

How-To

Weeding Your Wardrobe Soon, you may be moving into a college dorm or a small apartment with limited space for clothes. To make every garment count, take an afternoon to strip your wardrobe down to the essentials.

Step 1	Step 2	Step 3	Step 4	Step 5
Pull out clothes that you know you'll never wear again. Maybe they don't fit or are seriously out of style. Pile all these cast-offs in a box.	Pick out the items you wear all the time and put them to one side. These are definite "keepers." Add any items that you know you'll need in the future, like work clothes.	Pick out the items that need fixing. Perhaps some pants need to be taken up, or a shirt needs a missing button replaced. Put them in a separate "For repair" pile.	For each remaining item, ask yourself why you don't wear it. If it doesn't go with anything else you have, decide whether you want to get something new to make it wearable. If the answer is no, add it to the discard box. If it's something you haven't worn for a whole year, recognize that you probably won't wear it next year either and discard it.	Get rid of the items in your discard box. You can give them away, sell them, or trade them with someone. Just do it right away—otherwise that box might sit there for months.

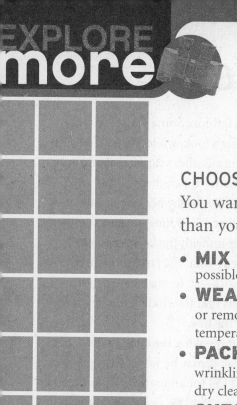

EXPLORE more

Traveling Light

CHOOSING CLOTHES FOR TRAVEL CAN BE challenging. You want everything you need, but you don't want to pack more than you can carry. Here are some tips:

- **MIX AND MATCH.** Choose pants that go with as many tops as possible, and vice versa.
- **WEAR LAYERS.** You can dress up or dress down an outfit by adding or removing a jacket. Layers are also good for adjusting to changing temperatures.
- **PACK CLOTHES THAT DON'T WRINKLE.** To reduce wrinkling, roll your clothes instead of folding them. Use white tissue paper or dry cleaning bags between layers. Unpack as soon as you arrive.
- **CHECK THE WEATHER.** Know what temperatures and conditions to expect at your destination and pack accordingly. Take an umbrella regardless.

Suppose you're going on a three-day, two-night trip, and you can only take one small bag. **FIRST**, choose a destination and describe the climate.

_____

NEXT, list the events and activities you'll need to dress for.

_____

_____

Based on this information, **IDENTIFY** six garments you would take. (Don't count underwear, nightwear, or socks.)

1. _____   4. _____
2. _____   5. _____
3. _____   6. _____

How many different outfits can you make with these six items? **LIST** them here.

_____

_____

Is it possible to get by with six articles of clothing? **YES / NO**

If not, what else could you squeeze into one bag that would stretch these items further?

_____

Fashion Sense

Let's face it—not everyone feels the same about fashion. Some people would be embarrassed to be seen in public wearing last year's look, while others are happy to ignore the trends completely and wear the same clothes year after year. You can probably guess which group spends more money on clothes!

Following fashion can be fun, but it's an expensive hobby because what's "in" changes so quickly. Styles, colors, or accessories that are sizzling hot this summer may be out by the time fall rolls around. Keeping up with the latest fads means replacing your clothes constantly—which is exactly what the fashion industry wants you to do. On the other hand, buying classics—styles that are worn year after year, even if they're never really "in"—means that the clothes you buy now will still be working for you a year or two down the line.

It's possible to join in on a fad for fun without breaking the bank to do it. For example, if bright orange is the hot color this year, it may be worth paying $15 or less for an orange T-shirt or tank top—but not $150 for an orange suit or designer shoes that will probably look outdated by next year. And no matter what the cost, don't jump on the orange bandwagon if you really don't like the color.

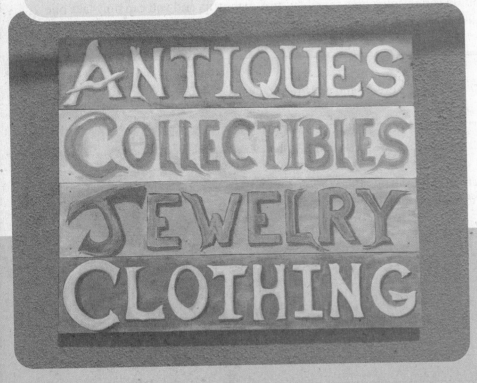

REAL CLOTHES FOR REAL BODIES

Flipping through fashion magazines can be depressing—not just because you can't afford all the great clothes, but because you can't see how you'd ever fit into them. If the fashion industry was your only guide, you might assume that everyone except you is tall, thin, and good looking. A quick look around you, though, will tell you that's not true. So why don't the models match up to reality?

Choosing gorgeous models helps make the clothes look good. But it doesn't take a genius to figure out that an outfit that looks great on a model or on a store mannequin isn't necessarily going to flatter a real person with a regular body shape. Instead of fretting about how you'd look in those high-fashion clothes, focus on the styles and colors that work best for the body you have.

Check the Net

Check the Net

Sizing Schemes

In a recent survey, 60 percent of Americans said they had trouble finding clothes that fit. Women have more problems than men because there is no standard sizing scheme for women's clothing. Visit the Web sites of several clothing retailers and see how their sizing charts compare. How much can a single clothing size vary?

KeyTerms: women's clothing, men's clothing

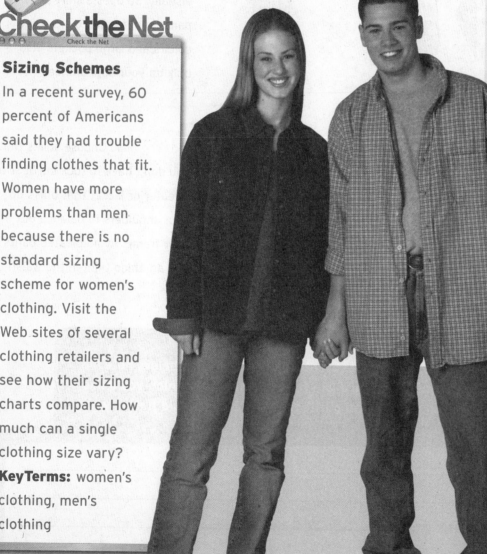

It's About Color

Have you heard of "having your colors done?" Personal color analysis is a method of determining which clothing colors work best with your skin, hair, and eyes. A color consultant analyzes your coloring and assigns you a "palette" of colors that are most flattering for you. Color consultants work in salons and department stores, and from their homes. You can also "do" your own colors with the help of a book on the subject.

FITS THAT FLATTER

You may not be built like a model, but with the right clothing choices, you can look more like one. Certain styles of clothing can shift the focus toward your best features and away from problem areas. In general, bright colors, shiny fabrics, big prints, and details such as pleats draw attention to an area. Check out the illustration for some more specific examples.

Look taller. As a rule, anything that makes you look taller also makes you look thinner, and vice versa. This includes up-and-down lines or an unbroken line of color—shirt, pants, socks, and even shoes in the same color. Deep v-necks rather than crew necklines lengthen the neck. Shoes with heels also give you a boost.

Look shorter. Lines going across the body add width and make you look shorter. A belt in a contrasting color makes you look shorter by cutting you in half visually. So does a shirt and pants in different colors. Wide collars and large pockets also bulk up your appearance.

Hide the hips. Skirts, dresses, and pants that fall straight from the hip are slimming. Look for fabrics that drape, and steer clear of clingy spandex. Jacket lapels and accessories worn near the face (such as a scarf or brooch) can draw emphasis away from the hips.

Hide the bulk. Choose shirts that you don't have to tuck in. Wear a sweater or jacket that bulks up your shoulders to balance out your frame. Avoid pleated pants and anything tight in the waist.

it's Your turn

What do you consider your best features? On the lines below, note which parts of your body you'd like to emphasize and which you'd like to downplay. Then describe an outfit that you think would flatter you.

I want to focus on my _____

_____

I want to draw attention away from my _____

_____

A flattering look for me would be _____

_____

Going Shopping

When it's time to shop for clothes, where do you go? Do you head for a department store or go cruise the thrift shops? Hit the mall, or hit the Web? By now, you've probably figured out which sellers have the kinds of clothes you like best. There's more to clothes shopping than where you shop, though. It also matters how you shop. With a little effort, you can save yourself time and money when you hit the stores.

Every time you buy a new garment, there are several questions you need to ask yourself:

Does it go with my other clothes? A great pair of green pants is just going to hang in the closet if it doesn't match any of your shirts. The most useful items will be those that go with several things you already own, so you can mix and match.

Is it well made?
A designer label or a high price doesn't guarantee quality. You need to look carefully at the garment. Make sure that the seams are straight and that trims and fasteners are attached securely. Check the fabric to see that it's in good condition, with no snags or puckers, and doesn't wrinkle too easily.

Does it look good?
A garment may fit you perfectly and still not be flattering. Maybe the color doesn't work for you or the style is all wrong. Even a cheap ten-dollar sweater is a waste of ten dollars if it doesn't look good on you.

Does it fit? Judge each item by how it actually fits, not by the size marked on the tag. If a garment fits well, you should be able to move freely in it—sitting, standing, reaching, and bending. The clothes shouldn't sag or pull or gape.

> "JUDGE EACH ITEM BY HOW IT ACTUALLY FITS, NOT BY THE SIZE MARKED ON THE TAG."

DID YOU KNOW?

Shoe Shopping The best time to shop for shoes is late in the day—your feet are actually larger then than they are in the morning.

**You Don't Have
to Buy**

Do you feel like you
have to buy something
whenever you enter a
store or outlet mall just
to justify your trip?
Think again! There's
nothing wrong with just
looking at the
merchandise and
scoping out new
fashions. If you don't
see what you want, you
can always come back
another time—and
maybe you'll even find
it on sale!

Check the Net

Check the Net

Coupon Codes

By knowing a retailer's
special coupon codes, you
can save money when
shopping online. Entering
a valid code might reward
you with free shipping or
$20 off a purchase. Check
out some of the special
sites on the Web devoted
to current coupon codes.
KeyTerm: coupon codes

BUYING ON A BUDGET

If you're like most people, you don't have an unlimited amount to spend on clothes. Luckily, there are lots of ways to stretch your clothing budget. For starters, you can shop at thrift stores or discount stores, where prices are generally lower. At these stores, you may have to check items with special care, since their quality can vary widely. If you keep your eyes open, though, you can pick up some real bargains.

You can also look for the best deals wherever you shop. For example, at department stores, you can buy "private label" clothes rather than designer brands. You can also wait for sales, use coupons, or buy items that have been marked down (reduced in price). Usually, the longer an item sits on the rack, the lower its price will drop. At factory outlets, you can buy irregulars (garments with minor flaws) or seconds (items with more noticeable flaws that may be fixable) at reduced prices.

SPECIAL HANDLING

The real cost of a garment is more than just the amount on the price tag. It also includes the cost of caring for the garment, whether that means putting it through the washer once a week or taking it to the dry cleaner once a month. Throwing an item in the wash with your other clothes isn't a big expense, but dry cleaning costs can add up fast. If you buy a suede jacket for $100 and then find it costs $40 or more to clean, in just a couple of cleanings you'll have doubled the total cost of the jacket!

Special care costs you time, as well. If a garment needs to be hand washed and line dried every time you wear it, you may decide it's just not worth the trouble and quit wearing it altogether. The money you spent on it will be wasted. So if you're the kind of person who can't be bothered with clothes that need to be dry cleaned or hand washed, be sure to check the care labels before you buy.

How-To

Calculating Cost per Wearing While it can be a real thrill to find a bargain, sometimes the shirt you thought was such a steal just hangs in your closet gathering dust. To figure out how good a bargain you've really found, you can calculate the cost per wearing. Here's how:

Step 1
Figure out the total price of the item, including tax and shipping if applicable.

Step 2
Estimate the number of times you might wear the item. For example, a prom dress might be worn only once, while a winter coat could be worn hundreds of times. Quality will affect this figure, since a well-made garment will last for more wearings.

Step 3
How much would it cost to keep the garment clean during that time? Add the cost of caring for the item to the total cost.

Step 4
Divide the total cost by the number of wearings expected. The result is the cost per wearing. The lower it is, the better the bargain.

What's It Made Of?

Natural fibers, such as cotton, silk, linen, and wool, often need special care. They may shrink if you put them in the dryer, or they may wrinkle and require ironing. Nonetheless, many people prefer these fabrics because they're so comfortable to wear. Synthetic fibers, such as rayon, nylon, and polyester, are often easier to care for. Some people find synthetics uncomfortably warm, however, so many fabrics used today are blends of natural and synthetic fibers. Cotton/polyester is one very popular blend. It combines comfort with ease of care.

Treat Your Clothes Right

YOU CAN HAVE A COLLECTION OF TERRIFIC CLOTHES, but if you keep them all in a heap on the floor, you're still going to look like a slob. Your clothes can only help you look good if you keep them looking good. That means hanging them up or folding them as soon as you take them off. If you're in too much of a rush for that, at least drape your clothes over a chair instead of leaving them crumpled up on the floor. That way, they'll be less wrinkled when you get back home.

KEEP IT CLEAN

To keep your clothes looking their best, you need to clean them regularly—and properly. Some clothes can simply go through the washer and dryer and come out looking as good as new. Others need special treatment. Before you put any garment in the wash, check the label to see what kind of care it needs. If the label says "hand wash," "line dry," or "dry clean only," take the instruction seriously. Hand washing or dry cleaning may be a bit of a hassle, but it's a lot better than throwing your favorite sweater in the dryer and having it come out two or three sizes too small!

Sometimes you'll check a clothing label and you may see a row of mysterious symbols. These are universal codes for washing instructions, but unfortunately, their meanings are not always obvious. The chart on the next page provides a translation. In general, any symbol with an X through it means "don't."

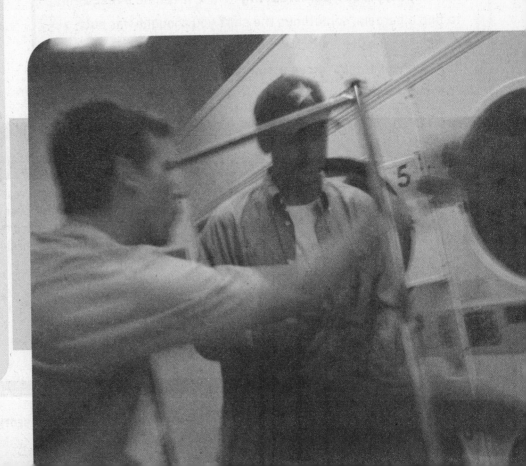

DECODING LAUNDRY

Symbol	What it means	How to do it
	Machine wash	Put the garment in the washer and select the right temperature. One dot means wash in cold water, two means warm, and three means hot.
	Gentle cycle	Select the correct cycle on the machine. One line means use the "permanent press" cycle; two lines mean use the "delicate" cycle.
	Hand wash	Put the garment in water and add a cleaning product that's labeled "safe for hand washables." Let it soak for a few minutes, then squeeze the suds gently through it and rinse it out completely.
	Bleach	Add bleach with the detergent. A white triangle means you can use any kind of bleach; a striped one means to use only non-chlorine bleach when needed.
	Tumble dry	Put the clothes in the dryer and select the right heat level. As with the "machine wash" symbol, more dots mean more heat, and more lines under the symbol mean to use a gentler setting.
	Line dry	Hang the garment up to dry. Don't put it in the dryer.
	Dry flat	Lay the garment out flat on a towel (in a place where it won't get stepped on) and let it dry that way. Don't put it in the dryer.
	Iron	Lay the item on an ironing board and iron it carefully with a hot iron. (Again, more dots mean more heat.) Make sure you iron every part, but don't leave the iron on any one spot for more than a few seconds.
	Dry clean	Take the garment to the cleaners and let the professionals handle it. Paying to clean an item is still cheaper than paying to replace it if it gets ruined in the wash.

How-To

Doing the Laundry Never done your own laundry before? Don't worry—this isn't rocket science. There are just a few simple points you need to keep in mind.

Step 1	Step 2	Step 3	Step 4	Step 5	Step 6
Sort it out. Put jeans and dark clothes in one pile, whites and light colors in another. Remember to check all the pockets as you place clothes in the washer—you don't want to end up with a shredded tissue stuck to your T-shirts or ink all over your pants.	Set the temperature. Hot water cleans clothes better, but it can shrink cotton, wool, and other natural fabrics. So use the warmest water possible for the type of fabric. However, if your clothes have stains, use cold water—heat may set the stains.	Set the cycle. Use "permanent press" or "gentle cycle" if your clothes call for it—or if you think they can't take rough handling.	Follow the loading instructions. You will either need to load the clothes first and then the detergent or vice versa. Don't overload the washer—it may seem like you're saving time and money by doing one mega-load, but clothes need to move freely to get clean.	Transfer clothes to the dryer. Make sure you pull out any items that shouldn't be machine dried, such as wool sweaters. A hotter setting will dry clothes faster, but it can also shrink them, so you may want to use one dryer setting for tougher clothes and another for knits.	Fold and hang. Remove clothes as soon as they're done and fold or hang them, smoothing out wrinkles with your hands. This step may save you the trouble of ironing later.

QuickTip

No Wrinkles

Perma press drying cycles have a built-in cool-down cycle. Don't skip this cycle or your clothes will come out wrinkled!

Handy Helpers

There are lots of new products that can help you keep your clothes in shape. If you're no good at ironing, you can try using a small handheld steamer filled with distilled water. An even quicker option is a spray-on product that releases wrinkles as you tug and smooth the fabric. For dry-clean-only clothes, you may be able to save money with a home dry cleaning kit. Just be sure to follow the directions carefully—you won't save any money if you turn an expensive shirt into an expensive rag.

Wash and... Whoops!

WHEN JASON LEFT FOR COLLEGE, he turned down his mom's offer to show him how to do laundry. It couldn't be hard to figure it out, he thought. He let his clothes pile up for a couple of weeks, and when he was down to his last pair of boxers, he took it all to the laundry room. He threw the clothes in a washer, added some soap, let it run, and then transferred everything to a dryer with the heat set on high. To his surprise, when he pulled out his clothes, his underwear and socks all looked gray and dingy, and some of his shirts were about half their original size.

YOUR IDEAS

1. What mistakes did Jason make?

_____
_____
_____
_____
_____
_____
_____

2. How could he avoid these problems in the future?

_____
_____
_____
_____
_____
_____
_____

Check the Net

Stain Stoppers

Did you know that hairspray takes out ballpoint pen ink and that an ice cube helps remove candle wax and gum? Knowing what to use on specific stains helps protect your clothing investment. Check the Internet to find more information on how to get out stains.

KeyTerm: stain removal

DEALING WITH DAMAGE

No matter how careful you are, accidents happen. You drop a piece of pizza on your new jeans, or a button comes off your favorite shirt. Don't let minor damage take your good clothes out of circulation. Deal with the problem promptly, and you can make the item almost as good as new.

For most stains, the key is to act as quickly as possible. However, the wrong treatment could actually make a stain worse. If you're not sure how to treat a particular type of stain, try cold water first—it may not help, but it probably won't hurt. If that doesn't work, a little detergent or pre-wash stain remover may do the trick. Wait a few minutes and then hold the area under running water. For stubborn spots, you may have to consult a reference to see how to handle that particular type of stain. And remember, heat can set some stains—so make sure the spot's really gone before you wash the item in hot water.

If you stain a garment that must be dry cleaned, be sure to point out the stain and explain what caused it when you take it to be cleaned. Dry cleaners have a variety of special cleaning products that they can use to remove stains.

A STITCH IN TIME

Have you heard the expression "A stitch in time saves nine"? This is literally true with ripped clothes. The sooner you stitch up a small hole, the less likely it is to turn into a big hole. Start by threading a needle and then making a knot in one end of the thread. If the rip is along a seam, fixing it is easy—just keep pushing the needle in and out and pulling the thread tight along the length of the tear.

If the hole is in the middle of the fabric, you may need to add a patch. There are two ways to do this. The easy way is to use an iron-on patch, which you can buy at a fabric store. It goes on with a hot iron, but may peel off over time and may not match your garment exactly. If you need a better match, and a more secure one, you may be able to cut a small piece of fabric out of the hem. Place it behind the hole, turn under the raw edges of the hole, and stitch the patch in place.

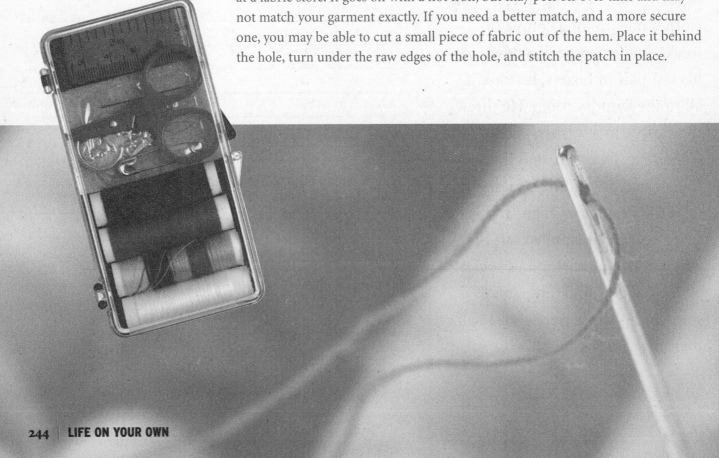

MINOR ALTERATIONS

Suppose you find a pair of pants that are on sale at a great price, but they're too long? Or maybe you gain or lose a few pounds, and some of your clothes don't fit anymore. At times like this, you'll need to make some minor alterations. If you've got a pair of pants or a skirt that isn't the right length, for example, it's fairly easy to take up or let down the hem. You can also take in the seams on clothes that are too loose or adjust the shoulder straps on a top.

Some alterations, like moving a button, are so simple that you can do them yourself at home. Hemming and adjusting seams are also pretty easy for someone with a bit of sewing experience. For more elaborate alterations than that, you can take your clothes to a professional. Many dry cleaners have someone on their staff who does alterations. You can also check your local phone directory under "tailors and seamstresses."

Button Up

Missing buttons are one of the easiest problems to fix. If you've saved the original button, you can sew it back in place by stitching through the holes in the button—in one and out the other—several times. Make sure to leave some play in the threads so that you have room to get the button through the buttonhole. If you don't have the lost button, you can probably find a good match for it at a drugstore or fabric store. Failing that, you can give the garment a different look by replacing all of the buttons.

PUTTING IT ALL TOGETHER

WORK CLOTHES

Suppose you've landed a new job as a runner for a law firm. You'll be acting as a messenger—delivering documents to clients, going to the courthouse, and helping with filing in the office. You want to look professional, but you don't have a fortune to spend.

1. **DESCRIBE** at least three characteristics your work clothes would have to have. Explain why each one would be important.

_____

_____

_____

_____

2. **LOOK** at pictures of clothes on the Web and in catalogs, magazines, or store flyers. Find two outfits that you would consider for your new job. Make sure the descriptions of the clothes include care instructions. If possible, tape the pictures below or make a sketch of the outfit. Then explain why you think each outfit is a flattering choice for you. Beside each sketch, write the estimated purchase price for the outfit.

Outfit A:

_____

_____

_____

_____

_____

_____

Outfit B:

_____

_____

_____

_____

_____

_____

3. **DESCRIBE** how you would take care of each garment you've chosen. Include washing, drying, removing wrinkles (if applicable), and cleaning (if applicable).

   Outfit A: _____

   _____

   _____

   Outfit B: _____

   _____

   _____

4. In the box below, **CALCULATE** the cost per wearing of each outfit. Include the total price of each garment and the cost of care. Estimate that you'll wear each outfit 30 times.

5. Assume you will be earning $8 per hour. How many hours would you have to work to pay for the new clothes?

6. After thinking about their cost and care requirements, would you stick with your original choices? **YES / NO**

   Explain why.

   _____

   _____

   _____

   _____

   _____

Navigating Your Careers

Life After High School

HIGH SCHOOL GRADUATION WILL MARK the end of an era. You'll leave behind the routine and purpose of twelve years and begin a new phase in your life. So now is the time to set a new direction and start planning your future.

You don't need to plan your entire future right now, of course, but you should start thinking about it. Sooner or later, you'll want to live on your own. That means that you'll need to get a job and earn a living. Because you'll probably spend a large portion of your adult life working, your career choices deserve serious thought.

it's Your turn

How well do you really know yourself? Discovering the "real you" is key to figuring out the path you'll want to take after high school. Your answers to the following questions will help you get a handle on your interests, your talents, and what you want out of life.

1. What are my favorite and least favorite school subjects? _____
2. What hobbies and activities do I enjoy? _____
3. What special skills or talents do I have? _____
4. Do I prefer to work alone or as part of a team? _____
5. Do I prefer to give direction or take direction? _____
6. Do I prefer to work indoors or outdoors? _____
7. What jobs have I liked? Why? _____
8. What jobs have I disliked? Why? _____
9. What do I hope to be doing in five years? In ten years? _____

Review your answers. What links can you make between your responses and possible career options?

_____

LIVING THE LIFE YOU WANT

What's important to you? What are your hopes and dreams for the future? What kind of lifestyle do you want? The career you choose will have a major impact on your life. It will affect not only how you spend your working hours and how much money you earn, but also where you live and how much free time you have.

Consider the examples of Serena and her brother Miguel. Serena is a flight attendant. She loves to travel and always dreamed of seeing the world. Serena is young and single and doesn't mind being away from home for days at a time. She enjoys living in a large city with an international airport. Miguel, on the other hand, lives in a small town, where he works at a local bank. Although he doesn't make much money, Miguel is happy with his job. It gives him plenty of free time to do the things he enjoys—spend time with family and friends, coach Little League, and volunteer at a nursing home.

Serena and Miguel have both chosen careers that allow them to have the kind of lifestyle they want. When you start thinking about careers, a good place to start is to think about what you want out of life—and what you'll need from your job in order to get it.

DID YOU KNOW?

Life Changes Many people change their minds about careers as they move through the life cycle. A job that involves travel may be attractive to a single, unattached young adult. That same person may find the work less appealing, however, when he or she marries and starts a family.

GETTING THE SKILLS YOU NEED

Although it's possible to get a job right out of high school, most jobs in today's workplace require some kind of additional education or training. There are many ways to receive this training. As you read about the options below, consider which one would best suit your needs.

At **colleges and universities**, students can earn a bachelor's degree after four years of study. Many high-paying professional jobs require at least a bachelor's degree.

Two-year colleges offer associate degrees in a variety of occupational areas. Evening and weekend classes are often available for students who work during the day.

Technical and trade schools provide training in specific professions, including automotive technology, electronics, plumbing, graphic design, and computer technology. Many schools offer both day and evening classes.

Apprenticeships give people a chance to earn money while learning a trade on the job from an experienced worker. Most apprenticeships are in skilled trades, such as carpentry and construction.

Going the Distance

If you want to go to college but can't attend traditional classes, distance learning might be the right choice for you. In a distance learning program, students take online classes from their home computers. Distance learning can help people who don't live near a college or who don't have transportation.

DID YOU KNOW?

College Pays Off In their lifetimes, people with bachelor's degrees will earn nearly twice as much as those with only a high school diploma. People who go on to receive doctoral degrees will typically have lifetime earnings nearly three times those of a high-school graduate.

Serving in the **armed forces** is one way to get free training in a wide range of technical fields, including computer technology, engineering, and aviation. However, it also requires a four-year commitment to active military duty.

The World of Work

NOW THAT YOU KNOW MORE ABOUT YOURSELF, you can start thinking about which careers would fit your interests, abilities, and personality. But with thousands of occupations to choose from, where do you begin? The U.S. Department of Education has simplified the process by organizing careers into "clusters," groups of occupations that share certain characteristics. If one job in a career cluster interests you, it's likely that other jobs in the same cluster would also appeal to you.

The chart below shows ten career clusters and sample jobs within each cluster, ranging from entry-level positions to those that require advanced education or training. Which jobs would you like to learn more about?

Career Cluster	Entry Level	Technical Level Jobs	Professional Level Jobs
Health & Medicine	Nursing aide, medical assistant, medical records clerk	Medical secretary, dental hygienist, registered nurse	Nurse practitioner, physical therapist, orthodontist
Agriculture & Natural Resources	Meat packer, logger, rigger	Farmer, forestry technician, derrick operator	Agricultural inspector, food scientist, petroleum geologist
Government, Law, & Public Safety	Postal clerk, police dispatcher, security guard	Paralegal, police officer, fire fighter	Urban planner, lawyer, fire investigator
Arts & Communication	Stagehand, photographer's assistant, reporter	Web designer, makeup artist, graphic designer	Cinematographer, musician, illustrator
Human Services	Camp counselor, nursing home aide, personal shopper	Child welfare worker, recreational therapist, consumer credit counselor	School social worker, family counselor, consumer fraud investigator
Education & Training	Student teacher, teacher assistant, administrative assistant	Preschool teacher, coach, test developer	High school teacher, corporate trainer, curriculum specialist
Business & Finance	Management trainee, bookkeeper, bank teller	Human resources manager, public relations specialist, stockbroker	Advertising manager, computer programmer, accountant
Hospitality & Tourism	Waiter/waitress, maid, lifeguard	Chef, travel agent, flight attendant	Catering manager, cruise director, tour director
Manufacturing & Engineering	Assembler, machine tender, equipment operator	Computer technician, welding technician, inspector	Metallurgist, civil engineer, electrical engineer
Housing & Construction	Real estate clerk, home furnishings salesperson, roofer	Landscape gardener, home inspector, plumber	Interior designer, architect, building inspector

On the lines below, write five jobs that you think you might like. Then figure out which career clusters these jobs fall into and list those as well.

Job: _____   Cluster: _____

Job: _____   Cluster: _____

Job: _____   Cluster: _____

Job: _____   Cluster: _____

Job: _____   Cluster: _____

What conclusions can you draw about which career clusters appeal to you?

_____

_____

_____

_____

DOING YOUR HOMEWORK

You might think that working with animals sounds like fun, but do you know how many years of education a veterinarian needs? Maybe you've dreamed about a career as a film actor, but do you know how competitive the field is? When you think about your career options, it's useful to find out as much as possible about the jobs you're considering. The more you know, the better you will understand which careers would suit you best.

To locate information about career clusters and occupations, start at the library. In the careers section, you'll find a variety of resources, including reference books, magazines, and videos. You can also use the library's computers to find career information online. Interviewing someone who works in a field that interests you is a good way of getting further information and insights.

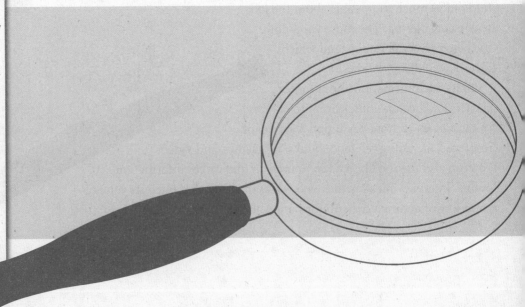

GETTING THE FACTS

It's important to research your career options carefully. Too many people waste time, money, and education or training on a career only to discover that it is the wrong one for them! Ask yourself about these factors when researching careers:

The nature of the work. What are the main duties and responsibilities of the job? What would a typical workday be like? Would I use computers or other technology?

Earnings and benefits. How much money can I expect to earn in this occupation? Would I be paid an hourly wage or a yearly salary? What types of benefits are common?

Working conditions. What sort of environment would I be working in? How many hours are in a typical work-week? Would I need to work nights or weekends? Would I work alone or as part of a team? Is the job physically or emotionally demanding?

Qualifications. What type of degree would I need to pursue a career in this field? What kind of skills and training should I have? Which high school courses or extracurricular activities would be valuable?

Employment trends. How many people hold jobs in this field? What businesses or industries employ most of these workers? Where are the jobs most likely to be located?

Employment outlook. What's the growth rate for occupations in this field? How competitive is the field? How will job openings be created in the future?

Check the Net

Online Career Guides

Several career guides published by the U.S. Department of Labor are available on the Internet. They provide a wealth of information about careers, including industry and occupation profiles. Go online to find more information about an industry or occupation that interests you.

Key Terms: Career Guide to Industries, Occupational Outlook Handbook, Occupational Outlook Quarterly

Learning About Careers

TAKE ANOTHER LOOK AT THE CHART on page 252.
Which of the ten career clusters most interests you?
Within that career cluster, which jobs do you find appealing? Use library and Internet sources to research two jobs
in that cluster. Fill in the chart below.

RESEARCHING CAREER OPTIONS

Factors to Consider	Career Option 1:	Career Option 2:
Nature of the work		
Working conditions		
Qualifications		
Earnings and benefits		
Employment trends		
Employment outlook		

After doing this research, which of these two career
options would you be more likely to pursue? Why?

_____

_____

_____

_____

No Pay, But Great Benefits Although most internships don't pay anything, they look great on your résumé, especially when you're just starting out. They show that you have some professional experience and that you're taking your job search seriously. Another benefit: some interns are offered paid positions after graduation.

SEE FOR YOURSELF

Doing research is a good first step for learning about different careers, but you can find out even more by getting some workplace experience. Working at different jobs can help you figure out what types of work you like—and what you don't like. It also gives you a chance to develop skills that you can use later in your career.

There are different ways to get work experience before you leave school. You can take a part-time job in the evenings or on weekends, or a full-time position during the summer. You can also learn about work by volunteering for a community organization, such as a soup kitchen, animal shelter, or museum. Although you won't be paid, you'll gain valuable experience while helping others.

To learn about a specific field, you might consider an internship—an opportunity to work at a company and gain practical experience under the guidance of experienced workers. Although most interns aren't paid, they can receive school credit for their work. Work-study programs are another type of job training for students. As the name suggests, people in these programs spend part of their time at school and part at work. Finally, you could try job shadowing—following a worker for a few days on the job. Observing a person going about a typical workday can give you a good idea of what the work involves.

THE DAILY GRIND

For many people, a workday means "nine to five"—9:00 a.m. to 5:00 p.m., Monday through Friday. However, many jobs allow for a more flexible schedule. The chart below shows some advantages and drawbacks of different types of work.

Type of Work	What It Means	Advantages	Drawbacks
Full-time	Typically, 7 to 8 hours, 5 days a week, possibly weekend or night work	Benefits such as paid vacations and health insurance	Hours have limited or no flexibility
Part-time	Less than 35 hours a week—may be a few hours per day or a few full days per week	Free time for other pursuits, such as going to school	Less pay and no benefits
Freelance	Self-employed workers hire out their services to one or more clients	Ability to set your own hours	Work isn't always steady; no paid benefits
Contract	Hired to work on a specific project	Steady work for a certain time period, such as 6 months	May be "down time" with no work between assignments
Temporary	Hired to help out during busy times or fill in for employees who are away	Offers a chance to sample different jobs	Work may not be steady; no benefits

DID YOU KNOW?

Outsourcing A growing trend in the business world is outsourcing, in which large companies eliminate some full-time positions and instead hire outside contract workers to do the work. This trend reduces the number of full-time jobs but opens up opportunities for people who work on a contract basis.

Looking for Work

ONCE YOU HAVE A GOOD IDEA OF THE CAREER PATH you want to follow, you'll need to prepare a résumé—a written summary of your work experience, education, skills, and interests. Many employers ask all job applicants to submit a résumé. It's best to prepare your résumé *before* you start your job search. That way, when you find a job opening that sounds promising, you'll be ready to roll.

SHOW YOUR STUFF

Before you prepare your résumé, think about the skills you can highlight. There are certain skills that employers in every field like to see in the workers they hire. These skills will help you on the job no matter what career path you choose. And, just as important, you can transfer these skills as you change jobs—or even careers—down the road. They fall into five basic categories:

Basic skills are the skills you learn in school. You'll need reading and writing skills to communicate with coworkers, understand manuals and schedules, fill out forms, and write memos and reports. Math skills will help you interpret charts and graphs, compute sales figures, or count change.

Thinking skills, such as reasoning, analyzing, and evaluating will help you make decisions, draw conclusions, and solve problems at work.

Technology skills involve using computers and other electronic equipment. For most jobs, you'll need a basic knowledge of word processing, e-mail, and online research. More advanced knowledge of computers and software may help you get ahead in today's high-tech workplace.

Interpersonal skills help you work effectively with others. They include communication skills, such as speaking and listening, and teamwork skills, such as cooperation and compromise.

DID YOU KNOW?

Résumés The word *résumé* comes from a French word meaning "to summarize." In some fields, a résumé is known as a *curriculum vitae*, or CV, from a Latin phrase meaning "the course of life."

Management skills— organizing, planning, establishing priorities, and managing resources— help workers in all positions do their jobs more effectively. They also increase your chances of being promoted.

it's Your turn

Answer the following questions to see how your employability skills measure up.

BASIC SKILLS

1. Which of the basic skills—reading, writing, or math—is your strongest? _____

Which is your weakest? _____ How could you work on improving this skill?

_____

_____

THINKING SKILLS

2. Describe a recent situation in which you used thinking skills to make a major decision.

_____

_____

3. Describe a recent situation in which you used thinking skills to solve a problem.

_____

_____

TECHNOLOGY SKILLS

4. List the technology skills that you currently have.

_____

_____

5. How could you strengthen your technology skills?

_____

_____

INTERPERSONAL SKILLS

6. Describe a recent situation in which you used communication or teamwork skills to accomplish a goal.

_____

_____

MANAGEMENT SKILLS

7. How do you use management skills in your daily life? Explain how these skills help you at home, at school, or at work.

_____

_____

YOUR LIFE ON PAPER

Your résumé is your first chance—and, in some cases, your *only* chance—to impress an employer. So give it all you've got! Use a computer to type up your résumé; most employers won't even look at a handwritten one. If you don't have a computer at home, use one at school or at the library. Make sure the paper you use is good quality and choose a neutral color—nothing flashy.

Most résumés contain the following sections.

Contact information. At the top of your résumé, put your name, mailing address, telephone number (with area code), and e-mail address.

Employment objective. Describe the type of work you want to find. This statement should fit the job you're applying for. You may need to change the objective if you applying for several different jobs.

Kayla McKinney
321 Elm Street
Littletown, PA 19000
(215) 555-6789
kmckinney@abc.com

EMPLOYMENT OBJECTIVE
To obtain a job with a photography studio.

WORK EXPERIENCE
June 2005–May 2006:
Sales Associate. Berkeley's Department Store. Worked part-time in electronics, assisting customers and operating cash register.

November 2003–May 2005:
Volunteer. St. Francis Hospital. Helped deliver flowers and mail and read books to children and elderly hospital patients.

EDUCATIONAL BACKGROUND
Kennedy High School, class of 2006
Two photography courses at Bigville Community College, summer 2005

SPECIAL SKILLS
Solid knowledge of digital camera equipment and digital photography. Proficient with both Macintosh and IBM-compatible computers.

AWARDS AND ACTIVITIES
• Received first place for photography in 2006 high school art competition.
• Took photographs for high school yearbook during junior and senior years.
• Served as photography editor for school newspaper during junior and senior years.

REFERENCES
Available on request.

Work experience. List all the jobs you've had, starting with the most recent and working backward. If you haven't had much paid experience, you can list volunteer work you've done.

Educational background. List the schools you've attended and your dates of graduation. Include any special courses or training related to the job you're applying for.

Special skills. Mention any skills or abilities you have that you could use on the job.

Awards and activities. If you've received any awards or participated in any activities that are relevant to the job, include them on your résumé.

References. References are the names of people that employers can contact to learn more about you. You can list your references on your résumé or write "Available on request." Just make sure that you actually have the references to provide if someone requests them!

 **QuickTip**

The Right References

Choose references who can give a positive description of your character and abilities. Former employers and teachers are usually good choices. *Don't* choose family members—employers tend to see them as biased and won't take their opinions seriously. Always ask permission before giving someone's name as a reference.

A résumé should be brief, so don't go over one page. Focus on your strengths, but don't lie about your background or exaggerate your skills and abilities. Eventually, the employers will catch on—whether it's at the interview or after you've gotten the job—and they'll be *less* impressed with you, not more.

In a recent survey, recruiters said that their number one pet peeve about résumés was mistakes in spelling, typing, and grammar. Don't be a statistic! Check and double-check your résumé for spelling and grammatical errors. When you're done checking it, ask someone else to proofread it for you, too.

Color Me Wrong

Some job applicants use brightly colored paper, such as hot pink or lime green, in an attempt to get their résumés noticed. This strategy can make a résumé stand out—but for the wrong reasons. Most employers prefer professional-looking résumés printed on good-quality white or off-white paper. It's better to make employers notice your résumé for the *right* reasons—your skills, your experience, and your professional presentation.

Check the Net

Check the Net

Résumé Formats

There are several ways to organize your résumé. The most common type is a chronological résumé, which lists experience and education in order by date. A skills résumé or functional résumé, by contrast, highlights skills and abilities. Search the Internet for more information and examples of these formats.

KeyTerms: chronological résumé, skills résumé, functional résumé

“ IN A RECENT SURVEY, RECRUITERS SAID THAT THEIR NUMBER ONE CRITICISM ABOUT RÉSUMÉS WAS MISTAKES IN SPELLING, TYPING, AND GRAMMAR. ”

LOOKING FOR LEADS

After preparing your résumé, you're ready to look for job leads, or information about specific job openings. One of the best ways to do this is by networking—using personal contacts to learn about job openings. Your network can include relatives, friends, neighbors, former employers, and local business owners. If you let these people know what kind of job you want, they may tell you about job openings where they work. They can also tell other people in *their* networks about you.

You can also find job leads in classified ads. The "Help Wanted" section of your local newspaper is one source, and business and professional journals are another. Job listings may also be posted on the Internet. On many Web sites, job seekers can search for jobs in a specific field or location. On some sites, you can also post your résumé for prospective employers to view.

Your school may have resources, such as a career counselor, to help you find job leads. Some schools hold annual job fairs, where local companies provide employment information and applications to students. You can also fill out an application at an employment agency. When companies have job openings, they can call one of these agencies, and the agency tries to pair up qualified applicants with job openings. Public employment agencies, which are run by state governments, provide their services free of charge. Private employment agencies charge a fee to either the employer or the job seeker.

Check the Net

Job Openings

When you search online, you can find job openings not only in your local area but also across the country or even around the world. Try searching the Internet for job openings in a career field that interests you. Look for jobs in a location where you might want to live someday.

KeyTerms: job listings, job search

Applying Yourself

YOU'VE PREPARED YOUR RÉSUMÉ and searched for job leads, and you've finally found a job opening that sounds just perfect. Now what? Well, your first goal is to get yourself an interview. Keep in mind that you'll probably be one of dozens or even hundreds of applicants. You need to take advantage of every chance to make yourself stand out. Each contact that you have with a prospective employer—by mail, by phone, or in person—is an opportunity to shine.

RELEASING YOUR RÉSUMÉ

To apply for a job, you'll need to send out a copy of your résumé. There are three ways to do this—by mail, fax, or e-mail. No matter which method you choose, you should make sure you use the correct contact information.

The most traditional way of sending a résumé is by mail. Many employers prefer this method. However, your résumé may take several days to reach its destination this way. You can get it there faster by faxing it. A faxed résumé may not look as crisp and clean as your original, though, and you won't have any choice in the paper that's used.

Some employers accept and prefer résumés by electronic mail. You simply attach the document file to an e-mail message, and the recipient can either print the file or view it on the computer. One drawback of this method is that the recipient may not use the same word processing software as you do. In this case, your formatting may be lost—or worse, the document may be unreadable!

DID YOU KNOW?

Virus Protection Not all employers accept résumés sent by e-mail. Some companies have a policy against opening e-mail file attachments from unknown sources because of the risk of computer viruses. So before e-mailing a résumé, check with the company to make sure that e-mail files are acceptable. Otherwise, your precious résumé might be deleted without ever being read!

FILLING OUT FORMS

When you apply for a job, you may have to fill out an application form. The form may ask for such information as your name, address, and phone number; Social Security number; employment history; education; and references. Much of this information is on your résumé, so have it and your list of references handy. Before filling out any form, read the instructions carefully. Write as neatly and clearly as possible. Answer all the questions, or write NA ("not applicable") if a question doesn't apply to you. When you're done, double-check the form for errors. Be sure to flip over the paper before you turn it in—some application forms have two sides!

COVER STORY

Along with your résumé, you'll need to include a cover letter. This letter should explain who you are, why you're writing, and why you think you would be a good candidate for the job. Your cover letter is nearly as important as your résumé. A well-written, error-free cover letter may get an employer intrigued enough to read your résumé—which, in turn, may result in an interview. A poor cover letter, on the other hand, could lead an employer to toss your résumé in the trash without so much as a glance. Keep your cover letter brief—one page at most—and have a friend or relative proofread it for errors. A sample cover letter appears on the next page.

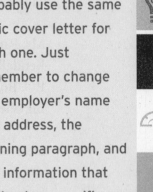

QuickTip

Time Saver

If you apply for more than one job, you can probably use the same basic cover letter for each one. Just remember to change the employer's name and address, the opening paragraph, and any information that relates to a specific company.

SAMPLE COVER LETTER

321 Elm Street
Littletown, IN 19000
(215) 555-6789
lmckinney@abc.com

May 8, 2008

Ms. Patricia Kendall
Kendall Portrait Studio
P.O. Box 478
Bigville, IN 19100

Dear Ms. Kendall:

I am writing in response to your ad in *The Gazette* for a photographer's assistant. This is just the kind of position I'm looking for. With my interests and experience, I could be a valuable asset to your studio.

I have been taking photographs for the past five years and have enhanced my abilities by taking classes in photography at the local community college. During my junior and senior year of high school, I took photographs for both the school newspaper and the student yearbook. This past March, one of my photographs received the top prize in a student art competition. The enclosed résumé provides more details about my skills and experience.

I am especially interested in working for Kendall Portrait Studio because of your fine reputation and the quality of your work.

I would be available for an interview anytime after my graduation on May 22. Thank you for considering me for this position.

Sincerely,

Kayla McKinney

How-To

Writing a Cover Letter Your cover letter is nearly as important as your résumé. Most cover letters follow a basic three- or four-paragraph format.

Step 1

Write your greeting. Whenever possible, find out the name of the person who does the interviewing and hiring, and address your cover letter to that person (for example, "Dear Ms. Jones"). If you don't know the person's name, you might use a title such as "Dear Customer Service Manager." As a last resort, use "To Whom It May Concern."

Step 2

In the first paragraph, explain why you're writing. Tell the employer where you heard about the job opening. Include the name of the person who told you about the job or the publication where you saw a classified ad.

Step 3

In the second paragraph, discuss the experience, skills, and qualities that make you qualified for the job. Refer the reader to your enclosed résumé.

Step 4

To conclude your letter, restate your interest in the job and mention your desire for an interview. If you won't be available to begin work until a certain date—the start of summer vacation, for example—say so here.

Step 5

Sign your letter—as neatly as possible. Attach your résumé and send it off!

it's Your turn

Check the classifieds section of your local newspaper, and find a job that looks interesting. Pretend that you're applying for this job. On the lines below, write a cover letter that you could send along with your résumé to the prospective employer. When you're finished, switch cover letters with a classmate and proofread each other's work.

Dear _____,

_____

_____

_____

_____

_____

_____

Sincerely, _____

Selling Yourself

AFTER YOU SEND OUT YOUR RÉSUMÉ AND COVER LETTER to prospective employers, it's time to play the waiting game. If you're lucky, the phone will ring a few days later with the call you've been waiting for—an employer asking you to come in for an interview. You know the employer must have liked your résumé, so you've passed the first test, but the interview is your real chance to sell yourself. Planning ahead will help you make the best impression possible.

BE PREPARED

You might think that there's no need to prepare for an interview ahead of time. After all, the interviewer's only going to ask you about your skills and experience—things you already know, right? Well, not quite. You can give yourself a definite edge by learning as much as you can ahead of time about the company. Check the company's Web site, the library, or local newspapers and magazines. If you know someone at the company, pump that person for information about what the company does and its goals for the future.

The day before the interview, make sure you have all the materials you'll need to take with you. Include several copies of your résumé, reference letters, a pen and notepad, your driver's license, and your Social Security Number. It's also a good idea to prepare a list of questions to ask the interviewer about the job and the company. You can stash these items in a small portfolio or binder to make them easier to carry.

DID YOU KNOW?

Discrimination The Civil Rights Act of 1964 makes it illegal for companies to discriminate against job applicants on the basis of race, color, religion, gender, or national origin. Other federal laws ban discrimination based on age or disability. This means that the company cannot hire, or refuse to hire, someone based on these factors. Nor may the interviewer ask you questions related to those topics.

FIRST IMPRESSIONS

As the saying goes, "You never get a second chance to make a first impression." Like it or not, the first look someone gets at you will give that person an idea of what you're like—an idea that can be hard to dislodge. So make your first impression a good one by looking clean, neat, and professional. Wear clean, pressed clothes, and make sure you're well groomed.

What exactly should you wear to an interview? That depends on the workplace. A good rule of thumb is to dress appropriately for the job you're applying for. If you interview for an office job, for example, you would probably want to wear a suit—or the closest thing you have to one. For an interview at a fast-food restaurant, you wouldn't need to dress up as much, but don't go *too* casual. Jeans, shorts, or sneakers are never appropriate for an interview. As a rule, it's better to be a little overdressed than to be underdressed.

Timing Is Everything

A good way to ruin an interview before it even starts is to show up late. Plan ahead to make sure you get to the interview on time—or even a little early. If your appointment is in the morning, set your alarm clock to allow plenty of extra time. Also, find out ahead of time how to get to the place where your interview is going to be, and how long the trip will take. If you're not sure, do a trial run the day before.

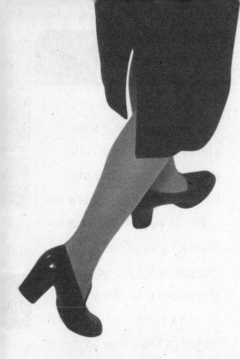

BEST FOOT FORWARD

You've done your homework, and you're looking your best. Now it's time for the actual job interview. When you meet the interviewer, be sure to smile, introduce yourself, and give a firm handshake. Even if you're nervous, try to project self-confidence and a positive attitude. While you talk to the interviewer, sit up straight, pay attention, and maintain eye contact. Don't fidget or chew gum, and if you have a cell phone, make sure it's turned off.

The interviewer may begin by telling you about the company and the position available. Then you will probably have to answer a series of questions—and some of them won't be easy. Even a question that seems simple, such as "Tell me about yourself," is tougher than it sounds. The interviewer doesn't really want to know about your personal life or your family. Stick to the facts that are relevant to the job opening, such as your education, skills, work experience, and career goals. Keep your answers focused and specific, but not too short to be useful.

it's Your turn

Here are some examples of questions that you may be asked during a job interview. How would you answer them? List your responses on the lines provided.

TYPICAL INTERVIEW QUESTIONS

1. What are your strengths? _____
_____

2. What are your weaknesses? _____
_____

3. Why do you want to work here? _____
_____

4. Why should I hire you? _____
_____

5. What are your career goals? _____
_____

6. Where do you picture yourself five years from now? _____
_____

7. Why did you leave your last job? _____

WE'RE SORRY...

Unfortunately, not every interview will end with a job offer. There are all kinds of reasons you might not get a job that you really wanted. Perhaps you just weren't qualified for the job—or maybe you were, but another applicant was even more qualified. There's also the possibility that you didn't make as good an impression as you wanted to.

In any case, try to make a rejection into a learning experience. If an interviewer calls to tell you that you didn't get the job, ask why—politely, of course. Some interviewers are willing to give you feedback that you can use to do better in future interviews. Maybe next time, you'll hear the magic words: "You're hired!"

QuickTip

Send a Note

After an interview, follow up by sending a note to thank the interviewer—whether you still want the job or not. Even if this job isn't the right fit, your note will leave a positive impression, which may help you if future opportunities come up at the same company.

Check the Net

Interview Questions

Interviewers ask questions that will enable them to get to know applicants better. Search the Internet for interview questions and then prepare answers you would use. The more you practice answering sample questions, the easier you will find it to answer questions during the interview.

KeyTerms: interview questions, job interviews

Your Questions, Please

During an interview, you will probably have a chance to ask questions about the company and the job. Here's where your research will come in handy. Let the interviewer know that you did your homework by asking intelligent questions that show you know something about the company. Although you'll probably be interested in the pay rate, do not bring up this subject. You can always ask about pay later if you receive a job offer.

QuickTip

Take Your Time
Accepting a job offer is an important decision, and it's worth taking your time to think it through. Thank the employer for the offer, but ask if you can have 24 hours to think about it before you decide. During this time, don't be embarrassed to call back and ask questions if there's anything you don't understand.

Do You Want the Job?

YOU JUST RECEIVED THE PHONE CALL that you've been waiting for—the job is yours! Before you jump at the offer, get the details. Two factors you'll definitely want to consider are pay and benefits. If these topics didn't come up during the interview, now is the time to ask about them. Don't focus just on these points, though; consider all aspects of the job and the company. Is it the kind of work you want? Do you think that you'll like the environment? Will you have the chance to learn new skills? Will there be opportunities for advancement? All these factors will affect your decision.

GETTING PAID

When deciding on a job offer, consider not just *how much* you'll earn, but also *how* you'll be paid. Will you receive an hourly wage or a salary? How often will your paychecks come—once a week, every two weeks, once a month? Will you be paid for working overtime, and if so, at what rate? If there is no overtime pay, is there some other form of compensation like extra vacation time?

Some companies offer incentives to reward employees for hard work or special achievements. For instance, workers may get a performance bonus for doing their jobs well. Another type of incentive is a profit-sharing plan, in which employees receive a share of the company's profits. Such plans encourage employees to help the company succeed.

Making Tough Choices

JILLIAN IS STUDYING to become a pediatric nurse. She's looking for a job at a doctor's office that will give her some experience and help her pay for night school. Last week, Jillian had interviews for receptionist positions at a pediatrician's office and a family physician's office. Both interviews went well, but Jillian really liked the pediatrician's office and hoped to get that job. Today, the other doctor's office called and offered her a job. Jillian isn't sure what to say.

YOUR IDEAS

1. What are the pros and cons of accepting the job?

_____

_____

_____

_____

_____

_____

_____

_____

2. How would you handle the situation if you were Jillian?

_____

_____

_____

_____

_____

_____

_____

A *cafeteria plan* may sound like it has something to do with lunch, but it's actually an employer benefit policy. Some employers allow their employees to choose which benefits they want, the same way you might pick out different foods in a cafeteria line. For example, an employee who is covered under her husband's health insurance plan might opt for extra vacation time instead of health insurance.

REAPING THE BENEFITS

For some people, benefits such as health care and retirement plans may be even more important than the pay rate. Benefits vary widely among workplaces, with large companies typically offering more extensive benefits than small ones. Benefits may include:

Paid vacation time

for full-time, salaried employees. Most new employees get two weeks of vacation time per year, plus national holidays and a certain number of sick days or personal days. People who have worked for a company longer may get more vacation time.

Health insurance for

employees and, possibly, for their spouse and family. Plans vary considerably and may require employee contributions.

Retirement plans

such as pensions and 401(k) plans. Many retirement plans have tax advantages for the employee.

Convenience benefits designed to

make life easier and less stressful for employees. Examples of convenience benefits include flexible work hours, on-site cafeterias, and on-site child-care centers for employees' children. Some companies also provide on-site health clubs or paid health club memberships for employees.

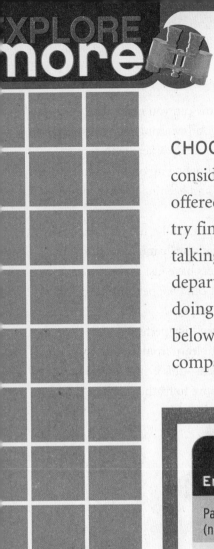

EXPLORE more

Company Benefits

CHOOSE TWO LOCAL COMPANIES that you might consider working for. Gather information about the benefits offered to full-time employees at each company. You might try finding this information on the company's Web site, by talking to employees, or by calling the human resources department of each company and explaining that you are doing research on company benefit plans. Use the chart below to compare the information you find about the two companies.

COMPARING BENEFITS

Employee Benefits	Company A	Company B
Paid vacation time (number of days)		
Paid sick time (number of days)		
Paid personal time (number of days)		
Health insurance (type, coverage, cost to employee)		
Retirement plan (type and employer contributions)		
Convenience benefits (description)		

Which company do you think provides better employee benefits? Explain why.

_____

_____

_____

_____

You can give yourself a good name at work by being a "team player." Be ready to jump in and help coworkers whenever they need a hand. If you get an assignment that you don't like, focus on how it will help the company. After all, you can't succeed if the company fails. If you receive a promotion, be gracious. It's okay to show that you're happy, but don't rub your success in others' faces. Similarly, if someone else gets a promotion that you thought you deserved, don't sulk. Give the person credit for doing a good job—and remember that every success benefits the team as a whole.

On the Job

ONCE YOU'VE GOT THE JOB YOU WANT, how can you make sure that you're successful? One crucial step is to establish good working relationships with coworkers and supervisors. For starters, treat all your coworkers with respect. Show that you're responsible and trustworthy by showing up on time, doing your share of the work, doing what you promise to do, and keeping private company information to yourself.

If you start to feel like your job is more than you can handle, use your management skills to set priorities and keep yourself focused. If it's really too much for you, don't be embarrassed to ask for help. Your coworkers have just as much reason as you do to want to see the project succeed, and that can't happen unless you all work together.

No matter how hard you work, you won't do everything perfectly. Accept criticism from your supervisors gracefully, and do your best to learn from it. And if you do make mistakes, don't try to hide them or blame others—this is sure to backfire. Instead, own up to your mistakes and take the initiative to fix the problem.

Lifelong Learning

AFTER YOU FINISH SCHOOL, you'll continue to learn new things throughout your life. You'll pick up some new skills on the job, and you may also receive additional training to help you do your job better. Some employers even pay for workers to take college courses that will give them skills related to their job.

Take advantage of any opportunities to gain knowledge and improve your skills. The more you know, the better your chances for advancement—and the higher earnings that come with it. And whenever you decide to change jobs, your knowledge and skills will be valuable assets that you can take with you. In today's fast-paced, ever-changing workplace, it's more important than ever to keep your skills sharp and up-to-date.

QuickTip

Moving On
Sooner or later, you'll probably decide to look for another job. It's best not to discuss your plans with your coworkers until you actually receive another job offer. When you do leave a job, leave on the best terms possible. For example, give your employer time to find a replacement for you. Don't burn your bridges behind you—you never know what the future might hold.

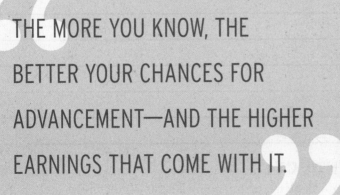

THE MORE YOU KNOW, THE BETTER YOUR CHANCES FOR ADVANCEMENT—AND THE HIGHER EARNINGS THAT COME WITH IT.

Putting it all together

GET A JOB!

You've just graduated from school, and you're looking for your first full-time job. You have a general idea what kind of work interests you, but you don't know what jobs are actually available in your area. You need to get your résumé ready and find a job you want to apply for. To narrow down your job search, pick a field that you'd like to focus on:

I'M LOOKING FOR A JOB IN

_____

_____

1. **START** by checking the want ads in the local papers. You can also check job listings online. Find a job opening that interests you, and follow the directions below as if you were actually applying for that position. Describe the position you found here:

_____

_____

_____

_____

2. **PREPARE** a rough draft of your résumé, using the sample résumé on page 261 as a model. You'll need to include your name, mailing address, phone number, and e-mail address, as well as your work experience, education, skills, and references. Make sure that the employment objective you list at the top of your résumé matches the job you're applying for.

3. **WRITE** a cover letter addressed to the person who's offering the job. Use the sample on page 266 as a model. When you're done, exchange résumés and cover letters with a partner and proofread each other's work.

4. Suppose that your application was successful, and you've been asked to come in for an interview. **USE** library and Internet sources to **LEARN** about the company—what it does, where it's located, how many people work there, and so on. Using your findings, prepare a list of questions to ask the interviewer. List your questions here.

_____

_____

_____

_____

_____

_____

_____

5. **CONDUCT** a mock interview with your partner. Decide which of you will be the first to apply for the job that he or she chose. The other person should play the interviewer and ask the typical interview questions from the list on page 270, as well as any other questions that might be relevant to the specific job opening. Afterward, switch roles so that each of you gets a chance to interview for the job opening of your choice.

6. When you play the interviewer, **TAKE NOTES** on how your partner performs. Did the applicant pay attention, make eye contact, and use good listening skills? Did he or she ask intelligent questions about the job? Write your impressions of your partner's interview here.

_____

_____

_____

_____

_____

_____

_____

_____

7. GO OVER your partner's notes on your performance during your job interview. Based on your partner's evaluation, do you think you would get the job? Why or why not? How could you better prepare for a real interview?

_____

_____

_____

_____

_____

_____

_____

_____

8. REFLECT on the process you completed. **DESCRIBE** what you did well and what you will want to improve for a future job search.

_____

_____

_____

_____

_____

_____

Glossary

Aerobic exercise Rhythmic activity that speeds up your heart rate and breathing.

Allowances Factors that affect the amount of income that is withheld from your pay.

Annual percentage rate (APR) Amount of interest paid per year on the balance in your credit card account.

Apprenticeship Training program in which a person can earn money while learning a trade from an experienced worker.

Bait and switch Deceptive practice in which advertisers attract buyers by advertising a product at one price and then try to sell them a higher-priced item instead.

Body composition The ratio between fat tissue and lean muscle tissue.

Body language Combination of facial expressions, gestures, and posture that can express a person's feelings.

Bond Certificate that indicates that you have loaned money to the issuer in exchange for an agreed interest payment by a certain date.

Budget A plan for spending and saving over a given period of time.

Calorie Measurement of the energy supplied by food and of the energy your body uses. Carbohydrates Sugars and starches that provide the body with ready energy.

Career cluster Group of occupations that share certain characteristics.

Certificate of deposit (CD) Certificate issued by a bank to indicate that you have deposited money for a certain amount of time in exchange for a specified interest rate.

Cholesterol White, waxy substance produced mostly in the liver that helps the body transport and digest fat.

Coinsurance Portion of insurance costs that you pay.

Commission Payment system in which salespeople are paid a percentage of every sale they make.

Communication The sending and receiving of messages.

Comparison shopping Comparing the prices and features of similar products to ensure that you get the best deal.

Conflict A clash of opposing ideas or interests.

Cover letter Letter that accompanies a résumé and that introduces a job seeker to a potential employer.

Credit card Card that enables the user to pay for a purchase and be billed for it later. Also allows a user to extend payment over a period of time and pay interest on the balance.

Credit limit Maximum amount you can charge on a credit card.

Credit rating Evaluation of a person's credit history.

Debit card Card that enables the user to make a purchase or obtain cash and have the money deducted from his or her bank account.

Deductible Set amount that you must pay for any loss before your insurance coverage kicks in.

Deduction Anything that is subtracted from your gross pay on a paycheck.

Dehydration Condition that occurs when the body does not get enough water.

Dovetailing Overlapping two or more activities in order to make more efficient use of time.

Eating disorder Disorder characterized by unhealthy and potentially dangerous eating patterns.

Ethical Fair, right, and just for all the people involved.

Etiquette Set of guidelines for how to behave in many different social situations.

Fats Nutrients needed to transport and store other nutrients, regulate growth, and provide a source of energy.

Food poisoning Illness caused by eating food contaminated by harmful bacteria. Also known as foodborne illness.

Fraud Deceitful conduct for personal gain.

Frequent shopper card Card that gives you discounts on certain items when you shop at a specific store.

Goal Something that gives your life direction and purpose and that you consciously work toward.

Grace period Period of time allowed to pay a bill after you receive it.

"I" messages Way of communicating in which a person focuses on his or her own feelings instead of criticizing somebody else.

Identity theft The illegal use of an individual's personal information.

Individual retirement account (IRA) Personal savings plan that enables workers to set aside pre-tax money for retirement.

Insurance Protection for which you pay regular premiums and that covers your expenses if you experience a major loss.

Internship Temporary, often unpaid, position that affords an opportunity to work at a company and gain experience.

Invest To commit money to stocks or bonds with the purpose of making a profit over time.

Job shadowing Process of following a worker on the job for a few days to learn what responsibilities the work entails.

Lease (i) Legal document that sets up the terms for renting a rental property. (ii) To pay a monthly fee in exchange for exclusive use of a vehicle for a certain period of time.

Listening The process of showing that you've heard another person's words and understood the feelings behind them.

Loan Sum of money made available to a borrower who agrees to pay it back, with interest, over an agreed period of time.

Management process A series to steps you can take to organize a major job into something you can handle.

Mass transit Public transportation systems designed to carry large numbers of people.

Mediation Process of resolving a conflict by bringing in a neutral third party who helps the two sides find a solution.)

Minerals Nutrients needed to form body tissue and keep body processes operating smoothly.

Minimum balance Minimum amount you must keep in an account in order to avoid paying fees.

Money market account Type of savings account in which the bank invests the money you deposit in order to earn higher yields.

Mutual fund Set of investments shared among many investors.

Nutrients The chemicals found in food that help the body work properly.

Online profiling Practice of collecting information about the Web sites a person visits and using it to tailor advertising to that person's interests.

Outsourcing System in which companies eliminate certain full-time positions and hire outside contract workers instead.

Overscheduling Taking on more than you can handle.

Overtraining Pushing your body past its limits by working out too hard and too often.

Premium Regular fee paid to an insurance company.

Priorities Your most important needs and wants; the things that you should deal with first.

Procrastination Putting something off until later.

Proteins Nutrients needed to build and repair tissues.

Resources All the things you can use in order to meet a goal.

Résumé A written summary of your work experience, education, skills, and interests.

Return policy Rules established by stores that govern returns and refunds.

Saturated fats Fats, found mostly in animal products, that are hard at room temperature.

Secure site Web site that uses special software that encodes personal information during transmission.

Security deposit Fee paid by a renter to cover the cost of any damage he or she may cause to a rental unit during the period of the lease.

Self-esteem Liking and respecting yourself.

Sexually transmitted disease (STD) Disease spread through sexual contact with an infected person.

Staples Basic food items, such as eggs and flour, that you always keep on hand.

Sticker price A dealer's initial asking price for a vehicle.

Stock Portion of the ownership in a particular company. Stocks are sold in units called shares.

Sublet To move out of a rental unit and rent it out to someone else in your place.

Support system All the people and groups you can turn to for help.

Time trap Something that prevents you from using time effectively.

Trans fats Fats, found mostly in products such as margarine or vegetable shortening, that are produced during the processing of liquid fats.

Unit price The price of an item per quart, pound, ounce, or other unit of measure.

Values Your beliefs about what is important.

Vitamins Nutrients needed in small amounts that help the body function properly and process other nutrients.

Warehouse club Store that buys products in bulk and sells them at a discount to customers who pay a membership fee.

Warranty A manufacturer's written promise to repair or replace a product if it doesn't work as claimed.

Work-study program Training program in which people spend part of their time at school and part of their time at work.

Index

Abuse, **48, 197**

Accidents. *See also* Safety.
    motor vehicle, **168**
    preventing home, **198**

Active listening, **35**

Advertising, **61-63**
    goals of, **61, 62**
    influence of, **61**
    techniques, **62, 63**
    types of, **62**

AIDS, **200**

Alcohol, **193**

Anorexia nervosa, **190-192**

Applications, job, **265**

Apprenticeships, **251**

Attitude, positive, **174, 178**

Auctions, online, **66**

Banking, **101-104**
    balancing a checkbook, **103**
    checking accounts, **102**
    credit and debit cards, **105-108**
    electronic transactions, **104, 112**
    online, **104**
    types of accounts, **101**
    using an ATM card, **104**

Behavior, avoiding risky. *See* Safety.

Benefits, employment, **272, 274**

Binge eating, **190-192**

Body composition, **179, 186**

Body image, **187**

Body language, **34, 35**

Body Mass Index (BMI), **186, 189**

Bonds, **118**

Budgeting. *See* Financial
    management and planning.

Bulimia nervosa, **190-192**

Calcium, **208**

Calories, **188, 209**

Car maintenance, **169**

Carbohydrates, **208**

Career clusters, **252**

Careers. *See also* Employment, Jobs.
    clusters, **252**
    college education and, **251**
    employability skills, **258-259**
    exploring options, **253-254**
    finding a job, **252-270**
    internships, **256**
    life cycle and, **250**
    lifestyle and, **250**
    researching, **254, 256**
    self-assessment, **249**
    skills needed for, **251**
    sources of information about,
        253-254
    working conditions, **254**
    workplace experience, **256**

Cell phone, choosing a, **72-73**

Certificates of deposit, **118**

Change(s)
    managing, **7-28**
    preparing for, **7**
    support systems and, **28**
    transition and, **28**
    types of, **7**

Checking account
    balancing a checkbook, **103**
    using a, **76, 101-102**

Cholesterol, **208**

Clothing, **229-247.** *See also*
    Sewing.
    appropriate dress, **229, 231**
    budget, **238**
    buying, **237-239**
    care of, **239, 240-242, 244-245**
    cleaning, **240-243**
    colors, **235**
    costs, **238, 239**
    dress codes, **231**
    evaluating wardrobe, **232**
    expanding wardrobe, **232**
    fashions, **234-235**
    fibers, **239**
    for special occasions, **231**
    for travel, **233**
    quality, **237**
    recycling unwanted, **232**
    shopping for, **237-239**
    sizes, **235**
    stain removal, **244**
    storing, **232**
    styles, **235, 236**
    wardrobe needs, **230**

Colleges
    advantages of a college
        education, **251**
    distance learning, **251**
    types of, **251**

Communication, **33-36**
    active listening, **35**
    barriers to, **36**
    body language and, **34**
    criticism and, **36**
    family and, **38**
    relationships and, **33**
    refusal skills, **45**
    tact and, **36**
    tone of, **36**
    using "I" messages, **34**
    without words, **35**
    workplace, **51**

Compensation package, **272, 274, 275**

Complaint, making a, **80-81**

Conflict, **54, 55**
    escalation in, **54**
    reasons for, **54**
    resolving, **55**

Consumer
    advertising and the, **60-63**
    choices, **59, 60**
    credit, **107-108**
    complaints, **80-81**
    fraud, **82**
    influences, **59, 60**
    payment options, **76**

privacy, **83**

publications, **69**

shopping options, **64-67, 69-71**

Consumer Reports, **69**

Conversation, starting a, **42**

Cooking, **217-219.** *See also* Food, Nutrition.

classes, **219**

equipment for, **217**

recipes, **218**

shortcuts, **217**

Cover letter

how to write a, **267**

purpose of, **265**

sample, **266**

Credit cards

comparing, **107**

dealing with debt, **108**

fees and terms, **107**

scams, **82**

using, **76, 105-106**

Credit ratings, **106**

Criticism, **36, 276**

Cuts, preventing, **198**

Dating, **46-50.** *See also* Relationships.

arranging a date, **46**

handling rejection, **47**

responsible behavior, **48**

rules of, **47**

Debit cards, **76, 105**

Decision making, **16**

ethics and, **21**

evaluating, **17**

managing, **22**

multiple roles and, **27**

process, **17, 19**

Deductions, payroll, **91**

Dietary Guidelines for Americans, **211**

Dietary supplements

for weight control, **189**

when needed, **211**

Discrimination, workplace, **268**

Disease

foodborne illness, **199**

getting treatment for, **202**

health insurance, **202-203**

preventing, **199-201**

sexually transmitted, **200-201**

Distance learning, **251**

Divorce, **41**

Dormitories, **123, 137**

Dovetailing, **24**

Dress codes, **231**

Driving. *See* Transportation, Vehicles.

Drugs

avoiding drugs, **194**

characteristics of drug users, **194**

drug slipping, **196**

Eating. *See* Food, Cooking, Nutrition.

Eating disorders, **190-192**

help for people with, **192**

risks associated with, **190**

symptoms of, **190**

types of, **190**

warning signs of, **192**

Eating out, **222-224**

cost of, **223**

healthy choices when, **224**

portion sizes and, **224**

Electrical shocks, preventing, **198**

Emergencies

auto, **168**

home, **144**

Emotional health, **174-175**

self-esteem, **175**

Emotions

controlling, **35**

expressing through body language, **35**

health and, **174**

misunderstandings and, **36**

Employability skills, **258-259**

Employment

employability skills, **258-259**

options, **253-254, 257**

outlook and trends, **254**

payment, **272**

benefits, **272, 274**

types of, **257**

Ethics, **21**

Etiquette, **37**

Exercise plan, **185**

Expenses, living, **126, 127**

Falls, preventing, **198**

Family

changes, **38-41**

communication and, **38, 40**

divorce and, **41**

expectations, **38**

moving away from, **39**

relationships, **38-41**

respect for, **40**

returning to, **40**

rules, **38**

staying close to, **40, 41**

Fashion

fads, **234**

keeping up with, **234**

Fats, **207**

Fibers, clothing, **239**

Financial management and planning, **89-121.** *See also* Banking, Money.

balancing a checkbook, **103**

banking, **101-104**

budgeting, **97**

credit and debit cards, **105-108**

financial goals, **95**

income taxes, **91-93,**

needs and wants, **94**

paychecks, **90, 91**

paying bills, **109-110, 112-113**

payment methods, **89, 90**

saving money, **95, 98, 99, 119**

saving vs. investing, **116-118**

types of investments, **118**

Fires, preventing, **198**

Fitness. *See* Physical health.

Food. *See also* Cooking, Meal planning, Nutrition.

eating out, **222**

money-saving techniques, **216**

preferences, **213**

preparation skills, **213**

safety, **220**

shopping for quality, **215**

shopping options, **214**

storage, **220, 221**

Food poisoning. See Foodborne illness.

Foodborne illness, **199, 220**

401(k) plans, **119**

Fraud
  combating, **82**
  types of, **82**
  warning signs of, **82**
Friendships, **42-45, 177-178**
  building new, **42, 177**
  changes in, **45, 177**
  ending, **45**
  long-distance, **43**
  maintaining old, **43**
  problems in, **44**
Furniture, **136-139**

Goals
  assessing, **12-13**
  long-term, **11**
  managing, **22**
  purpose of, **10**
  resources and, **14, 15**
  setting, **12-13**
  short-term, **11**
Gym, joining a, **182-183**

Health, **173-203**
  disease prevention, **199-201**
  emotional, **174**
  exercise, **180-185**
  healthy habits, **173**
  healthy weight, **186-189**
  nutrition and, **180**
  physical, **179-185**
  safety and, **195**
  social, **177-178**
Health-care system. *See* Health
  insurance.
Health club. *See* Gym, joining a.
Health insurance
  how it works, **202**
  managed care plans, **202**
  paying for, **203**
Home
  moving away from, **39**
  returning to, **40**
  sharing a, **52**
  shopping from, **65-66**
Homes, **123-151.** *See also* Housing,
  Living space.
Homesickness, **38**
Housing. *See also* Living space.
  choices, **124**
  emergencies, **144**

expenses, **126-127, 135**
leases, **128-129**
locations, **125**
neatness and cleanliness, **140-142**
options, **130**
responsibilities, **124**
safety, **143-145**

Identity theft
  preventing, **84**
  techniques, **84**
"I" messages, **34**
Income, **89, 272**
Income taxes, **91-93**
Individual retirement accounts
  (IRAs), **119**
Information
  career, **254**
  judging reliability of, **25**
  managing, **22**
  sources of, **25, 211**
Injuries, avoiding, **185**
Insurance, **114-115**
  auto, **165-166**
  costs, **114**
  legal requirements, **165-166**
  rates, **166**
  renters, **126**
  types of coverage, **115, 165**
Internet
  safety, **196**
  shopping, **65-66**
Internships, **256**
Interviews, **268-271**
Investing, **116-118**
Iron, **208**

Jobs
  accepting an offer, **272**
  applying for, **265**
  changing, **277**
  compensation package, **272, 274**
  giving notice, **277**
  handling rejection, **271**
  interviewing for, **268-271**
  networking, **267**
  openings, **263**
  samples of entry level, **252**

samples of professional level, **252**
samples of technical level, **252**
sources of leads, **263**

Kitchen
  cleanliness, **140**
  equipment, **217**
  food storage, **221**
  safety, **220-221**

Laundry
  doing the, **240-242**
  symbols, **241**
Lease
  auto, **159**
  housing, **128-129**
Listening, active, **35**
Living space. *See also* Housing.
  caring for, **140-142**
  choosing, **125**
  decorating, **136-139**
  furnishing, **136-139**
  paying for, **126-127, 135**
  sharing, **132-135**
Loneliness, **40**
Loss, dealing with, **28**

Maintenance
  auto, **169**
  home, **141-142**
Management process, **22**
Management skills
  change and, **7-8**
  consumer, **69-71**
  decision making, **17**
  clothing, **229-232**
  financial, **94-100**
  food, **212-124**
  goal setting, **10, 11**
  health, **173-174**
  housing, **134-135, 140-142**
  multiple roles and, **26-27**
  transportation, **153-164**
  workplace, **268-270, 276**
  time, **23-24, 27**
Manners, **37**
Marriage, **49**
Mass transit, **153-154**
Meal planning, **212,**
  planning a potluck, **219**

Mineral, **208**
Minimum wage, **89**
Misunderstandings, **36**
Money. *See also* Financial
   management and planning.
   budgeting, **97**
   financial documents, **111**
   financial goals, **95**
   keeping track, **111**
   paying bills, **109-110, 112-113**
   saving, **95, 98, 99, 119**
   saving vs. investing, **116-118**
Moving, **146-148**
Mutual funds, **118**

Needs, **59-60, 94**
Negotiation, **81**
Networking, **263**
Nutrients, **208**
Nutrition, **207-211**
   balanced approach to, **207**
   basic nutrients, **208**
   getting information about, **211**
   physical health and, **180**

Online shopping, **65-66**
Outsourcing, **257**
Overscheduling, **24**
Overtime, **89**

Paycheck, **90, 91**
   components of, **90**
   types of deductions, **91**
Peer pressure
   resisting negative, **44-45, 60**
Physical activity, **180, 181**
Physical fitness. *See* Physical health.
Physical health, **179-185**
   body composition, **179**
   developing an exercise plan, **185**
   endurance, **179**
   fitness, **179**
   flexibility, **179**
   joining a gym, **182-183**
   nutrition, **180**
   physical activity, **180, 181**
   sleep, **180**
   sports, **184-185**
   strength, **179**
   weight management, **180**
Poisoning, preventing, **198**

Possessiveness, **44**
Priorities, **8-10**
   decision making and, **16**
   financial, **94, 95**
   roles and, **27**
   setting, **10, 23**
   values and, **12**
Privacy, **83, 84**
   consumer, **83**
   health care, **83**
   protecting, **84**
Problem solving, **19-21, 22**
   consequences and, **20**
   ethics and, **21**
   resources and, **20**
Procrastination, **24**
Protein, **208**
Public transportation. *See* Mass
   transit.

Rape. *See* Sexual assault.
Recipes, **218**
References, **261**
Refusal skills, **45, 48**
Relationships, **33-57.** *See also*
   Friendships.
   abusive, **48**
   communication and, **33-36**
   conflicts in, **54, 55**
   control in, **47**
   ending, **50**
   positive, **49**
   successful, **49**
   types of, **33**
   with coworkers, **178, 276**
   with friends, **177**
   with roommates, **52, 178**
   with supervisors, **51**
   workplace, **51**
Resources
   human, community, material,
     natural, **14**
   managing, **22**
   types of, **14**
   using wisely, **15**
Restaurants, **222-224**
Résumé
   format, **262**
   preparing, **258, 260-262**
   sending out, **264**

Retirement, saving for, **119**
Roles, **26-27**
   balancing multiple, **26-27**
   types of, **26**
Roommates
   relating to, **52-53, 132-135,**
     178
   rules for, **52**

Safety
   equipment, **167**
   food, **220**
   home, **143-145, 195, 198**
   Internet, **196**
   outdoor, **198**
   sexual assault, **197**
   staying safe, **196**
   when driving, **166-167**
Salary, **272**
Security check, **195**
Self-protection, **196**
Service providers
   choosing, **71, 74**
   evaluating, **75**
   getting the most from, **75**
Services
   evaluating, **75**
   shopping for, **71, 74-75**
Sewing, **244-245**
   alterations, **245**
   repairs, **244**
Sexual assault
   date rape, **48**
   preventing, **197**
   surviving, **197**
Sexually transmitted diseases
   (STDs), **200-201**
   avoiding, **201**
   characteristics of, **200**
   getting tested for, **200**
   myths and facts, **201**
Shopping. *See also* Consumer.
   buying secondhand, **66-67**
   catalog, **65-66**
   comparison, **69**
   coupons and rebates, **70**
   for clothes, **237-239**
   from home, **65-66**
   money-saving techniques, **216**
   online, **65-66**

options, **64-67, 69-71**
payment options, **76**
returns and exchanges, **77**
sales, **70**
secondhand sources, **66-67**
services, **71, 74-75**
stores and outlets, **64**
strategies, **70**
Shyness, **42**
Sleep, **180**
Social health, **177-178**
Social Security, **91, 119**
Sports, **184, 185**
benefits of, **184**
safety, **185**
Stain removal, **244**
Stocks, **117, 118**
Stress, **174, 175**
emotional health and, **174**
managing, **175**
Support systems, **28**

Teamwork, **276**
Time
dovetailing tasks, **24**
managing, **22, 23-24, 27**
overscheduling and, **24**
planning schedules, **23-24**
procrastination and, **24**
Tobacco, **193**
Transition, **28**
Transportation, **153-171.** *See also*
Vehicles.
carpooling, **154**
mass transit, **153-154**
options, **153-155**
safety, **166-168**
vehicle ownership, **155-156**

Values, **7-8**
careers and, **250**
decision making and, **16, 19**
priorities and, **12**
Vehicles
comparing, **158**
costs of ownership, **155-156,
158**
dealing with emergencies, **168**
depreciation, **159**
equipment for, **167**

financing, **156**
insurance, **165-166**
leasing, **159**
maintenance, **169**
used vs. new, **159**
responsible driving, **166-167**
shopping for, **158-164**
Vitamins, **208**

Wages, **272**
Wants, **59-60, 94**
Warehouse clubs, **217**
Warranties, **79**
Water, **208**
Weight, **186-189**
benefits of healthy weight, **186**
body composition, **186**
body image, **187**
Body Mass Index, **186**
calories and, **188, 209**
defining healthy weight, **186**
underweight teens, **189**
weight gain, **189**
weight loss, **187-188**
Weight gain, **189**
Weight loss, **187-188**
Workplace. *See also* Careers,
Employment.
discrimination, **268**
environment, **254**
experience, **256**
family-friendly policies in, **27**
relationships, **178**
schedules, **257**
working conditions, **254**